INEQUITY IN THE TECHNOPOLIS

T0313466

EDITED BY

JOSEPH
STRAUBHAAR

JEREMIAH SPENCE

ZEYNEP TUFEKCI

ROBERTA G. LENTZ

INEQUITY IN THE TECHNOPOLIS

RACE, CLASS, GENDER, AND THE DIGITAL DIVIDE IN AUSTIN

University of Texas Press, *Austin*

Requests for permission to reproduce material from this work should be
sent to:
  Permissions
  University of Texas Press
  P.O. Box 7819
  Austin, TX 78713–7819
  www.utpress.utexas.edu/about/book-permissions

♾ The paper used in this book meets the minimum requirements of ANSI/
NISO Z39.48–1992 (R1997) (Permanence of Paper).

LIBRARY OF CONGRESS CATALOGING-IN-PUBLICATION DATA

Inequity in the technopolis : race, class, gender, and the digital divide in
Austin / edited by Joseph Straubhaar . . . [et al.]. — 1st ed.
    p.   cm.
Includes bibliographical references and index.
ISBN 978-0-292-75438-6
  1. Digital divide—Texas—Austin. 2. Information technology—
Government policy—Texas—Austin. 3. Information technology—Social
aspects—Texas—Austin. 4. Austin (Tex.)—Social conditions.
I. Straubhaar, Joseph D.
  HN80.A934I54 2012
  303.48'330976431—dc23   2011035819

This book is dedicated first to a dear departed colleague in the project that culminated in this book, Ozlem Okur, who helped create some of its central concepts: techno-disposition, techno-capital and techno-habitus.

It is also dedicated to another dear departed colleague, Ana Sisnett, who as longtime director of the Austin Free-Net inspired many of us to work harder on behalf of those who were and often still are excluded from access to the benefits of digital life in the technopolis of Austin.

Finally, it is dedicated to the dozens of talented undergraduate and graduate students at the University of Texas, particularly in the Radio-Television-Film Department, who worked on this project over the years 1999–2010.

CONTENTS

This book was very much a team effort, in its research, writing, and editing. The most centrally involved appear as editors and authors, but many others contributed ideas, research work, interviews, mapping, and coding. Even more people in the community contributed their time patiently to teach us things, be interviewed, let us observe them at their work and learning, and inspire us by their examples.

The people most central to us, outside the research team and participants in seminars that did much of the research, were Ana Sisnett of the Austin Free-Net (AFN) and Jorge González of the Universidad Autónoma de México. Ana was one of the driving forces behind many, if not most, of the most effective digital inclusion projects in Austin. We worked directly with her on the project that is described in Chapter 4. We began the resource mapping that turned into Chapter 2 at her instigation; she wanted to know whether the resources were in the right places. And she is a primary protagonist of much of the history described in Chapter 6. Right behind Ana were her longtime colleague Dale Thompson, now director of AFN, and Rondella Hawkins of the City of Austin's Telecommunication Policy Office, who is the sort of patient but passionate advocate for digital inclusion that more cities should have.

Jorge González is in many ways the chief intellectual architect of several of the theories and particularly the methods that we employ in this book. We drew on his writings from the first and then increasingly got him to Austin to lead seminars and courses to train and inspire many of those who worked on this project. We adapted his ideas of how to map resources over time, which drive Chapter 2, and his ideas on the value of interviewing multiple generations of families to see how those resources were used, which drive Chapter 9.

This project began with paired graduate and undergraduate seminars at the University of Texas in 1999. Upon arriving in Austin in 1998, Joseph Straubhaar, the lead editor, was struck by how much East Austin was also plagued by the digital divide that he had been observing in Brazil. He wanted to get students not only reading about it but also researching it hands on, and volunteering to work with it. Those courses were a mutual learning process between professor, graduate students, and undergraduate students, who often had as much passion and insight as the graduates. Many of the graduate students in that first seminar ended up being the coeditors and authors of this book, which gives us unusual continuity in an edited volume.

Many people collected the information analyzed here. Specifically, we would like to acknowledge the work in observation and interviewing put in by the following students in 1999–2000. Graduate students involved included Carol Adams-Means, Loreto Caro, Miyase Christensen, Yinan Estrada, Elissa Fineman, Christine Giraud, Karen Gustafson, Lisa Hartenberger, Roberta Lentz, Ozlem Okur, Viviana Rojas, Debasmita Roychowdhury, and Zeynep Tufekci. That list includes many of our eventual coauthors and two coeditors. Undergraduate students involved included Monem Adel, Ben Archey, David Benrey, Forrest Black, Kathy Bolton, K. Bonnicksen, Cara Bradley, John Brending, John Brooks, Theresa Chevas, Karen Cooke, Jon Duffey, Lisa Eisenstein, Cris Hogenson, Orlando Kell, Yangsu Kim, Blake Jones, Molly Lepeska, Corey Lieberman, C. Luncesford, Stan Main, Leean Matson, Jenn Mosley, Molly Norling, Brian Prestwood, Rene Rhi, Hyun Rhim, Griselda Salinas, R. Schimkowitsch, Michelle Schultz, Evan Scruggs, Bryan Shaw, Ryan Starus, Vanessa Vega, Melanie Villarreal, and Kerstin Wiggins. We would also like to acknowledge and thank the administrators, teachers, parents, and students at Johnston High School who let us interview and discuss issues with them.

We would also like to thank all the staff and volunteers in the Capital Area Training Foundation (CATF) at Reagan and Travis high schools that we interviewed and all the trainees that we interviewed and observed in their programs in 2000–2003, parts of which are reported and analyzed in Chapter 4 by Zeynep Tufekci. We acknowledge the financial support of the U.S. Department of Education and the extraordinary contributions of the CATF, AFN, Austin Community College, and Knowbility in that project.

We would like to acknowledge the work in observing and interviewing put in by the following students in 2003: Dan Abram, Carolyn Cunningham, Holly Custard, Emelia Violeta Dominguez, Lauren Haddock, Yeon Jin Ku, Gunho Lee, Mia Moody-Hall, Juan Piñon, Maria Rios, Jeremiah Spence, Joseph Villescas, Chongxiang Wang, Lindsay Welter, and Andrea Whiteis. Several of these students became part of the next wave of researchers and authors for this book. We would also like to thank all the staff and volunteers in the more than forty-three organizations dedicated to digital inclusion, access, and training that we interviewed.

We would like to acknowledge the work in mapping resources, observing, and interviewing put in by the following students in 2004. Graduate students involved included Nada Danielle Antoun, Carlos Martinez, Juan Piñon, and Andrea Whiteis. Undergraduate students involved included Christopher Babiak, Brewer Baker, Sarah Beachy, Mia Bhimani, Justin Bohls, Jami Bernice Broad, Roger Brown, Celeste Caballero, Isis Cerda-Clay, Robert Dahlem, Angelique Disher, Anthony Fernandez, Nicolas Foladare, Amie Gay, Abram Gonzalez, Janice Heffernan, Benjamin Jacob, Bobby Jones, Mario Lara, Michael Mann, Dorothy Menton, Monika Merola, Ivan Neel, Matthew Norris, Rolando Perez, Raven Platt, Jack Prather, James Price, Matthew Rogers, Emily Ryan, Julie Sowa, Erik Stark, John-Michael Torres, Jennie Trower, Salina Vela, Jared Womack, and Brook Zbylot.

We would like to acknowledge the work in mapping resources, observing, and interviewing put in by the following undergraduate students in 2005: Andres Saul Alvarez, Timothy Dennis Amerson, Eduardo Arzola, Lisa Marie Avendano, Marilyn Baird, Katherine Bartle, Alfred Ruben Cantu, Matthew Choi, Kristen Coale, Spencer Dean, Sergio Delgado, Ricardo Diaz, Lauren Edleson, Jacob Esquivel, Elry Falkenstein, Nicolas Gomez, Christine Graves, Frank Guida, Elizabeth Harvey, Claire Huie, Jose Francisco Lozano, Joy Lucas, Lauren Lunecki, Jessica Madsen, Chris Marquard, Brian Mitchell, Thomas North, Russell Nye, Lindsey O'Neal, Brandi Perkins, Daniel Setiawan, Taylor Seyer, Steven Stromberg, Wancha Talla-Takusi, Lindsay Tobias, Stephen Torres, Taryn Waldman, and Jessica Werner.

We would also like to acknowledge the work in mapping and creative programming skills provided by Utku Bozsoy, whose vision, along with Jeremiah Spence's, was the foundation for the online mapping system used to visualize the mapping data collected for Chapter 2 of the book as part of the Austin Memory Project.

We would like to acknowledge the work in observing and interviewing put in by the following students in 2009. Graduate students involved included Ji-Hyun Ahn, Paul Alonso, Stephanie Appell, Daniel Axelbaum, Dianna Beltran, Maria Boyd, Leonardo Cardoso, Yongdong Chen, Alexander Cho, Teresa Correa, Daniel Darland, Racquel Gonzelez, Dominique Harrison, Ricky Hill, Shih-Hsien Hsu, Gabino Iglesias, Stephen Janise, Kyung Sun Lee, Caitlin McClune, Vijay Parthasarathy, Monique Ribeiro, Esme Rodriguez, Mabel Rosenheck,

Judy Thomas, and Jacqueline Vickery. Several students also became much more involved as authors in this book, notably Stuart Davis, Laura Dixon, and Dean Graber, and several others are involved in ongoing research for related projects.

Undergraduate students involved in 2009 included Jonathan Anderson, Yurij Bryndzia, John Cano, Roger Chavez, Jose Angel De Luna, Brandon Drenon, Blas Garcia, Jordan Garcia, Jose Garza, Darrell Lieck, Joie Lopez, Thomas Meek, Alexander Milan, Joseph Mitchell, Larissa Montes, Nelly Mota, Rhea Rivera, James Sayre, Sasha Tollette, Chelsea Vernon, Erica Weaver, and Dustin Wise. Several of the undergraduates got much more involved in subsequent coding and analysis too. Those included Braulio Alvarez, Philip Clark, Laura Covarrubias, and Michelle Mejia.

JOSEPH
STRAUBHAAR

ZEYNEP TUFEKCI

JEREMIAH SPENCE

VIVIANA ROJAS

CHAPTER 1

DIGITAL INEQUITY IN THE AUSTIN TECHNOPOLIS

AN INTRODUCTION

This book comes from a ten-year-long study of the digital divide in Austin, Texas, that gradually turned into a broader inquiry into Austin's history as a segregated city, its turn toward becoming a technopolis, what the city and various groups did to try to address the digital divide once it was identified as a major issue in the 1990s, and how various groups and individuals were affected by those programs, as well as by the larger history of Austin.

Austin is widely admired and emulated as a successful example of a technopolis. Often, however, too little attention is paid to the lives of the digital have-nots. This book attempts to remedy this by presenting theoretically informed findings from a ten-year study of the digital divide, or digital inequity, in Austin, covering the period through the dot-com boom and beyond. It examines Austin's turn toward becoming a technopolis by situating it in its history as a segregated city and examines the impact of efforts by the city administration and other groups to address the digital divide.

In terms of policy, the book examines the impact of digital inclusion programs that were created in the 1990s nationally and for the state, as well as the aftermath when those programs were gradually cut back by conservative administrations in both the nation and state after 2000. It also examines how the City of Austin persisted in its own efforts at digital inclusion, working with public libraries and a number of local nonprofits, like the Austin Free-Net, and the positive impact those programs had.

Theoretically, building on the work of Michel de Certeau (1984), the book examines the structuring of cultural geography in the city as planners intentionally structured first a residentially segregated city and then an economic technopolis from above, while other groups and individuals reworked many of those structures from below to make them more livable and equitable. The book also proposes and examines the concepts of techno-field and techno-capital, building on Pierre Bourdieu's (1984) ideas of fields of struggle and competition to gain and use resources, like technology access and skills. This book grew out of collaboration between the editors and graduate and undergraduate students at the University of Texas, as well as a variety of groups and individuals around Austin. It was a unique opportunity to study a crucial national, even global, issue in the unique conditions of the city where we lived.

There is a tendency to speak of the digital divide, or, more recently, digital inequality (DiMaggio et al. 2004), in reference to all things digital. But we want to recognize very explicitly that digital technologies are not a completely new thing. They layer over earlier technologies, and digital skills build on analogous ones learned at home or in the classroom. Further, even a hip, creative city like Austin, considered one of the most wired in the country, has to deal with the legacy of segregation, radically reinforced by city planners in 1928. This book will try to deal with these issues, to see how older layers of history and development affect new efforts and how the many intriguing efforts in Austin to increase access, teach skills, improve learning, and reimagine the economy have worked out. We will look beyond Austin at the broader implications of the interplay of digital media with society, families, and individuals, and within Austin at the policy implications of the information-technology-oriented social and government program interventions.

How important are new digital technologies to questions of social change and social equity? How much do the impacts of these new technologies depend on earlier patterns of who got a good education and who did not, who had access to earlier waves of technology and who did not? Many popular and scholarly authors view digital technologies as crucial to an emerging information or creative economy. The focus of Austin planners on information, creative, and high-technology industries has transformed it more than many other places, contributing strongly to the doubling of its population between 1980 and 2005, and to a striking shift in the types of jobs many people have in the city. Austin leaders deliberately planned the transformation of the city into a technopolis—a city whose economy focuses on recent technological developments and industries. It is important, therefore, to think about the impacts of this transformation on *all* the people of Austin—not just the technologically privileged.

THE TECHNOPOLIS AS A NEW FORM OF CULTURAL GEOGRAPHY

As we have thought about how to make sense of Austin's experience, both historical and contemporary, of striving to become a technopolis, and the effects of that experience on Austinites' social and economic well-being, we have considered the city as a complex cultural, economic, and social geography that has built up over time. Parts of that geography were planned from the top down, like the reinforcement of segregation in the 1920s and the planning of Austin as a technopolis from 1970 on. Other parts were structured or planned from the bottom up by nonprofits, schools, and groups operating at a more grassroots level.

Theoretically, we want to build on de Certeau's concepts of cultural geography (1984); on Bourdieu's concepts of capital, field, and habitus (1984); on Anthony Giddens's concept of structuration (1984); on Raymond Smilor, David Gibson, and George Kozmetsky's ideas about the technopolis and how it was to be built (1988); on Jorge González's concepts and methods of mapping resources available to people over time, paired with family histories with media and capital (1986); and on Paul Bertaux's concepts and methods of observing family social mobility over time (Bertaux and Thompson 1997). We also take a critical look at Everett Rogers's theory of diffusion of innovations (1983) and the policies that explicitly or implicitly rely on it.

De Certeau (1984) argues that the cultural geography of a city is constructed from both above and below. He notes that political leaders, planners, industrialists, and others make many strategic decisions from the top down. The history of Austin features three moments of top-down geographic structuring that had powerful impacts on the city. Austin was structured first as a brand new political capital for the state of Texas in the 1800s (Humphrey 1997). Second, it was structured powerfully as a racially segregated city in 1928 (Orum 2002; also discussed in Chapter 2 of this volume). The third major restructuring came in the 1970s with both desegregation (discussed in Chapter 2) and the top-down planning of Austin as a technopolis (discussed in Chapter 3).

The remaking of Austin as a technopolis lends the most obvious new shape to the city. However, we will argue that the city is also still profoundly, deeply structured (beneath the visibility of many current residents) by the previous creation of segregated structures of education, work, housing, transportation, and so on from the 1920s to the 1970s, which were not really undone by desegregation after the 1970s. Much of the first third of this book (Chapters 2–4) will directly address these key moments of top-down structuring and their effects on how current Austinites live, work, and go to school. In these chapters, we take a primarily historical view, using maps we found, maps we created from original data (following González's concepts and tools), and considerable economic data about work.

There was a fourth key moment in Austin of top-down planning and attempted change starting in the 1990s, aimed precisely at remedying some of the problems caused by the shift to the technopolis economy. At the national, state, and local levels, a number of decision makers, from President Clinton down to the staff of the City of Austin, became concerned that the overall shift in the United States toward an information economy and technology use, accentuated particularly in Austin, was creating a new layer of social stratification between social classes, races, genders, and ages—a digital divide (Irving 1999). Chapters 5–7 in this volume discuss different aspects of that analysis and the programs that came out of it. We will look at these issues in a variety of ways, with historical analysis, policy analysis, interviews about the nature of the digital divide, and participant observation in libraries and community centers to see who uses public access.

Going back to our theoretical framework, we see that those who live in and use these city spaces make tactical decisions on the ground that can, to some degree, redefine what the place's users do with the space and what practices they evolve (de Certeau 1984). Many people in Austin fought against segregation and worked to undo it, although de facto segregation of housing, schools, work, and access to digital resources remains in many parts of the city (Orum 2002). Although the technopolis economy was planned by city, university, and business officials, drawing resources from national planners who wanted to see such development (Smilor, Gibson, and Kozmetsky 1988, xiii), others affiliated with the city, university, and community were worried about how to implement this idea in a way that mitigated some of its potential downsides. By the mid-1990s, one of their main solutions was to provide computer and Internet access, training, and skills to address the question of the digital divide. Chapter 6 of this book discusses how a variety of groups began to plan and implement local programs, often calling on resources that were becoming available through national and state programs, discussed in Chapter 5. Chapter 7 focuses on how libraries in particular came to be a focus of access to new digital resources and education. Chapter 8 discusses how enthusiasm for wireless Internet began to draw attention away from more traditional community access programs, perhaps reflecting a return to worrying about the young, mobile, creative people who were seen as critical to the technopolis project. Chapter 9 looks at how a variety of people responded to access and training as it became available. All of these chapters in different ways look at what de Certeau would call the structuring or modification of structures from below, by those actually living in the planned technopolis.

One of the main questions for this book is how much impact these efforts to structure (or restructure) the technopolis from below, and to make its benefits more widely accessible, actually had on those who needed them most. (Chapters 7 and 9 look particularly at those use and impact questions.) The other main question for this book is how to understand the struggle among a variety of people in Austin not just to gain access to digital tools but also to develop what we call techno-capital (the knowledge and skills required to use digital media capably), as well as what we call techno-disposition (an understanding of digital media's usefulness). Both are discussed below and in Chapter 9.

TECHNOLOGY AS A COMPETITIVE FIELD

Bourdieu (1980, 1984, 1993a) introduces the concepts of *field*, *capital*, and *habitus* to elaborate the continuity, regularity, and regulated transformation of social action, such as technology use by individuals and groups. He describes the tensions and struggles individuals face in their daily life in societies, such as the technological gaps between majorities and minorities. Bourdieu's relational theory, which focuses on the interaction between people (as social agents) and structures (like school systems or the economy), can help us to understand what other factors beyond their economic class operate in the environment in which Austinites live their lives.

Bourdieu's theoretical framework, also known as the theory of practice or theory of symbolic power (Brubaker 1993; Garnham 1986), is based on a distinction between several kinds of capital, notably economic, cultural, and social. Cultural capital, which is separate and relatively autonomous from economic capital, is defined as the possession of certain cultural competencies and bodies of cultural knowledge, typically acquired from parents and schooling, that provide for distinguished modes of cultural consumption (Bourdieu 1984). Just as economic relations that express the networks of power are quantified as economic capital, the cultural relations that express different levels of learned and empowering potentialities constitute cultural capital.

Cultural capital is distributed differentially throughout society and is accumulated and transferred from generation to generation, just like economic capital. Bourdieu argues that in modern societies, the accumulation of cultural capital requires a long-term investment of time and education. Although they are not reducible to each other, economic and cultural capitals are convertible (Johnson 1993). Rephrasing the popular idea that education lets people get ahead, Bourdieu would say that education helps one acquire cultural capital, which can be converted into economic capital by, for example, getting a better-paying job using one's expanded knowledge of favored norms of behavior.

Bourdieu discusses social capital as resources encapsulated in a set of social relations. The concept refers to "the aggregate of the actual or potential resources, which are linked to possession of a durable network of more or less institutionalized relationships, of mutual acquaintance and recognition—or in other words, to membership group—which provides each of its members with the backing of the collectivity-owned capital, a 'credential' which entitles them to credit, in the various senses of the word" (Bourdieu 1985, 249). Social and cultural capitals are employed in the reproduction or change of social stratification. They often combine, as when a Harvard degree gives not only an educational qualification but also access to an exclusive social network.

Bourdieu uses the term *field* to account for the concrete social situations within which people as agents operate, accumulating and using different forms of capital. A field is defined primarily by the particular form of capital present and secondarily by the relations developed around it as agents struggle to acquire or maintain that capital. Fields, whether economic, political, cultural, technological, or educational, are hierarchically organized and relatively autonomous but structurally homologous with each other. The economic and educational fields, for instance, are related to each other in the sense that people with economic capital also tend to acquire educational capital, and vice versa.

In this scheme, individuals (as agents) act in the different social fields with the capital they have accumulated and used—knowledge, financial resources, social connections, and so on—in the course of their life trajectory. Bourdieu uses the analogy of a game to explain why people participate or invest in a particular "field of forces" in which they compete or struggle for resources, including access to jobs. According to their class habitus, people make specific investments in the fields in which they participate, such as sports, work, education, or computer technology skill.

The habitus can be defined as a set of dispositions that generate similar practices and perceptions among members of the same group or class. It is a product of history and is internalized in the mind of the actors. It is an individual and collective process at the same time since it produces individual and collective practices. Members of the same group are the product of the same objective conditions and share a habitus without realizing that their practices are harmonized beyond what they as individual agents know or wish. Habitus, then, implies a certain knowledge and recognition of the stakes in the field and generates the strategies of action with which people participate in the field (Bourdieu 1993b; Kvasny 2005).

As Austin's economy changed toward being a technopolis, the fields of both education, broadly defined, and information technology access, knowledge, and skill became far more crucial to residents seeking to get ahead in life. In the U.S. economy overall, education has increasingly been associated with obtaining better jobs and higher wages over the course of one's life: "In 1975, full-time, year-round workers with a bachelor's degree had 1.5 times the annual earnings of workers with only a high school diploma. By 1999, this ratio had risen to 1.8" (Day and Newburger 2002). Education's importance for workers is even higher in a technopolis like Austin. The importance of technology skills and knowledge has been harder to measure, but a consensus is growing that technology access, disposition (willingness to use), knowledge, and skill are also crucial, particularly in the kind of information, knowledge, and creative industries that Austin has come to specialize in (Van Dijk 2005). One could argue that in an economy like Austin's, pretty much all residents are involved in competition in the fields of education and technology, whether they realize it or not.

TECHNO-DISPOSITIONS, TECHNO-CAPITAL, AND TECHNO-FIELD

Based on Bourdieu's concepts of capital, field, habitus, and disposition, we identified three interrelated concepts that can help in understanding people's attitudes, perceptions, knowledge, and uses of technologies of information. An individual's relationship with information technology not only depends on how much they know about it or whether they have the resources to access it. People's dispositions to technologies, or techno-dispositions, interact in a reciprocal and complex relationship with techno-capital, a specific form of cultural capital encompassing the acquired knowledge and skills to use information technologies in ways that are considered personally empowering or useful. For example, accumulation of cultural capital related to computers may lead to the formation of techno-capital, which in turn affects one's disposition toward the use of technology. However, if alternative social and cultural influences communicate that computer use is not socially relevant or desirable, then an individual's techno-disposition will direct her or him away from computer use. Both techno-disposition and techno-capital operate within a specific techno-field of human endeavor. In the case of East Austin, where much of the disadvantage in the fields of education and technology is concentrated because of segregation and other historical reasons, the techno-field is the site, or structured space, where struggles over media access are enacted by appropriating resources (access, knowledge, or techno-capital).

Techno-dispositions are delineated by such indicators as social practices, perceptions and attitudes, technical education, awareness of technology, desire for information, job requirements, social relations, community interactions, and geographic location. Social practices include an individual's and family's history of technology use, especially the Internet and other information and communication technologies (ICTs), as well as their patterns of mass media consumption (e.g., radio, television, and film).[1] Also key are respondents' thoughts and evaluations about ICTs and how they are perceived as a component of individual, family, and community life. Education incorporates both formal institutional education and less formal technology training and vocational studies. Technological awareness refers to the understanding among community members of the potential value of ICTs for economic mobility. Desire for information involves the relevance of various kinds of information and the related use of ICTs to conduct searches in everyday life. Individuals' dispositions toward technology are affected by job requirements and workplace propensities toward ICTs. Social interactions within the community and community organizations themselves, with their capacity to foster an environment that encourages ICT use, may also affect people's techno-dispositions. Finally, the geographic location of the place itself, particularly East Austin, structures the interplay of people's agency with technology through its relative lack of infrastructure and basic resources as a site of struggle over media access.

Techno-capital, then, is a product of techno-dispositions that lead people to invest time and energy, or not, in learning about technology. It provides certain competencies and resources to negotiate within the techno-field. As a structured space, the techno-field is analyzed as an arena where human agency is enacted in relation to other social forces—political, economic, social, cultural, and so forth. Techno-competencies, the acquired skills for and knowledge about ICTs, are shaped by the interplay between techno-capital on the one hand and the other forms of capital (social, economic, cultural, symbolic) on the other. In East Austin, the logic of the techno-field is contingent upon the interaction between individual techno-competencies and such social factors as attitudes toward information technologies, minority status, the emergence of Austin as a technopolis (and its attendant need for information workers), local income scarcity, and spotty educational and living standards in different parts of the city. Sources of cultural capital include education, family traditions, and other social resources. Sources of social capital include extended family ties, immigration history, perceived social mobility, community relations and neighborhood interactions, and peer groups. Finally, economic capital is composed of occupation, income, family size, and geographic location. The interactions between these fields of power will be analyzed to bring to light the concept of techno-capital, crucial for reconceptualizing the digital divide in a way that goes beyond physical access to information and computer technology (Van Dijk 2005).

We looked at this in several ways. We got a baseline for what kind of capital and needs people had by interviewing students and parents in 1999, and a ten-year comparison by interviewing families in 2009.

We also did interviews and participant observation in libraries and access centers in 1999, 2003, and 2009 to see who was using computers there. As government programs, local nonprofits, schools, and so on structured learning and access for those in need, we interviewed policy makers and activists, as well as examined documents and news stories, to see what they were trying to provide and why.

MAPPING CHANGE OVER GENERATIONS

In this research, we have followed some theoretical and methodological directions not only from Bourdieu (1984) but also from Paul Bertaux and Paul Thompson (1997) and González (1986), who have elaborated many of Bourdieu's concepts and come up with interesting ways of studying them in practice. We have worked particularly closely with González, adapting methods he and several teams used in Mexico to map out where information and cultural resources were being placed over time. He stresses the value of mapping out both where populations live and where the information, educational, cultural, and media resources that they might seek to use are located (González 1986). He stresses picking key years that bracket major changes in where the resources are placed to see what is being made available to whom and where. So we picked years (1910 and 1940) before and after segregation was imposed in Austin in 1928. We also picked years (1970, 1990, and 2000) before, during, and after desegregation and the buildup of the technology economy. That enabled us to see how resources available to people, particularly the poor and ethnic minorities, were shaped by planners who were changing the cultural geography of Austin by locating schools, libraries, community centers, and places of work. This is reflected in a number of chapters in this book, particularly in the history presented in Chapter 2.

González also stresses that we should look over time and across generations among families and social groups to see how people were using the resources at their disposal (1995). In his theoretical conception, mapping resources and seeing how families used them over time permits an understanding of complex cultural and social practices (1994). In doing this, he builds on the sociology of Bertaux (1981), who used life histories to understand how people acquired the cultural and other kinds of capital they needed to navigate and compete in the fields most important to them. Both clearly build on Bourdieu (1984) in their use of fields and capital. We, in turn, use their theories and methods to focus on the fields of new media use, education, language (which has also become a competitive field for Latinos and other immigrants in the United States), and technology employment. Bertaux also worked with Thompson and others (Bertaux and Thompson 1997) to look at factors contributing to social mobility across generations. We used González's adaptation of their methods in Chapter 9 to analyze how families accumulate capital in fields over generations, what their strategies are, and what is passed on successfully, or not, in education, language, and media use.

DEFINING THE TECHNOPOLIS

Smilor, Gibson, and Kozmetsky helped plan the Austin technopolis strategy, and they define the concept this way:

> The Technopolis is an innovative approach to economic development that involves linking technology commercialization with effective public and private sector initiatives for economic growth, diversification and global competitiveness. The *Technopolis Phenomenon* presents ideas, programs and initiatives that accelerate the creation of smart cities, fast systems and global networks. It focuses on the development and implementation of an innovative and effective infrastructure for technology commercialization and economic growth for global competitiveness in the 1990s. (1988, xiii)

In this book, however, we explore the implications for a city or a nation that decides to transition itself into a new type of society, focused economically, socially, and politically on an information or creative economy, fueled in part by industries specifically focused on computers, the Internet, and digital telecommunications. This kind of planned transformation is based on theories of a transition from industrial-type economies, in which earnings are based on capital and labor, to an economy in which information-technology-related skills are most rewarded and provide social mobility, increased job opportunities, and economic benefit to their holders (Bell 1973). The creation of video games, digitally recorded music and film, websites, other kinds of software, and various kinds of hardware from chips to computers to cell phones seems, on the surface, like an ideal economic base for a projected information society (Castells 1996). Scholars like

Richard Florida (2002) emphasize that cities like Austin are more correctly seen as creative economies, thus including music, film, and other intellectual or creative endeavors, rather than as information economies per se.

By many accounts, Austin is the very definition of success in the modern, information-technology-oriented economy. It has managed to transform itself from a "sleepy college town" in the 1960s to one of the highly touted "technopolises" of the United States. In fact, Kozmetsky, one of Austin's indigenous business intellectuals and the founder of the IC² Institute (Innovation, Creativity and Capital Institute) at the University of Texas, coined the term *technopolis* (Cardella 1999, 44). It has also maintained what many residents consider an excellent quality of life. Named the third-best metropolitan area for businesses and careers in 2005 by *Forbes* magazine (Badenhausen 2005), Austin boasts good jobs, easy living, a mild climate, a lively nightlife with a spirited live music scene, and many parks and outdoor recreation facilities. Florida (2002) considers it a prototype of how a city can and should function as a magnet for attracting the "creative class" that drives the current style of creative or information economy. In addition, a number of cities, from Boise, Idaho, to Curitiba, Brazil, have studied Austin as a model for how to become a creative economy city (Bishop 2000).

Austin is home to many technology companies, including Dell Computers. The city started by attracting U.S. government support for computer chip research, then chip manufacturers, then other technology companies. The trend accelerated in the 1990s with a whole variety of web and software companies. Even more remarkable than the growth, however, is that Austin planned all of this—way back in 1957:

> In 1957, Austin Area Economic Development Foundation created a "blueprint of the future" that set out to recruit industry that matched Austin's existing economic structure. A team of public and private leaders built upon UT's [University of Texas] research programs by attracting manufacturers of electrical and scientific equipment. Austin's success in the 1960s and 70s in making the transition from government to high technology manufacturing was built on the traditional factors of relatively low-cost land, a high-skilled workforce at reasonable wages, and a desirable quality of life. (Humphrey 1997, 25)

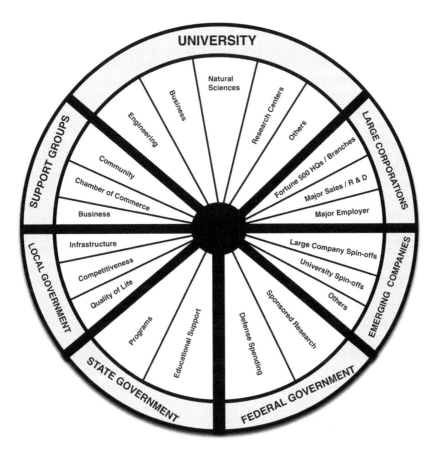

Figure 1.1. The technopolis wheel (Source: R. W. Smilor, D. Gibson, and G. Kozmetsky, "Creating the technopolis: High-technology development in Austin, Texas," *Journal of Business Venturing 4(1, 1989): 51).*

This techno-economic enthusiasm seems to have assumed that changing the Austin economy toward the technopolis model would benefit all, or most. The sectors to be most involved with this new economy in Austin are shown in what Smilor, Gibson, and Kozmetsky (1988) called the technopolis wheel (Figure 1.1).

THE TECHNOPOLIS AND WORK

Inherent in the technopolis model is the premise of changing educational requirements, technology skills, and economic rewards in a city like Austin. Daniel Bell's theory of postindustrial society makes specific predictions about the relationship between work, skill, and reward, following from the key premise that information and the tools for accessing and manipulating information form the critical resource, and thus the main path to social mobility. This form of social mobility now stresses overall higher education as well as technology skills (Webster and Robins 1986, 32–48; Giddens 1984, 21). More people will be engaged in information or creative work, which will be better rewarded since it now forms the key economic resource, while blue-collar or other industrial-era skills will be downgraded in importance and less rewarded.

One Austin critic of the technopolis model noted in 1991, "Many non-high-tech employees will have a difficult time finding their place on the technopolis wheel. For example, despite the fact the authors consider the research university the 'nucleus' of the technopolis, the only category under 'university' in which students might fit would be 'other'" (Henson 1991, 5). Further, in the major paper by Smilor, Gibson, and Kozmetsky (1988), there is no mention of income equality or increased breadth of jobs. This is not surprising since most early anticipations of the information economy and technopolis were very optimistic, assuming a positive transformation for all. Only in the mid- to late 1990s did policy planners, like those in the Clinton administration, along with academics, nonprofits, and some in the city government in Austin, begin to worry about a digital divide between those with technology access and skills and those without, those with good jobs in the technology economy and those without.

However, there was an assumption that the information sector, at least in Austin, would create new manufacturing jobs as well. In the implementation of technopolis planning in Austin, there was considerable early attention to encouraging high-technology manufacturing plants, such as Sematech or AMD, to locate in East Austin near the African American and Latino communities, in order to make work there more accessible. But not everyone in East Austin considered them a positive development, given that they came with potential pollution from the chemicals involved in chip manufacture. Further, in reality, many of these jobs were deskilled and relatively low paid, as described in Chapter 4.

How broadly have gains actually been shared in terms of jobs, income, education, and social mobility under Austin's emergence as a technopolis? Who has been left behind, and how does such neglect occur? How much can be attributed to preexisting disadvantages in education, work skills, income, and geography? For example, while Austin is considered a hip town with a proud music scene and lots of new high-technology jobs, it also still reflects the legacies of racial segregation on the east and southeast sides of town, where black and Latino communities are concentrated and where schools are noticeably worse than those on the west, and largely white, side of the city. One historically black and Latino school on Austin's east side, Johnston High, was one of the first schools in Texas to be closed for poor performance. It is examined in Chapters 2 and 9 of this book to see how its failure can help us understand the persistence of inequity in the Austin technopolis.

Beyond historical issues like racial segregation that still affect many in a technopolis like Austin, what are some of the contemporary issues that accompany a technology-oriented development agenda? If information technologies are so crucial to local, national, and even global economies, what happens to people who lack access to them or who don't know how to use them strategically to obtain higher-paying technology jobs? For that matter, how many "good" new jobs have actually been generated in Austin when compared to lower-income service jobs that seem to have grown even faster?

These and other questions are addressed in Chapters 2–4 of this book. We focus on the extent to which the Austin technopolis has grown equitably. Is it raising the average levels of education, income, and standard of living? Is it doing the things planned developments are supposed to do? We also examine the impact of a technology-oriented development agenda on education and other public services that affect the general standard of living in Austin.

REASONS FOR THE PERSISTENCE OF INEQUITY IN AUSTIN

Austin has many faces. It has a growing music and film economy. It has a diverse computer-oriented tech sector that pulls people from across the United States, Europe, and East and South Asia. It has an enormous university, the University of Texas, with over fifty thousand students. For undergraduates, mostly from Texas, Austin offers both a good school and a party environment. For graduate students, from all over, it offers a world-class university. For Latin American immigrants, it offers growing construction and service sectors to work in. For many longer-term Latino and African American residents, it offers a conundrum of both opportunity and frustration, as most of the best jobs created bypass them and their children.

Even in the midst of some of the most impressive booms of the modern U.S. economy, the city had a significant portion of its population living under conditions of poverty. What is striking about this development is that high poverty rates persisted even when the official unemployment rate in Austin fell to 2.6 percent in 1999—much lower than the historically low national unemployment rate of 4.4 percent. While employment in general was growing until 2000, income in the computer-related sectors grew much faster. A 2003 analysis notes,

> The *average* computer-related job in Austin was $100,000 per year in the year 2000. The average wage for workers not in the computer industry was $33,000. And despite the flush economic times that existed in the last part of the 1990s, computer-related jobs have far outpaced other jobs as an engine of growth in the region. Adjusted for inflation, non-computer workers have seen their wages raised by 17% between 1988 and 2000, while computer workers' wages doubled. (Robbins 2003, 5–6)

The year 2000, it turns out, was the best of times. The numbers were much bleaker whenever the economy of the area took a downturn, as it did in the mid-1980s, or after 2000, or again in 2008. Broken down by race and ethnicity, Austin's poverty levels paint a picture of a divided city. Between 1980 and 2007, poverty among white (non-Hispanic) people in Austin tended to go down slightly. Poverty among Hispanics went up slightly during that period, and poverty among African Americans, which declined in the 1990s boom, went up strongly by 2007, even before the Great Recession began in 2008 (Table 1.1).

Looked at another way, the poverty figures show that the technology-economy boom of the 1990s alleviated poverty among all groups, but was unsustainable. Employment went down after the 2000 dot-com bust, when many start-up companies in web services, information technologies, and other new technologies declined or went out of business. This national technology-economy decline hit Austin particularly hard, along with other information-technology-centered regional economies like Silicon Valley.

The longer 1990–2007 trend raises the question of how a city can be one of the most successful technopolises of the 1990s and early 2000s, yet maintain such bleak poverty levels? How is it that 2.6 percent unemployment, reached in 1999, was not enough to eliminate

Table 1.1. Percentage of People Living Below the Poverty Line in Austin Between 1980 and 2007

Race	1980	1990	1999 (2000 census)	2007
All races	15.8	17.9	14.4	17.5
Whites	13.7	14.9	11.1	13.0
African Americans	24.6	26.2	19.5	31.9
Hispanics	22.0	26.3	20.9	23.1

Source: City of Austin 1993; U.S. Census with data from the Decennial Census; 2007 American Community Survey

or drastically reduce poverty in a city that embraces a development-plan based on information and communication technology sectors—the very industries that are often touted as the most wealth-creating and successful industries? Since then, unemployment numbers have taken a turn for the worse, reaching 4.1 percent in 2008 and as high as 6.1 in 2009 (Texas Workforce Commission 2009). These are still fairly low levels of unemployment, however, and unemployment in Austin has remained below the national trends, so the Austin economy is creating and maintaining more jobs than many others.

Yet, as can be seen in the poverty numbers, a large proportion of Austin residents, especially Austin residents of color, continue to live below the poverty level—as high as one in three of African American and one in four of Latino residents. The combined interpretation of unemployment and poverty levels suggests that the technopolis continues to generate structural inequalities and that the rising tide of high-income creative employment does not lift all boats; on the contrary, it may make the lives of low-income residents harder by pushing up property prices and other costs of living. Alarmingly, but not surprisingly, these disparities continue to follow historical trends of racial inequity, with African Americans and Latinos faring worst in the high-tech city.

THE LEGACY OF RACIAL SEGREGATION VERSUS TECHNOLOGICAL PROGRESS

Some of the reasons for the persistence of poverty in the technopolis of Austin may be found through an examination of Austin's history and the structures of race and class that generations of both de jure and de facto segregation have left in place. Another big question for Chapters 2–4 of this book is this: if you create a technopolis in a place that has been previously segregated, how is the technopolis then affected by previous structural issues (i.e., segregation into structured racial enclaves)? Even if the technopolis is planned to respond to and help ameliorate the segregation that was previously imposed, how much of its original impact on education, skills, and so on can be changed?

Austin has been the focus of a great deal of academic research, city and nonprofit project development, and community activism related to what has often been referred to as the digital divide. The team of scholars who wrote this book began in 1999 to look at the most basic question of the digital divide: which kinds of people had access to computers and the Internet. We found far fewer computers in East Austin schools. (East Austin has traditionally been a lower-income area, populated primarily by African Americans and Latinos. It was in fact the segregated area designated for African Americans in the city plan of 1928.)

One of the authors, Joseph Straubhaar, got to know East Austin better in 1998 when his two sons began attending two magnet schools that had been placed there as part of the school desegregation plan of the 1980s. He recalls his initial shock at seeing much lower information technology capacities in East Austin schools like Johnston High School and Kealing Middle School than in other Austin area schools, despite the presence of the magnet schools in those two schools. Although public schools had been a target priority for several of the digital divide programs we examine in this book, the public schools were a weak link in Austin's citywide efforts, with clearly unequal resources in East Austin, evident from the fieldwork we started doing in 1999 at Johnston High (reported in Chapter 9). That inequity is intimately related to the history of school and housing segregation in Austin (discussed in Chapter 2).

In our interview and observation work with schools, community centers, and other groups in Austin starting in 1999, we discovered that fewer African Americans and Latinos had computers and Internet access. We also initially found lower usage of computers and the Internet and less understanding of the role of new technologies, or techno-disposition, among African Americans and Latinos, although that began to change in the early 2000s. For example, Straubhaar observed an example in 1999 at the Austin public Fourth of July fireworks, one of the few occasions when people of all races, classes, and occupations gather together. He watched a twenty-something Latina sounding out the words on a banner towed behind an airplane over the event that said, "Jobs@Living.com." Quite understandably for anyone not using e-mail or the Internet, she did not understand what the "@" symbol or the "dot" in ".com" meant, so she hesitantly said, "Jobs living com?" This observation is not intended as any slight to her or her family, but it was clear that her schooling and background had not given her the knowledge necessary to understand. By contrast, one could see the advantages, especially for life and work in a technopolis, held by a young mother in a middle-class white family nearby who clearly did understand the message, as she also sounded out the banner: "Jobs at living dot com." Bourdieu (1984) would call this a difference in cultural capital: what we have learned at home, at school, at work, and from peers that enables us to compete in competitive fields of endeavor, like education or technology-oriented work, in a rapidly changing society.

In the 1990s, the increasingly visible transformations brought about by the widespread diffusion of information technology in the economy and in everyday life led to the theorization that this process could result in the persistence and deepening of inequality caused by a "digital divide." This was a gulf in access to and skills in the use of computers and the Internet, conceived in terms of differentials by minorities, women, older people, rural residents, and those living below the poverty line.

A national study at Vanderbilt University (Hoffman and Novak 1998) found that not only was there a gap between minorities and nonminorities regarding computer and modem ownership and Internet usage, but the gap was greatest among high school and college students. The study also revealed that more than income disparities were at play in explaining the gap. As the *Austin American-Statesman* reported, "Until now, researchers had assumed any inequality in Internet access could be explained by differences in income and the ability to afford expensive personal computers, modems and online connection fees. Several experts said they were surprised that the racial gap persisted even when incomes were equal" (Hotz 1998).

This finding once again highlighted the fact that race could not simply be seen as a proxy for income or class status. It had a particular resonance in heavily segregated places such as Austin. To find and examine the equivalent data for Austin, we did qualitative, in-depth interviews in 1999 and 2009. We drew on the in-depth interviews in Chapter 9 to understand why people were or were not using computers and the Internet, and what kinds of dispositions and capitals they had acquired or were seeking to acquire to navigate the field of information technology in their lives.

In 1998, when the digital divide started being discussed in policy circles, the Clinton administration was in power. The Federal Communications Commission assumed an interventionist stance and planned to respond relatively aggressively to the growing findings that minorities and low-income populations were lagging in Internet access and computer use. The national debate was encapsulated nicely in the pronouncements of Larry Irving, President Clinton's top telecommunications advisor, who explicitly recognized the racial and ethnic aspects of the divide. In a speech he gave in June 1998, Irving stated,

> Most kids would rather grow up to be Michael Jordan than Bill Gates and spend time on a basketball court than in a computer room. . . . Our children should know as much about Paul Allen (the co-founder of Microsoft and owner of the Portland Trailblazers [NBA team]) as Paul Pierce [the Boston Celtics first-round draft pick], and as much about Michael Dell [founder of Dell Computers] . . . as Michael Jordan. . . . And our children should have a shot—better than a three-pointer—at being one of those computer success stories.

Thus, from the beginning, the digital divide was pushed to the forefront of the national agenda, with a dual focus on lack of access and differential infrastructure in minority households, and on cultural factors, including dispositions and habitus, that were assumed to be retarding adoption of these new technologies by minorities—as Irving noted about the lack of technology role models.

The question of the digital divide rests fundamentally on an understanding of what these new technologies mean. Are they mainly new forms of entertainment, such as television; new forms of connectivity; or essential new economic tools? Most policy makers and social theorists agreed that all three roles apply, with the bulk of the disagreement being relegated to the entertainment and consumer aspects of these technologies. In Austin, as nationally, there seemed to be a near consensus that information technology is essential to economic mobility. Unspoken in the national debate was the implicit assumption that technological diffusion in the workplace was resulting in the up-skilling of labor, an assumption that was to heavily influence attempts to redress inequity and lack of mobility. Chapters 4–5 of this book look at the discourse around that idea.

One of the coeditors, Roberta Lentz, observed in an earlier work that access to specifically digital technologies is only the top layer of the problem:

> The term "digital" focuses attention on the technological aspects of inequities. However, where one is located relative to this digital dividing line is a consequence of historical and structural factors. A person's family trajectory, access to schooling and subsequent job opportunities, and degree of geographic mobility to pursue opportunities in the "new" economy are all aspects of everyday life that play a role in how interested in and capable one might be in using information technologies. (2000, 356)

RESPONSES TO THE DIGITAL DIVIDE AS A KEY ISSUE OF THE TECHNOPOLIS

As disparities within the technopolis locally and in the information society nationally became apparent in the 1990s, what were the responses of national, state, and local authorities? We observe how the city undertook providing access and training to digital technologies in Austin. As city, nonprofit, state, and university initiatives attempted to directly affect the development of providing access and building human capital in education and training, were there substantial widespread benefits? How did those change over time?

Initially, both the national government under the Clinton administration and the Texas state government started programs to provide more access to excluded groups and, in some cases, training in how to use the technologies as well. The federal government started several programs in school, library, and community center access and job training. The state government started an innovative program called the Texas Infrastructure Fund. Austin also initiated several local programs. (Chapter 5 examines these programs in some detail.)

Local organizations actively sought federal and state (Texas) funds.

In fact, Austin came to be seen by a number of experts as one of the most innovative sites in the country in terms of programs aimed at increasing what came to be referred to as "digital inclusion." There were very strong Austin programs to provide public access that stood out as models nationwide, as documented by John Horrigan and colleagues (2001) and Lisa Servon (1999). There were strong programs early on, by the mid-1990s, in public libraries and some community centers. The team of scholars involved in this book began to systematically examine what had been done in Austin to increase digital inclusion. That is covered in more detail in Chapters 6 and 7.

STRUCTURING ACCESS

We were very interested in how institutions like libraries were restructured to deal with new roles and tasks as part of the response to the digital divide. Along with the perspectives on de Certeau's ideas about planning and structuring cities from above and below (discussed earlier), we used Giddens's (1984) structuration theory to guide examination of processes by which the connectivity gap is created and perpetuated in the larger political and economic sphere. Giddens offers several useful concepts that help with macro- and microanalysis of how specific policies and institutions might unwittingly contribute to structuring aspects of the digital divide. He sees rules as constraints on, and resources as opportunities for, social actors.

One of the first responses in Austin and in most U.S. cities was to turn to city libraries as the primary sites of public access. Initially, the City of Austin and the public libraries formed a partnership with the Austin Free-Net (AFN), a nonprofit organization that provided the connections (with city, state, and federal funding) and did most of the training. The Austin model, as some referred to it in the 1990s, was somewhat more expansive than the focus on libraries that eventually took place in most American towns and cities. AFN also worked with a variety of other community centers, housing projects, job-training centers, and other organizations to try to reach people who did not necessarily go to libraries. One of the first studies that the team involved with this book did in 1999 was to observe who went to libraries to use public access computers. We wondered whether the libraries were structured to meet the needs of the poorest users and began to realize that many people, including some specific groups, like minority teenage boys, did not find them friendly.

We also interviewed librarians and other public access operators in 1999, 2003, and 2009 to see how their programs and ideas were developing.

In 2003, at the peak of these efforts, we found there were over forty programs in East and South Austin that worked with disadvantaged groups, from racial minorities to the poor and unemployed to those with physical disabilities, to help them access and learn how to use computers and the Internet. The range and background of those programs is described in Chapters 6 and 7, while Chapter 4 examines one of the training and work-oriented programs in the context of how skill requirements for workers developed in Austin as it turned into a technopolis.

From the 1990s on, many skeptics began to comment on such government interventions; several even viewed the idea of specific new digital inequities as insignificant, likely to pass quickly as most people gained at least some access to new digital technologies, at school, work, or public libraries (Compaine 2001). That skeptical approach has become policy for the U.S. government after 2000 and for many states, including Texas, more recently. Many of the public access programs in Austin were funded by U.S. federal and Texas state programs. They were gradually shut down between 2001 and 2003, which began to limit what the Austin-based programs could do. As federal and state funds began to be withdrawn, because of ideological changes in both federal and state policy, the City of Austin concentrated on public access in its public libraries, which it had its own funds to support. Fortunately, the city's efforts were supplemented by a series of timely grants from the Dell Foundation, which gave computers for online catalogs and access stations, then funding for Wired for Youth centers, and most recently laptops for a library-based laptop-checkout program called Connected Youth.

As the issue of subsidizing public access was debated and programs eliminated, other scholars pointed out that physical access to computer and Internet hardware was no longer the primary issue, and perhaps never had been. Jan Van Dijk (2005) pointed out that as the divide between those who do and do not have physical access gets smaller, the divide between those who do and do not know how to use the technology to their own advantage actually grows deeper, with perhaps more severe implications for lasting social stratification. In Austin, it seems that educational divides, income divides, and geographic separation or segregation (by income and race) may actually be growing as the city transforms itself into a technopolis. For example, we began to discover that although local efforts as well as federal, state, and local financing had created a number of access points, many of the poorest, least advantaged people were not using them. We therefore studied several kinds of public access centers and training programs, as well as the recent focus on wireless access, to see what reasons existed for many of those in need not using public access (see Chapters 6–9).

By 2004–2005, we began to discover that much of the enthusiasm that had once existed for providing access to digital resources, particularly computers and the Internet, in libraries and other public centers was being refocused on providing wireless access around Austin. In Chapter 8, Martha Fuentes-Bautista and Nobuya Inagaki examine that shift of policy attention and resources to wireless access by the City of Austin and many of the nonprofit actors involved in digital inclusion. They also map out where public free wireless was available, as of 2007, and show that it was concentrated heavily in West Austin, and that almost the only providers in the minority areas of East Austin were, once again, the public libraries.

One of the key issues touched on in both Chapters 5 and 8 is how technologies spread—how they influence people and their work or education, but also how technologies are shaped by society and by individuals. Chapter 5 takes a critical look at what is often referred to as the diffusion of innovations (Rogers 1983). In that view, technologies tend to be pushed outward into society by business or government, but are ultimately adopted and used by individuals, who decide when and how to start using them. While accurate in many ways as a description of the process, that analysis has two problems. One is that it places responsibility for learning about technology with the individual, which means that the digital divide or related issues can be seen as the fault of people too lazy or ignorant to take up what is obviously good for them. That ignores many of the problems we have discussed so far, such as structural problems like segregation or widespread, nonvolitional problems like the lack of techno-capital in many neighborhoods and among many specific groups. The other major problem with the diffusion analysis is that it makes the process seem inevitable if one waits long enough, ignoring all the increased stratification and lost access to resources that some groups may have to endure in the meantime as they wait for technology to trickle down to them (Shingi and Mody 1976).

However, as explored in Chapter 5, several authors and officials, including some behind the framing of U.S. policy after 2000, thought that it was not up to policy to address problems in the diffusion of innovation (Compaine 2001), and cut back the resources that had been put into place previously: "On Feb. 6, 2001, Federal Communications Commission Chairman Michael Powell commented on the digital divide by giving the comparison of owning a computer to owning a luxury car. 'I think there is a Mercedes divide,' he said. 'I would like to have one, but I can't afford one'" (Clewley 2001). Clearly in that era, policy makers did not see computers, Internet access, or the education and training necessary to use them as economically or socially important, or as likely to contribute to social stratification in a way that required policy address.

HOW PEOPLE USE AND CONSTRUCT COMPUTERS AND THE INTERNET IN AUSTIN

Besides looking at the structures providing wired and wireless access, as well as training, we started looking more directly at the reaction of the intended users of these services. Since Austin is a best-case scenario for public access to and education in the use of computers and the Internet, we also had an opportunity to see what problems remained even when the city, state, and various nonprofit groups had created a variety of programs for digital inclusion.

Our first initiative in this area was to interview ninth grade students and their parents at Johnston High School in 1999–2000 to see how students and families at one of Austin's poorest and most resource-deprived high schools were using or not using the new digital tools and what they thought of computers and the Internet. We found that very few of the children or parents used computers or the Internet much, although several of the parents did think such use was important for their children's education.

One of the ways we came to understand that lack of usage by some was in terms of the need to help them build capacities and cultural capital. Many people we interviewed then and later did not have much understanding of the information or digital economy and how it was evolving. However, one of our studies also showed that many poor people who went through training still did not find jobs in this area because of the limited number of entry-level positions available and the broad array of skills, education, and cultural capital required, beyond computer skills, for such jobs. But trainees did learn valuable cultural capital regarding how to employ information and communication technologies in their personal lives or sometimes in the jobs they did have (see Chapter 4).

We returned again to interview people about these issues in 2004–2009. In 2004, we interviewed both majority and minority (African American and Latino) people in Central, East, and South Austin to see what kinds of differences persisted. In 2005, we interviewed more people in these groups in Austin but focused on trying to interview two or three generations of the same families, to see how generations were changing and how much impact family patterns of using media and new media had on the different generations. We found in both years that the same patterns we had seen in 1999–2000 tended to persist. In 2006, we interviewed recent immigrants to Austin, since it was clear that among those who we interviewed in 2004–2005, many suffering the worst divides in access, cultural capital, competencies, and knowledge about how to use information technologies to their own benefit were recent immigrants. In 2009, we did a more in-depth examination of generational differences among three-generation families, comparing Latino, black, white, and Asian populations.

CONCLUSION

This introduction lays out the theoretical schema of the book, introduces the most important historical themes and issues, discusses how we studied them in 1999–2009, and shows how different chapters tie into the overall argument and analysis. The overall theme, guided by theoretical perspectives from de Certeau (1984) and Giddens (1984), examines how the city was structured first as a small, segregated political capital and university town, then restructured by a new generation of planners as a technopolis, building on the capabilities of the university and the determination of national and local authorities to retake the initiative (from Japan) in computer and related technologies. In defining the city as a technopolis, planners defined a new field of work, education, and competition for resources focused on technology and related education and skills. To examine what we call the techno-field of Austin, we invoke a layer of theory by Bourdieu (1984), which looks at fields as social spaces where new occupations, new degrees and study programs, new social programs, institutions, and related funding all get redefined by nations, states, and cities in ways that also define and redefine life in Austin, both for those in the new technology economy and those who serve it in other ways. People in the techno-field struggle for cultural capital, which we call techno-capital, that enables them to compete in the new field. They form dispositions to thought and action (or inaction), which makes them more or less competitive. Those dispositions group together among similar people to form what seem like class dispositions, which Bourdieu calls the habitus. As we studied these processes over time in the city, we used mapping protocols and ideas based on González (1986), as well as his ideas on examining social processes via multigenerational interviewing.

Chapter 2 by Spence, Straubhaar, Tufekci, Cho, and Graber takes up the story begun here. It focuses on the early history of Austin, before the city focused on the new digital industries and becoming a technopolis. It focuses on the initial crucial structuring of the city by its planners as a segregated city and the lasting consequences that flowed from that top-down decision. It examines how the structure of housing and education evolved in Austin from the late 1800s. It particularly looks at how segregation in both education and housing, most specifically implanted in the 1928 zoning plan, affected Austin's subsequent efforts to develop an economy that required a very educated workforce, a theme also discussed in Chapter 3 by Hartenberger, Tufekci, and Davis. Using maps created for this study, Chapter 2 shows graphically how the changes of 1928 radically shifted the population around, damaging the educational system for Austin's African American and Hispanic minorities in a way that could not really be undone by desegregation when it began fitfully in the 1950s–1970s.

After that, Chapter 3 discusses the structuring of Austin as a technopolis, and Chapter 4 by Tufekci examines the unintended consequences, especially for work and education, of that shift. In the process, we examine and critique the theories of work and education associated with the information society by Bell (1973) and others, as well as beginning to examine some of Austin's specific efforts to address those issues with technological-skills training. These efforts have begun to constitute a new layer of restructuring, under the name of addressing the digital divide, that responds to some of the new inequalities created by the American information society in general and by the specific form of the technopolis in Austin. The question of the digital divide, how to define it in both academic and policy terms, and how to address it in both policy and programmatic terms by U.S. federal authorities is examined in Chapter 5 by Lenert, Christensen, Tufekci, and Gustafson.

Chapters 6–10 address much more specifically the bottom-up response by city authorities, schools, and nonprofits to the social problems of the technopolis, defined in the 1990s as a digital divide, and also address many other related issues. The focus on the digital divide began to change to a focus on digitally related inequalities (DiMaggio et al. 2004), which had other (often deeper) roots and implications. So the main programs described in Chapter 6 by Cunningham, Custard, Straubhaar, Spence, Graber, and Letalien as responses to the digital divide shifted somewhat after 2000, in part because of policy and resource changes. To create more locally sustainable programs in computer and Internet access, capability building, and training, the City of Austin refocused on its own libraries, as noted in Chapter 7 by Lentz, Straubhaar, Dixon, Graber, Spence, Letalien, and LaPastina, while local nonprofits like AFN, senior centers, public housing centers, and church programs managed to hang on. As Fuentes-Bautista and Inagaki show in Chapter 8, city and local activist attention shifted somewhat as the field of access to the Internet was redefined with a new focus on creating wireless access (Wi-Fi), which is of much more use to creative professionals and students with laptops than to the poorer, minority-centered clientele of the public access programs at libraries and centers.

Chapter 9 by Rojas, Straubhaar, Spence, Roychowdhury, Okur, Piñon, and Fuentes-Bautista returns to the Bourdieu-related perspective on how people in Austin navigated the new, rapidly emerging and changing field of technology and the related field of education. This chapter elaborates and develops our own ideas about techno-field, techno-disposition, and techno-habitus. Comparing 1999 with 2009, we found that techno-dispositions and group techno-habitus were changing rapidly. Many minority youth who might have been wary of computers in 1999 were caught up in the youth generation's turn to digital technologies by 2009, even though they still lacked much of the techno-capital that many more-advantaged youth had.

Finally, Chapter 10 by Straubhaar draws conclusions about what the history of the technopolis has to tell both those who live there and those who are interested in understanding the larger global phenomenon it represents. It also examines some of our key theories to determine how useful they have been in our quest to understand the various structurings, restructurings, and responses from below by the key actors and agents in the city's history.

NOTES

1. For Bourdieu, practices are the strategies agents use to play in different fields, such as the techno-field. Perception, awareness, and desires form part of the habitus that is a cognitive and motivational structure. Starting from simple indicators, we build a definition of *techno-disposition*, which inasmuch as it is widely shared across the group, constitutes a class habitus.

REFERENCES

Badenhausen, K. (2005). Best places for business and careers. *Forbes.com*. Retrieved May 5, 2005, from http://www.forbes.com/bestplaces/.

Bell, D. (1973). *The coming of post-industrial society: A venture in social forecasting*. New York: Basic Books.

Bertaux, D. (Ed.). (1981). *Biography and society: The life history approach in the social sciences*. Beverly Hills, CA: Sage.

Bertaux, D., and P. Thompson. (1997). *Pathways to social class*. Oxford: Clarendon Press.

Bishop, B. (2000). In tech era, cities setting the pace for prosperity. *Austin American-Statesman*, February 20.

Bourdieu, P. (1980). *The logic of practice*. Trans. Richard Nice. Stanford, CA: Stanford University Press.

———. (1984). *Distinction: A social critique of the judgement of taste*. Cambridge, MA: Harvard University Press.

———. (1985). The forms of capital. In J. G. Richardson (Ed.), *Handbook of theory and research for the sociology of education*, pp. 241–258. New York: Greenwood Press.

———. (1993a). *The field of cultural production*. New York: Columbia University Press.

———. (1993b). *Sociology in question*. London: Sage.

Brubaker, R. (1993). Social theory as habitus. In C. Calhoun, E. LiPuma, and M. Postone (Eds.), *Bourdieu: Critical perspectives*, pp. 212–234. Cambridge, UK: Polity Press.

Cardella, R. A. (1999). The Austin computer software industry: An engine for economic development. University of Texas at Austin.

Castells, M. (1996). The information economy and the process of globalization. In *The rise of the network society*, pp. 92–147. Malden, MA: Blackwell.

Clewley, R. (2001). I have a (digital) dream. *Wired*, April 27.

Compaine, B. M. (Ed.). (2001). *The digital divide: Facing a crisis or creating a myth?* Cambridge, MA: MIT Press.

Day, J. C., and E. C. Newburger. (2002). The big payoff: Educational attainment and synthetic estimates of work-life earnings. *Current population reports*. Washington, DC: U.S. Census Bureau.

de Certeau, M. (1984). *The practices of everyday life.* Berkeley: University of California Press.

DiMaggio, P., et al. (2004). Digital inequality: From unequal access to differentiated use. In K. Neckerman (Ed.), *Social inequality.* New York: Russell Sage Foundation.

Florida, R. (2002). *The rise of the creative class: And how it's transforming work, leisure, community and everyday life.* New York: Basic Books.

Garnham, N. (1986). Extended review: Bourdieu's *Distinction. Sociological Review* 34(2): 423–433.

Giddens, A. (1984). *The constitution of society: Outline of a theory of structuration.* Berkeley: University of California Press.

González, J. (1986). Y todo queda entre familia. *Revista Estudios Sobre las Culturas Contemporáneas* 1(1): 135–154.

———. (1994). La transformación de las ofertas culturales y sus públicos en México. *Revista Estudios Sobre las Culturas Contemporáneas* 6(18): 9–25.

———. (1995). Coordenadas del imaginario. *Revista Estudios Sobre las Culturas Contemporáneas,* Época II I(2).

Henson, S. (1991). The technopolis and you: On the role of research universities. *UT Watch—Polemicist* 2(5): 12–13.

Hoffman, D. L., and T. P. Novak. (1998). Bridging the digital divide: The impact of race on computer access and internet use. Retrieved July 21, 2006, from http://www.eric.ed.gov/ERICWebPortal/contentdelivery/servlet/ERICServlet ?accno=ED421563.

Horrigan, J. B., et al. (2001). *Cities online: Urban development and the Internet.* Washington, DC: Progress and Freedom Foundation/Pew Internet Project.

Hotz, R. L. (1998). Blacks get less access to Internet, study finds: When education, income equal, whites still surf web more. *Austin American-Statesman,* April 17.

Humphrey, D. (1997). Austin: A history of the capital city. Texas State Historical Association, Austin.

Irving, L. (1998). Refocusing our youth: From high tops to high-tech. Remarks at the National Urban League and the National Leadership Council on Civil Rights Urban Technology Summit, June 26, 1998. Retrieved from ntia.doc.gov/ ntiahome/speeches/urban62698.

———. (1999). Falling through the Net: Defining the digital divide. National Telecommunications and Information Administration. Retrieved from ntia.doc. gov/ntiahome/fttn99/introduction.html.

Johnson, R. (1993). Editor's introduction. In P. Bourdieu, *The field of cultural production,* pp. 1–25. New York: Columbia University Press.

Kvasny, L. (2005). The role of the habitus in shaping discourses about the digital divide. *Journal of Computer-Mediated Communication* (10)2. Retrieved from http://jcmc.indiana.edu/vol10/issue2/kvasny.html.

Lentz, R. G. (2000). The e-volution of the digital divide: A mayhem of competing metrics. *Info* 2(4): 355–377.

Orum, A. (2002). *Power, money and the people: The making of modern Austin.* Austin: Resource Publications.

Robbins, P. (2003). Environmental business—Introduction. Austin, TX, Sierra Club, Lone Star Chapter. Retrieved from www.texas.sierraclub.org.

Rogers, E. (1983). *Diffusion of innovations*, 3rd ed. New York: Free Press.

Servon, L. (1999). Case study: Austin, Texas. Center for Urban Policy Research.

Shingi, P. M., and B. Mody. (1976). The communication effects gap: A field experiment on television and agricultural ignorance in India. *Communication Research* 3(2): 171–190.

Smilor, R. W., D. V. Gibson, and G. Kozmetsky. (1988). Creating the technopolis: High-technology development in Austin, Texas. University of Texas at Austin.

Texas Workforce Commission. (2009). 2009 Annual report, Texas Workforce Solutions. Retrieved from www.twc.state.tx.us/news/ar09.pdf.

Van Dijk, J. (2005). *The deepening divide*. Thousand Oaks, CA: Sage.

Webster, F., and Robins, K. (1986). *Information technology: A luddite analysis*. Norwood, NJ: Ablex.

JEREMIAH SPENCE

JOSEPH
STRAUBHAAR

ZEYNEP TUFEKCI

ALEXANDER CHO

DEAN GRABER

CHAPTER 2

STRUCTURING RACE IN THE CULTURAL GEOGRAPHY OF AUSTIN

The formation of Austin, Texas, as a technopolis has built upon a complex and frequently overlooked history of purposeful racial structuration of the city in the early twentieth century (Giddens 1984; Cohen 1989). Austin's history of top-down (de Certeau 1984) planned development is not limited to its plans to attract high-technology industries. Until roughly the mid- to late 1970s, Austin took steps to maintain racial segregation in the face of an expanding legal environment of civil rights. Despite an outside, top-down attempt by the federal government to restructure educational segregation via mandated school closings and busing, and legal challenges to real estate transaction rules favoring white owners, segregation seems to have become self-perpetuating. Segregation, as a crucial feature of the background environment in which a high-tech development strategy was implemented, has played a strong role in constraining the possible outcomes of this development, particularly for the acquisition through education of critical cultural, economic, and techno-capitals (Bourdieu 1984).

The picture of Austin as burgeoning technopolis in the final decades of the twentieth century is not complete without attention to the structuring effects of de facto and de jure segregation in Central Austin over the past ninety years. Despite Supreme Court rulings explicitly outlawing segregation and civil rights laws designed to encourage integration, some of Austin's civic leaders spent the better part of the twentieth century, up until the 1970s, engineering an explicit scheme of racial segregation—one that has had a tenacious hold on the city to this day. It is across this landscape that Austin's tech economy was mapped out, and with predictable results. Lower-performing schools are located still in predominantly minority neighborhoods, the tech industry's dirty by-products pollute minority neighborhoods disproportionately, and minorities with lower skill sets end up occupying the tech industry's low-skill and low-paying factory jobs, or even lower-paying service jobs (see Chapter 4).

To some degree, the history of segregation in Austin reflects larger trends in the United States, particularly in the South. In 1885, Austin citizens organized an "Anti-Colored Movement" to push out the last black city council member (Humphrey 1977), who had come in with Reconstruction after the Civil War. This echoes political movements in other southern states to reverse black political representation achieved under Reconstruction. Measures varied somewhat across the South, but included efforts to restrict black voting, remove any remaining black office holders, and begin to segregate housing, restaurants, and public services. Housing segregation ordinances grew across the South after 1910, despite rulings against them, including a Supreme Court ruling in 1927 (Myrdal 1944). Residential segregation in Austin accelerated, as it did across the South, from 1880 to 1930, through deed restrictions, selective advertising, and the 1928 city plan that created an East Austin "negro district" (Koch & Fowler 1928).

This chapter maps out where people lived, focusing on the racial and ethnic groups that have been most deprived of access to information, educational, cultural, and media resources. Starting in 1875 and going through the 1970s, we examine, first, where African Americans and Latinos were located prior to overt segregation efforts in the mid-1920s; second, the results of the initiatives to segregate Austin during 1935 to 1954, as indicated in the 1940 household maps; third, the efforts both juridical and communal to integrate both neighborhoods and schools in Austin, as indicated in the 1970 household maps and the school integration tables; and, finally, how these findings provide a baseline showing how residential and educational segregation, as well as the deliberate segregation of resources, set the stage for the cultural geography of information, educational, cultural, and media resources in the development of Austin. This analysis provides a framework for understanding how the cultural geography of information was structured by the cultural geography of race and ethnicity in Austin, and more specifically how systemic, historical inequality contributed to the structuring of the technopolis, as explored in the other chapters of this book.

MAPPING EDUCATION AND STRUCTURED SPACE

This study builds on the theoretical and methodological framework of cultural practices and cultural fields (Galindo 1994; González 1986, 1991, 1995a, 1995b, 1997, 2000; Maass and González 2005), which examines the household within a social space. The space is a conceptual frame for a whole that contains multiple subsystems (work, cultural legitimacy, education, health, religion, media, entertainment, resources and restaurants, etc.), each with their own rule sets and rhythms that must be navigated by each person in a household and the household as a whole (González 1997, 139). Once an individual has gathered sufficient cultural, economic, or social resources, which can be seen as capital (Bourdieu 1984), he or she may transmit those resources to another member of the household.

Cultural resources are broken down into six cultural fields (religion, education, health, art, media, and leisure) that provide a base for understanding the availability of cultural resources. These fields function as areas of struggle to acquire or use capital, such as social, economic, cultural, or technological (Bourdieu 1984). Cultural fields are examined within a set geographic space or community, through interviews with members and historical mapping of the spaces of those fields. A multidimensional map of cultural resources is formed utilizing three methodological tools. First are cultural cartographies, which map the current and past cultural resources in the set geographical space to form a time-series map of cultural resources that are broken down into the six cultural fields categories (González 1995b). Second are family histories, which are gathered in the form of in-depth interviews with several members of a family, ideally across three generations to explore cultural practices, or cultural genealogies, which are visual representations of family histories using a genogram visualization technique (González 1995a), and life histories, which are gathered in the form of an in-depth interview with a community member to explore cultural practices and trends in accessing cultural resources (Galindo 1994). Third is a survey about cultural habits and practices (González and Chávez 1996). Jorge González summarized this as the FOCYP (Formation of Capitals and Publics) method. While the FOCYP project has media and cultural institution use across generations at the core of both the theoretical and methodological frameworks, this chapter has the relationship between education as a cultural resource and the construction of spatial frames along racial and ethnic lines as its major focus. The family history element of the methodology is explored in Chapter 9. More specifically Chapter 9 uses life histories to explore how people have understood and used information and communication technologies. (The cultural habits survey element is just now being completed. All three elements will be integrated in subsequent work to come.)

An extension of this analysis is to consider the impact of the relationship between both segregation and subsequent integration of the cultural field of education and the structural racial space on the transmission, or lack thereof, of social, economic, and cultural capital (Bourdieu 1984). The engineered, purposeful, and persistent inequality in the distribution of wealth in the Austin area can be viewed as a textbook example of the "possessive investment in whiteness" (Lipsitz 2006). This thesis, which relies on the dual premises of the purposeful guarding of white privilege for its monetary entitlements and the safeguarding of the transfer of this wealth across generations, can explain why segregation has such a lasting effect in Austin.

George Lipsitz observes, "The appreciated value of owner-occupied homes constitutes the single greatest source of wealth for white Americans" (2006, 33). By including discrimination in the 1928 city plan, in spite of a direct federal mandate to the contrary, Austin's white elite did everything they could to preserve their real wealth in terms of real estate by reinforcing the segregation of minorities to less-desirable property. Many of the earliest African American settlements in Austin were located on the edges of creeks, such as Wheatsville, in low-lying lands, such as Clarksville, or on bluffs and hilltops, such as Pleasant Hill or Gregorytown. For example, as Jennifer Ross (2003) explains, it was precisely the lack of desirability of the Clarksville land that allowed the community to continue intact in West Austin through the 1960s.

Legal scholar Cheryl Harris (1995) asserts that whiteness can be thought of as property itself, including rights of possession, use, transfer, and enjoyment, and the right to exclude others. By asserting their property rights in this manner, Austin's white city framers structured a built-in advantage into the fabric of the city. This real advantage in terms of economic capital can be traced across generations, and although Austin's minority youth today may manage to enroll in a higher-performing school and access better jobs through the accumulation of social, technological, and cultural capitals, they still have to contend with the fact that, on average nationally, white people will inherit seven times more money than blacks (Shapiro 2005), making it that much easier for their white classmates to secure high-barrier-to-entry creative-class jobs or continue on to postsecondary education.

MAPPING RESOURCES OVER TIME

González recommends mapping out resources for people by key years that reflect times before and after major changes in local or national history that affected those resources and the numbers, types, and locations of people who were trying to access and use them. Researchers from both the media studies and Mexican American studies departments at the University of Texas first examined this issue in 2002–2003 with the help of González, who provided a series of seminars to outline his methodology. The researchers subsequently assisted in the initiation of an Austin-based project, which resulted in several chapters in this book. We decided to look at the following years:

- 1910—Before 1910, Austin was a small state capital with a population of white Texans who had settled there because of the capital. They brought African American slaves with them. There was no prior Mexican American or Hispanic settlement before Austin was created to be a capital city, unlike San Antonio or other cities that were created before the white Texan settlers came. In 1910, the population was concentrated in what is now the center of town and included white Texans; African Americans, who lived near where they worked; and a few Mexican Americans, drawn by work, who lived in less desirable flood plain areas near the Colorado River and Waller Creek.
- 1940—From 1910 through the 1920s African Americans lived throughout the city center with a concentration along the eastern side of downtown, while Mexican American households were concentrated in a neighborhood in the southwest of downtown. While some Mexican American households remained downtown through the 1940s, most Mexican American families arriving in Austin moved into the Latino neighborhood east of downtown—just south of the African American neighborhood—between current-day East 10th Street and Cesar Chavez Street, and later down to the Colorado River banks.

- 1970—The results of the struggles for integration were slow to be seen for the African American community. This is indicated by the limited migration of African American households out of the traditional neighborhood. Mexican American neighborhoods, by contrast, grew rapidly outside of the East Austin neighborhood.

- 1990—Between 1970 and 1990, Austin's economy was transformed by the growth of high-technology industries, which expanded as the historical population of Austin grew rapidly and added all levels of skill and income to the workforce. However, there was a noteworthy lack of parallel social and economic mobility among the poorest of the African American and Latino communities remaining in the East Austin neighborhoods. While the Latino community of Austin grew throughout the city, a significant number of African American households, especially the poorest and least educated, remained in the East Austin neighborhood.

- 2000—When this study began in the early 2000s, Austin had expanded exponentially by most measures. The technology-oriented economy was the predominant sector in manufacturing, production, and sales in Austin at a time when Austin was considered to be one of the premier cities in the United States in terms of access to and use of information technology, as a transformative tool both for developing the city and for responding to the social challenges facing Austin. Austin was seen as one of the nation's most wired cities. In addition to efforts to improve schooling and other resources in Austin, the 1990s saw a marked effort by the city, the schools, and a number of nonprofit organizations to extend public access to, and education and training in, new media technologies. Several chapters in this book examine major parts of that effort and how successful they were.

THE EARLY HISTORY OF AUSTIN

The history of race in Austin is a complex and frequently ugly picture, reflecting the prevailing trends in race relations in the southern states associated with the Confederacy during the U.S. Civil War and with the most virulent racism and racist public policy. Throughout the South, Jim Crow laws were used to create, maintain, and reinforce segregation following the end of Reconstruction in 1877 (Briseno 1999; Schott 2000). As de jure segregation became harder and harder to defend in courts and to practice, many cities in the South adopted laws, policies, ordinances, and customs that were designed to result in de facto segregation, thus circumventing legal restrictions (Schott 2000).

Austin was a small frontier town from the early days of its founding by Judge Waller at the behest of the leaders of the Republic of Texas until the 1890s. At the end of the Civil War, a large population of freed slaves migrated from rural areas to regional centers in Texas, such as Dallas, Fort Worth, Waco, Corsicana, Tyler, Beaumont, Houston, and Galveston.

From 1875 to 1910 the population of Austin grew rapidly as the state government of Texas grew in size and the University of Texas expanded its presence in the city. Austin also began to develop its own economic base. This economic growth was complemented by a significant influx of immigrants from Germany, Mexico, and Sweden in addition to the arrival of several Jewish and Lebanese families. There was also a notable increase in African Americans in Austin and the surrounding communities during this period, and by 1900 there were 7,478 African Americans living in and around Austin (Manaster 1986) (Figures 2.1, 2.2).

Throughout the period from 1875 to 1910, there was a certain "natural" segregation, or more precisely an aggregation of ethnic groups into their own neighborhoods. African Americans arriving in Austin tended to settle in existing neighborhoods, and Mexican Americans tended to settle in the "Old Mexico" neighborhood in the southwestern part of town, what is now the "Warehouse District."

African Americans, particularly those who did not live near their places of work, tended to settle on the cheapest land in the city along the banks of Waller Creek and Shoal Creek, or in one of the freedmen communities on the periphery of Austin. Between 1880 and 1910 nine distinct communities, eight of which had their own community schools, could be identified: Wheatsville, Clarksville, West Austin, Red River, South Austin, Robertson Hill, Pleasant Hill, Masontown, and Gregorytown (Mears 2009). Residents either commuted into town by foot, horse, or carriage or worked on farms near their communities (Figure 2.1).

The decade of 1910 to 1920 signified a major period of transition for Austin, with a rapidly growing population, an expanding economy, and a major investment in infrastructure. The completion of the Tom Miller Dam and Longhorn Dam effectively guaranteed the stability of the city, protecting it from major floods and providing drink-

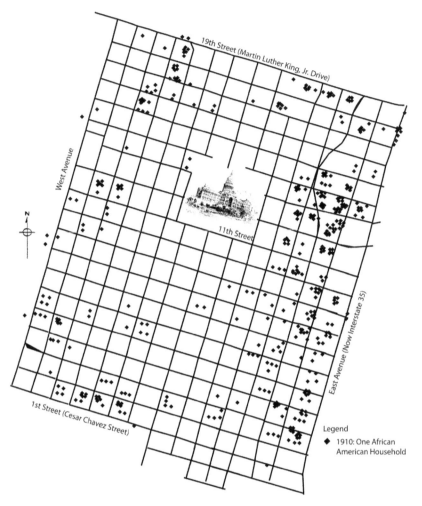

Figure 2.1. African American freed-slave communities in Austin, 1880–1910 (map drawn by Jeremiah Spence, 2011; data from numerous sources, including Mears 2009; capitol image from Lossing 1912)

ing water and irrigation (Orum 1987). Additionally, the completion of the Congress Avenue Bridge cemented the connection to the southern bank of the Colorado River and signaled the expansion of Austin southward.

A side effect of the dam completion was an increase in the value of the Warehouse District land, which at that time was home to more than one hundred Mexican families. The increasing value of the

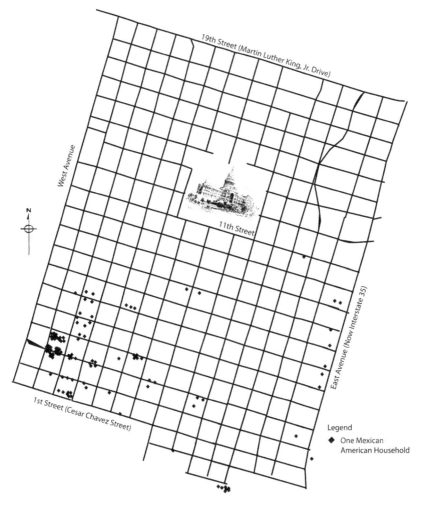

Figure 2.2. Mexican American households in Central Austin, 1910 (map drawn by Jeremiah Spence, 2011; data from Manaster 1986; capitol image from Lossing 1912; capitol image from Lossing 1912)

Warehouse District land, no longer subject to flooding, and the availability of land that didn't flood past the eastern limits of the city led to the relocation of the Mexican population from the Warehouse District to land beyond the eastern edge of the city, south of the primary area of African American settlement. This relocation was further encouraged by the relocation of community resources such as the Our Lady of Guadalupe Catholic Church and a community school, and by

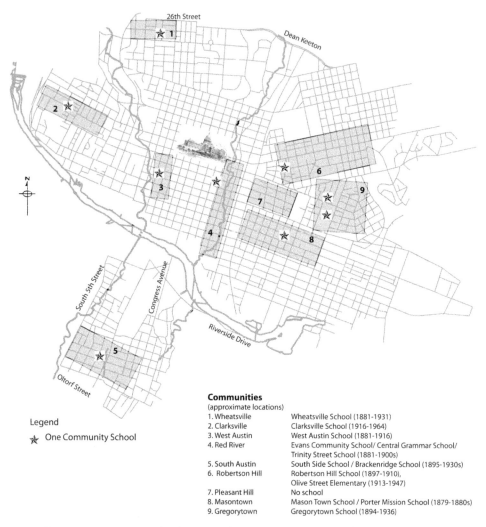

Figure 2.3. Community schools in Central Austin, 1910 (map drawn by Jeremiah Spence, 2011; data from Manaster 1986; capitol image from Lossing 1912)

more restrictive city ordinances (Connell 1925; Hamilton 1913; Humphrey 1997; Manaster 1986).

STRUCTURED SEGREGATION, 1920S–1950S

During the years 1910 to 1920, institutionalized racism and the oppressive Jim Crow laws, originally developed in the 1870s and 1880s (Briseno 1999; Schott 2000), were reexamined and reinforced by policy makers throughout the United States and especially the South. Repeatedly the Supreme Court handed down decisions prohibiting specific forms of institutionalized racism, such as in the case of *Buchanan v. Warley* (1917). Notably, throughout the United States, racist policies, while specifically targeted at the African American population, were also peripherally applied to other minority groups, including Hispanics, Native Americans, Asians, and at times Jews.

As the African American population was naturally migrating toward East Austin, the existing white households, businesses, and churches changed hands from white to African American owners. This created a great deal of resentment throughout the region and in February 1927 resulted, in part, in the Texas legislature passing a law providing Texas cities with the power to create their own ordinances to "foster the separation of white and Negro in the interest of peace, safety, and welfare" (McDonald 1993, 235; Ross 2003, 21–22). This law was later overturned by the Texas Court of Appeals, which prompted the City of Austin's planning commission to contract a consulting firm, Koch & Fowler, to develop a master plan for the city. The purpose of the master plan was to "provide for anticipated growth and serve as a basis for the establishment of policies concerning land use, public works, education, zoning, transportation, and parks and boulevards" (Feagin 1985, 33, cited in Schott 2000, 7). The master plan also included a brief section responding to the concerns of the city officials regarding the reinforcement and expansion of segregation of African Americans from "white Austin" (Koch & Fowler 1928). More specifically, the report identified an existing and developing "negro district," composed of the burgeoning communities of Gregorytown, Masontown, and Robertson Hill, and recommended that all African Americans in Austin be "encouraged" to live there and not elsewhere in the city.

The 1928 zoning plan pushed African Americans into East Austin by denying them access to resources in Central or West Austin and exclusively locating resources like libraries and schools for them there. The Mexican American population had grown considerably as people were pushed north out of Mexico by the Mexican Revolution of 1910–1920 and its aftermath of economic and social dislocation. By the 1940s the Mexican American families living in the "Old Mexico" neighborhood downtown were pushed into East and South Austin after the value of their land increased because of the successful damming of the Colorado River.

Throughout the period, the relationship between segregation laws

Figure 2.4. African American households in Austin, 1940 (map drawn by Jeremiah Spence, 2011; data from numerous sources, including Austin Human Relations Commission 1979; capitol image from Lossing 1912)

and the two groups (African American and Mexican American) was disparate. Whereas African Americans were obliged to move into the African American neighborhood, the Mexican American neighborhood developed in a less structured manner, as the 1940 maps indicate (Figures 2.4 and 2.5).

As the consultants, Koch & Fowler, acknowledged—indeed, lamented—there were no legal means of establishing segregation: "There has been considerable talk in Austin, as well as in other cities, in regard to the race segregation problem. This problem cannot be solved legally under any zoning law known to us at present. Practically all attempts of such have proven unconstitutional" (Koch

Figure 2.5. Mexican American households in Austin, 1940 (map drawn by Jeremiah Spence, 2011; data from numerous sources, including Austin Human Relations Commission 1979; capitol image from Lossing 1912)

& Fowler 1928). Instead, they decided that the best course of action would be to try to make life easier for African American people in one designated zone:

> In our studies of Austin, we have found that Negroes are present in small numbers, in practically all areas of the city excepting the area just east of East Avenue and south of the City Cemetery. This area seems to be all Negro population. It is our recommendation that the nearest approach to the solution of the race segregation problem will be the recommendation of this district as a Negro district, and that all the facilities and conveniences be provided

the Negroes in this district, as an incentive to draw the Negro population to this area. This will eliminate the necessity of white and black schools, white and black parks, and other duplicate facilities for this area. (Koch & Fowler 1928)

Measures implemented to enforce and reinforce geographic segregation included real estate deed restrictions and city ordinances that prohibited African Americans and Mexican Americans from buying or renting homes anywhere in Austin outside of East Austin, as well as denying access to city utilities to African American homes outside this neighborhood. African American institutions were encouraged and provided with permits as long as they were located in East Austin, and discouraged and denied permits if they located elsewhere.

The city also voted to build its housing projects in ways that would reinforce segregation. In the 1930s, three segregated housing projects were built in Austin: one for whites, one for blacks and one for Mexican Americans. In the 1950s, the city council voted to locate a large public housing program in East Austin. When additional units for whites and Hispanics were later built outside East Austin, housing designated for blacks was still located there to further concentrate African Americans in the area. Because these facilities were constructed where ethnic groups were already concentrated, they reinforced segregation (Schott 2000).

Likewise, churches and schools originally serving the African American and Mexican American communities that were located in the western end of the city center were literally moved to the East Austin neighborhood. The relocation of schools will be explored in more detail in the educational segregation section.

By 1940, African American households had been substantially relocated from Central Austin to East Austin (Herrera 1990; University of Texas–BRSS 1941). The African American neighborhood in East Austin came to be seen as an African American ghetto. This lasted until 2000 when city growth, urban development planning, and real estate gentrification began to open the area first to students and then to young, affluent white residents.

AFRICAN AMERICAN AND HISPANIC
HOUSEHOLDS IN AUSTIN, 1940–1970

Although desegregation efforts began in certain fields, such as access to libraries, in Austin in the 1950s, residential segregation had

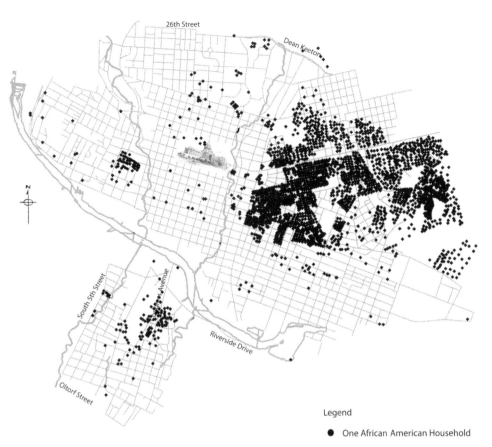

Figure 2.6. African American households in Austin, 1970 (map drawn by Jeremiah Spence, 2011; data from numerous sources, including Austin Human Relations Commission 1979; capitol image from Lossing 1912)

not changed much by 1970. The cultural distance between the African American and Latino communities between East Austin and "white" Austin increased significantly with the destruction of East Avenue and construction of Interstate 35 in the 1960s, which created a permanent concrete barrier between the two communities.

Figure 2.6 shows that the African American population in 1970 continued to be densely concentrated east of Interstate 35 in what were then poor and working-class neighborhoods, mostly in the historically African American community between East 19th Street and East 12th Street, with a few pockets around the northeastern St. John's area and in West Austin including the Clarksville neighborhood. By contrast, Figure 2.7 shows considerable expansion by La-

Figure 2.7. Mexican American households in Austin, 1976 (map drawn by Jeremiah Spence, 2011; data from numerous sources, including Austin Human Relations Commission 1979; capitol image from Lossing 1912)

tinos to many parts of the city, especially to the south and southeast, although the core of the Hispanic community, particularly in terms of churches, shops, and so on, remained in the southern part of East Austin along Cesar Chavez Street (Feagin 1985; Shipman 1978).

SEGREGATED SCHOOLS IN EARLY AUSTIN, 1880S–1950S

The early history of schools in Austin begins with one-room school-houses and quickly expands into small and medium-sized community schools that were mostly exclusively designated for African American (in period documents, Negro or colored), Latino (in period documents, Mexicans or Mexican American), or white children. The geographic distribution of schools in Austin mirrored the distribution of households, as discussed above. Schools were distributed throughout the city, as well as around the periphery of the city. As discussed throughout this chapter, there were notably different historical narratives that created the segregation patterns of African American and Mexican American families. In light of this, this section will examine the history of school segregation between the two groups separately.

African Americans between 1880 and 1910 lived in a number of freedmen communities throughout the Austin area (see Figure 2.3). Most communities featured their own community school (Atkin 1951; Brewer 1940; Jackson 1979; Long 1952; Mears 2001, 2009):

- Wheatsville—The Wheatsville School operated from 1881 until 1931, when the neighborhood no longer had a significant African American population, and the remaining students transferred to E. H. Anderson School in East Austin.
- West Austin—The West Austin School served African American students from 1881 until 1916, when the school board decided that the school should be used for the Mexican American population in the area. All African American students were then transferred to the Clarksville School.
- Clarksville—The Clarksville School operated from 1916 until 1964. In 1964 the school was closed and all students were transferred to Matthews Elementary School during the desegregation process (Ross 2003).
- Red River—The Evans Community School, which became the Central Grammar School and later the Trinity Street School, was open between 1881 and the early 1900s. The school closed as the African American population migrated eastward into the Robertson Hill community.
- South Austin—The South Side School and later the Brackenridge School served the South Austin population from 1895 through the 1930s. Michelle M. Mears (2009) notes that even after 1928 most African Americans south of the river stayed where they were.
- Pleasant Hill—The smallest of the East Austin freedmen communities, Pleasant Hill lacked its own community school and was quickly absorbed into the Robertson Hill neighborhood.
- Gregorytown—This community, which marked the eastern edge of town in the early Austin period, had its own school—the

Gregorytown School (1894–1936)—and was home to the Tillotson College and Normal Institute (1881–1952), which offered junior and senior high courses as well as college preparatory courses to both male and female African American students.

- Masontown—Cut crosswise by the East 5th Street railroad tracks, this community was the industrial district closest to the African American neighborhoods of East Austin and had its own school— the Mason Town School, later known as the Porter Mission School—open briefly between 1879 and the late 1880s.

- Robertson Hill—This neighborhood quickly absorbed the other neighborhoods as the African American population moved into East Austin between 1910 and 1930. It boasted several schools, including the Robertson Hill School (1897–1910), Olive Street Elementary (1913–1947), Samuel Huston College (1878–1952), and the Robertson Hill High School (1889–1907), which went on to become E. H. Anderson High School (1907–1938) and L. C. Anderson High School (1938–1971), before being closed by court order during the desegregation process.

Documentation of Latino schools during this period is much sparser; however, Carol Adams (1997) provides an overview based on what evidence is available (Austin Public Schools 1954; Cromack 1949):

- The first school for the Latinos of Austin was the "First Ward Mexican School," later the Garland School, which was open briefly between 1897 and 1900. The school was located at 2nd and Nueces streets (Barkley 1963).

- The West Austin School (or in some sources the West Avenue School) that previously served the African American community was converted to a school for Mexican American students in 1916 and continued through 1945. Presumably, the West Austin School was closed because of the gradual out-migration of Latinos from the West Austin neighborhood to East and South Austin neighborhoods.

- The East Austin equivalent was the East Avenue School, later named Comal Street School, which was opened in 1923 as a segregated Mexican American community school. All Mexican American students previously attending Palm, Metz, and Bickler were transferred to the Comal Street School.

- The Zavala School opened in 1936 and again all the Mexican American students attending Palm, Metz, Bickler, and Comal

Street schools were transferred to Zavala. Comal Street School was then closed in 1936.

In the 1930s the community schools were by and large closed, and students were transferred to segregated public schools. As the population of Austin, including African Americans and Mexican Americans, doubled between 1930 and 1950, the public school district had to respond in kind with the rapid construction of new schools. The school district decided to maintain the status quo of single-ethnicity schools as new schools were built.

TOWARD AN INTEGRATED SCHOOL DISTRICT, 1954–1972

The movement toward school desegregation in Austin began at the University of Texas. In 1946, Heman Marion Sweatt filed a lawsuit against university president Theophilus Painter and other school officials for denying him admittance into the University of Texas School of Law because he was an African American. He gained admission in 1950 (Keeton 2009). That same year, the Austin city council abolished racial segregation in the central library on Guadalupe Street downtown and the Carver Branch Library ("New Libraries Held Needed" 1951).

Desegregation efforts in K–12 schools officially began in Austin, as elsewhere in the South, with the 1954 Supreme Court decision in *Brown v. Board of Education of Topeka*, which concluded that the institution of separate but equal schools, which had been the norm in Austin for more than seventy years, was unconstitutional. In 1954, the Austin chapter of the NAACP petitioned for the "immediate abolition" of segregation in public schools ("School Desegregation Drive Looms" 1954). The school board then ordered that racial barriers be removed at the city's high schools ("Change Starting at Top" 1955). In 1955, thirteen African American students integrated three of Austin's high schools—seven at Austin High, five at Travis High, and one at McCallum High ("3 High Schools Get 13 Negroes" 1955). Representatives of Austin's African American community were in litigation with the Austin Independent School District (AISD) throughout the 1960s and 1970s seeking full integration of public schools.

Mexican Americans were notably absent from the *Brown* decision that initiated the public-school integration process. As a result, Austin's Mexican American community sued AISD and the Texas Education Agency repeatedly in federal district court in the late 1960s and early 1970s (*United States of America v. Texas Education Agency et al. [Austin Independent School District]*) to have Mexican American segregated schools and school populations included in the integration process.

Integration slowly moved down into lower school levels. In 1957, integration of Austin's junior high schools was proposed but postponed because of overcrowding ("Crowded Schools Delay Junior High Integration" 1957). The sixth grade was partially integrated in 1961 ("500 Negro 6th Graders Can Enter White Schools" 1961). All of grades 1–12 were allowed to desegregate in 1963 ("Grades 1 through 12 Affected in September" 1963). Despite these efforts, almost all schools, including elementary, junior high, and senior high schools, continued to be segregated up through 1970. Notably, there were no schools where African American children and white children were integrated. There were four schools where Latino children were integrated with white children; however, all four were predominately Latino (Ortega Elementary School, Allison Elementary School, Allan Junior High School, and Johnston Senior High School).

In 1967, students at the exclusively African American Anderson High (not the current Anderson High) were given the choice of attending any school. In 1969, all African American students in predominantly African American areas were given the choice of attending any school in AISD. As a researcher at the University of Texas noted in 1998, "Integration during the late fifties and the sixties meant integrating on the terms of white interests. White students were never asked to attend African-American schools and often integration consisted merely of redrawing attendance zones to mix African-American students and Mexican-American students together" (Arriola 1998). That plan of desegregation was considered inadequate later by the U.S. Department of Health, Education, and Welfare, which found that AISD violated the 1964 Civil Rights Act because it had eight predominantly African American schools ("School Hearing Concludes" 1970). AISD proposed to address the issue by upgrading those schools, but one local group pushed for mandatory two-way busing, which would take white students to African American schools as well as enable African American students to go to largely white schools. However, the schools that were considered heavily minority in their makeup in 1970 continued to be on the east side of Austin: "During the 1970–71 school year, there were 8 high schools, 11 junior high schools, and 55 elementary schools in Austin. At that time, 65% of the student population was white, 20% was Mexican-American, and 15% was African-American" (Arriola 1998; Table 2.1).

Table 2.1. Austin Independent School District, Ethnic Composition of High School and Junior High School Students, 1970–1971

Senior High Schools	Total Students	African-American Students as a Percentage of Total	Mexican-American Students as a Percentage of Total	White Students as a Percentage of Total
Anderson	938	98	0.5	1.5
Austin	1378	15	19	66
Crockett	2313	1	6	93
Johnston	1919	32	62	6
Lanier	2300	1	3	96
McCallum	1934	0.1	3.9	96
Reagan	2605	11	2	87
Travis	1297	3	30	67
Total Senior High Students	14684	14	15	71

Junior High Schools	Total Students	African-Americans Students as a Percentage of Total	Mexican-American Students as a Percentage of Total	White Students as a Percentage of Total
Allan	1039	42	54	4
Burnett	1152	0.1	3.9	96
Fulmore	974	3	32	65
Kealing	739	98	1.9	0.4
Lamar	837	0.1	5.9	94
Martin	818	11	83	3
Murchison	838	0	1	99
O'Henry	862	5	10	85
Pearce	1277	13	7	80
Porter	1303	2	8	90
Webb	940	7	13	80
Total Junior High Students	10779	15	19	66

Source: United States of America v. Texas Education Agency et al. (Austin Independent School District), 467 F.2d 848 (United States Court of Appeals, Fifth Circuit, Aug. 2, 1972), http://ftp.resource.org/courts.gov/c/F2/467/467.F2d.848.71-2508.html#fn19, derived from Defendants Exhibit No. 23

One of the consistent problems was that Austin officials denied that any segregation existed for Mexican American students. In fact, the city classified Mexican Americans as white, which meant that schools consisting of Mexican American and African American students could be considered already integrated (Arriola 1998). The number of schools in East Austin expanded to serve the growing population there, but the facilities and educational programs in those schools were widely considered inferior to those offered to the largely white populations in Central, West, and Northwest Austin.

During the 1970s a strong push to desegregate Austin schools was made, under federal court order, after initial efforts to let African American students attend other schools (noted above) were considered inadequate, since a number of schools remained predominantly African American in population. Federal courts ordered the closing of two predominantly African American schools: Anderson High and Kealing Junior High School (Table 2.2). Court-ordered two-way busing began in 1971. In a study (Wells et al. 2009) of desegregated schools in six U.S. cities, including Austin, researchers found that traditionally black and Hispanic schools were the first to be closed when school systems were required to comply with desegregation orders.

From the perspective of African American leaders, the closure of Anderson High School in East Austin (1971) and the opening of a "new" Anderson High School (1973) in mostly white northwestern Austin was particularly insulting and reinforced the idea that schools in black neighborhoods were inferior. Researchers (Wells et al. 2009) found that white officials and parents clearly gave little thought to the symbolic meaning of the failed effort to desegregate Anderson High School, which was the black community's pride and joy. Anderson's East Austin supporters had hoped the school's traditions as an all-black school would be honored but were disappointed to learn that memories such as plaques and sports trophies from the East Austin school were not welcome at the mostly white location (Wells et al. 2009, 87–90).

An African American graduate of Austin High School said she would have gone to Anderson if it hadn't been closed before she began ninth grade:

> They closed that school back in the seventies and kept the name
> but moved it to the west side of town so the white kids could go
> to it. I felt bad about that and I felt robbed . . . because all those old

Table 2.2. AISD Plan Approved by Court that Includes Closing Anderson High School and Kealing Junior High School and Redistricting Districts Following 1973 Plan in 1971 with Limited Transportation.

High Schools	Total Projected School Population	Number of African-Americans in the School	Percentage of African-Americans in the School
Austin	1185	189	15.9
Crockett	2794	278	10
Johnston	1686	332	19.7
Lanier	2854	287	10.1
McCallum	2451	361	14.7
Reagan	3065	554	18
Travis	1477	100	6.8

Junior High Schools	Total Projected School Population	Number of African-Americans in the School	Percentage of African-Americans in the School
Allan	773	195	25.2
Burnett	1252	116	9.3
Fulmore	1086	62	5.9
Lamar	1008	161	14.9
Martin	852	127	14.9
Murchison	947	100	106
O'Henry	770	39	5.1
Pearce	1254	163	13
Porter	1419	131	9.2
Webb	1052	160	15.2

Source: United States of America v. Texas Education Agency et al. (Austin Independent School District), 467 F.2d 848 (United States Court of Appeals, Fifth Circuit, Aug. 2, 1972), http://ftp.resource.org/courts.gov/c/F2/467/467 .F2d.848.71-2508.html#fn19, derived from Defendants Exhibit No. 37

black schools were torn down. They won all the state championships and all that stuff, and I wanted to go and be a part of that. My mother went to Anderson High School. I wanted to go to Anderson High, but they moved that school out of the east side of Austin. (Wells et al. 2009, 90)

ONGOING STRUGGLES TO ACHIEVE DIVERSITY
IN AUSTIN PUBLIC SCHOOLS AFTER 1970

AISD also moved to create more schools with adequate facilities in East Austin. It proposed to build several new elementary schools: Williams, Sanchez, and Houston. It also submitted proposals for a new southwestern high school and northeastern junior high, but the government objected to both, insisting on the integration of white schools rather than just the building of new schools in minority neighborhoods ("Desegregation Chronology" 1977). Formal moves were made to begin to desegregate schools after 1977, but the de facto segregation of East Austin schools continued through 2000. The government also argued that Hispanic schools were de facto segregated. The Fifth U.S. Circuit Court of Appeals ruled three times that AISD intentionally segregated Hispanic students ("Desegregation Chronology" 1977). Some of the issues were resolved in 1980 when U.S. district judge Jack Roberts approved a consent decree settling Austin's decade-long desegregation suit ("Judge Puts OK on AISD Busing Plan" 1980).

The consent decree resulted in large-scale busing in the 1980s. By 1990, critics in the anti-busing camp argued that programs such as priority schools, magnet schools, more minority hiring, and more multicultural programs were helping to ensure equal education in Austin (Garcia 1990). AISD trustees stopped busing elementary school students in 1986. Busing programs wound down and stopped altogether in 1999, leaving largely minority population schools in place on the east side of Austin. In 2004 a reporter observed,

> Five years after the district stopped busing for integration, Austin schools again are no more diverse than the neighborhoods in which their students live. Minority students make up 70 percent of the district's enrollment, and Austin schools are more segregated than they were 20 years ago. . . . Of the Austin school district's 106 regular, non-alternative elementary, middle and high schools, today, 13 have student enrollments that are more than 70 percent white. Another 48 schools have student enrollments that are more than 90 percent black and Hispanic. Overall, the district's student population is 30 percent white, 53 percent Hispanic, 14 percent black and 3 percent Asian and other. (Alford 2004)

One of the few lasting victories against de facto segregation was the location of magnet schools on the east side, which took place as the result of parent and school initiatives. The Science Magnet was started at LBJ High School in East Austin in 1984. The Liberal Arts Academy was founded at Johnston High School (five miles away in Southeast Austin) in 1987. The Science Magnet has thrived, absorbing the Liberal Arts Academy courses in 2002. However, the magnet became disconnected from LBJ in 2007 and became a separate high school, thus undoing the desegregation effort. The regular LBJ High School suffered and was placed on the state's list of unsatisfactory schools and threatened with possible closure in 2009. One of the African American schools closed under desegregation, Kealing Junior High School (in 1986), was reopened as a magnet school for both science and liberal arts (in 1993). The magnet remains open but has become disconnected from the regular school, which is also on the low-performing list. Several elementary magnet schools were opened and then closed as many parents strongly preferred to keep elementary-age students in neighborhood schools.

The number of schools in East Austin has grown to serve the growing population there. Efforts were made to improve the quality of education in East Austin schools, but a number of factors combined to make these programs lag behind others in more prosperous parts of town. When members of a student team led by Straubhaar began observing conditions and interviewing students and parents at Johnston High School in East Austin in 1999, it became readily apparent that teacher preparedness and experience levels, and the quality of physical facilities and information and communication technology facilities, were much lower than at schools in Central, Northwest, or West Austin.

In 1960, Johnston High School was built in the heart of East Austin. Mostly Hispanics who had attended either Anderson High School or Austin High School began attending the new school. Thus, after the construction of Johnston High School, Austin High School was left with a predominantly white student body and Anderson High School with a predominantly African American student body. Johnston High was successful in some areas, particularly band and some athletics, calling itself "the pride of the East Side," but its academic achievement level was always low (Chote 1991). After the integration of the Liberal Arts Academy magnet school with Johnston High, some parents felt that their students had been given new chances to participate in high-quality academic programs, while others worried that the higher grades of the magnet students masked over substantial problems in the nonmagnet academic program (as Straubhaar discovered through conversations with parents at PTA meetings during 1998–2002).

In 1999, when the research team began to examine it closely, Johnston High was full of struggling students and teachers. Local reporters found that the three zip code areas that fed into the school had the highest teen pregnancy rates in Austin, and that "one out of 20 Johnston High School students is either a parent or has a child on the way" (Kurtz and McEntee 2000). Nearly half of Johnston students lived in poverty, and most of the students worked full time. According to data from the Texas Education Agency, 47 percent of Johnston High students were eligible for free or reduced-priced lunch, compared to 31 percent of students at AISD high schools overall. The school had the highest dropout rate among AISD's ten regular high schools. It was considered one of thirteen low-performing schools in AISD according to 1998's TAAS (Texas Assessment of Academic Skills) test scores (Kurtz and McEntee 2000).

The student body at Johnston was diverse in 2000; nearly 30 percent of the high school's students were Hispanic, 20 percent were African American, and 17 percent were white. Almost all of the white students attended the Liberal Arts Academy, which was located at Johnston and shared a number of classes and all extracurricular activities with it. The existence of a Liberal Arts Academy that drew more affluent and competitive students from throughout the district masked some problems in the rest of the school. In 2000 only 241 of 1,774 students were seniors, and in 1999 only twenty-five regular (non–Liberal Arts Academy) students took the SAT.

CONCLUSION

The history of racial segregation in Austin shows how powerful and lasting certain kinds of top-down geographic structuring can be (de Certeau 1984). Both residential and school segregation created lasting structures of inequality that have resisted a variety of both top-down and grassroots efforts to undo them. Top-down restructuring efforts by federal desegregation orders in the 1950s–1990s did not change the structures of de facto segregation. Neither did local legal suits by African American and Latino groups. They were effectively countered by other grassroots efforts, including largely white parents' groups and anti-busing groups, as noted in the histories of the 1980s-1990s above. These can be seen as power struggles for hegemonic control (Gramsci 1971), which were won by those who already had entrenched power and economic, social, and cultural capital (Bourdieu 1984).

Theoretically, that triumph can be interpreted as an example of the power of the possessive investment in whiteness (Lipsitz 2006; Shapiro 2005); that is, the entrenched power of accumulated economic capital held by whites, in terms of the value of their housing, as well as their entrenched social capital (Bourdieu 1984), which lends itself to effective local organizing, resisted changes that would have reduced their own power and economic advantage. (This is particularly true of whites compared to African Americans. The outcomes for Latinos have been somewhat more varied, but the overall dynamic seems similar for the poor among Latinos as well.) This reinforces inequalities in some of the fields that we have defined as crucial for social mobility in an economy redefined as a technopolis: economic capital (which tends to be associated with access to technology, as we shall see in Chapter 5), cultural capital, and techno-capital.

This created a very unequal set of trajectories for competing in various fields for individuals and families in these different groups. This was particularly true as the Austin economy gradually turned into a technopolis, as Chapter 3 discusses, and the fields of education and technology became ever more critical for economic success and social mobility. Despite efforts to locate technology manufacturing jobs in East Austin (discussed in Chapters 3–4) and to assist minority populations in building techno-capital (discussed in Chapters 6–9), crucial fields like education, economic value of homes, and technology access and knowledge remain segregated.

REFERENCES

Ade, C. (1987). A demographic atlas of Austin: A report for the Urban Services Policy Research Project. Edited by David Eaton. Lyndon B. Johnson School of Public Affairs, University of Texas at Austin.

Adams, C. (1997). The history of Mexican-American schools in Austin: From Reconstruction through World War II. Class paper for MAS 374–Chicano Educational Struggles.

Akin, C. R. (1951). A study of school boundaries in East Austin, Texas. Master's thesis, University of Texas at Austin.

Alford, A. (2004). Brown at 50—An Austin perspective on the landmark ruling that desegregated schools across the nation. *Austin American-Statesman,* May 16. Retrieved from http://www.s4.brown.edu/cen2000/othersay/statesman _051704.pdf.

Arriola, E. (1998). Austin schools project: An investigation into the quality of education being provided, under the governance of the Austin Independent School District, to the African-American and Latino (Hispanic/Latina/o) children of the City of Austin. University of Texas Law School, Austin. Retrieved from http://www.womenontheborder.org/AUSTINschools.htm.

Austin Human Relations Commission. (1979). Housing patterns study of Austin, Texas: A report. May.

Austin Public Schools. (1954). *Seventy-three vital years: Public education in Austin, 1881–1954: Source book of research material.* Austin: Centennial Committee on Instruction and Research, Austin Public Schools.

Barkley, M. (1963). *History of Travis Country and Austin, 1839–1899.* Austin: Steck.

Bourdieu, P. (1984). *Distinction: A social critique of the judgement of taste.* Cambridge, MA: Harvard University Press.

Brewer, J. M. (1940). *An historical outline of the Negro in Travis County.* Austin: Samuel Huston College.

Briseño, V. D. (1999). Does Austin's growth management policy benefit all Austinites? The impact of Austin's smart growth initiative on East Austin: An analysis. University of Texas at Austin.

Change starting at top. (1955). *American-Statesman,* August 9.

Chote, J. B. (1991). Desegregation of the Austin Independent School District: A question of balance. Master's report, University of Texas at Austin.

City of Austin. (1993). Strategic choices.

Cohen, I. J. (1989). *Structuration theory: Anthony Giddens and the constitution of social life.* New York: St. Martin's Press.

Connell, E. M. (1925). The Mexican population of Austin, Texas. Master's thesis, University of Texas at Austin.

Crowded schools delay junior high integration: Board postpones act until situation eases. (1957). *Austin Statesman.* June 11.

Cromack, Isabel. (1949). Latin Americans: A minority group in the Austin Public Schools. Master's thesis, University of Texas at Austin.

de Certeau, Michel. (1984). The practice of everyday life. Trans. Steven F. Rendail. Berkeley: University of California Press.

Desegregation chronology. (1977). *Austin American-Statesman,* November 22.

Desegregation in Austin. (1975). *American-Statesman,* August 17.

Feagin, J. R. (1985). Delivery of services to black East Austin and black communities: A socio-historical analysis: Final report on Hogg Foundation grant.

500 Negro 6th graders can enter white schools. (1961). *Austin Statesman,* July 11.

Freeman, A. D. (1995). Legitimizing racial discrimination through antidiscrimination law: A critical review of Supreme Court doctrine. In K. Crenshaw, N. Gotanda, G. Peller, and K. Thomas (Eds.), *Critical race theory: Key writings that formed the movement,* pp. 29–45. New York: New Press.

Galindo, J. (1994). Historia de vida: Guía técnica y reflexiva. *Revistas Estudios Sobre las Culturas Contemporáneas* 6(18).

Garcia, J. E. (1990). After 10 years, outcome of AISD plan still disputed. *Austin American-Statesman*, September 2.

Giddens, A. (1984). *The constitution of society*. Berkeley: University of California Press.

González, J. (1986). Y todo queda entre familia. *Revistas Estudios Sobre las Culturas Contemporáneas* 1(1): 135–154.

———. (1991). Ferias, memorias urbanas y frentes culturales. Revistas Estudios sobre las Culturas Contemporaneas, 4(4): 392–421.

———. (1995a). Y todo queda entre familia: Estrategias, objeto y método para historias de familias. *Revistas Estudios Sobre las Culturas Contemporáneas*, Epoca II, 1(1): 135–154.

———. (1995b). Coordenadas del imaginario: Protocolo para trabajar las cartografias culturales. *Revistas Estudios Sobre las Culturas Contemporáneas* 1(2).

———. (1997). The willingness to weave: Cultural analysis, cultural fronts and the networks of the future. *Media Development* 44(1): 30–36.

———. (2000). Cultural fronts: Towards a dialogical understanding of contemporary cultures. In J. Lull (Ed.), *Culture in the information age*. London: Routledge.

González, J., and Chávez, G. (1996). La cultura en México I, cifras clave. CNCA and Universidad de Colima, Mexico.

Grades 1 through 12 affected in September. (1963). *Austin Statesman*, June 15.

Gramsci, A. (1971). *Selections from the prison notebooks*. New York: International.

Greenberger, S. (1997). City's first zoning map plotted neighborhood of minorities, hazards. *Austin American-Statesman*, July 20.

Hamilton, W. B. (1913). A social survey of Austin. Bulletin of the University of Texas 273, Humanistic ser. 15, March 15.

Harris, C. I. (1995). Whiteness as property. In K. Crenshaw, N. Gotanda, G. Peller, and K. Thomas (Eds.), *Critical race theory: Key writings that formed the movement*, pp. 276–291. New York: New Press.

Herrera, J. (1990). Recording history: A history of Our Lady of Guadalupe Parish Church. Master's report, University of Texas at Austin, 1–14, 78–81.

Housing pattern linked to deeds. (1973). *Austin American-Statesman*, May 12.

Humphrey, D. (1997). Austin: A history of the capital city. Texas State Historical Association, Austin.

Jackson, R. (1979). East Austin: A socio-historical view of a segregated community. Master's thesis, University of Texas at Austin.

Judge puts OK on AISD busing plan. (1980). *Austin American-Statesman*, January 3.

Keeton, W. P. 2009. *Sweatt v. Painter. Handbook of Texas Online*. Retrieved August 5, 2009, from http://www.tshaonline.org/handbook/online/articles/SS/jrs1.html.

Koch & Fowler Consulting Engineers. (1928). *A city plan for Austin, Texas*. Repr., Austin: Department of Planning, 1957.

Kurtz, M., and McEntee, R. (2000). Hard times at Johnston. *Austin American-Statesman*, January 23.

Lipsitz, G. (2006). *The possessive investment in whiteness: How white people profit from identity politics*. Philadelphia, PA: Temple University Press

Long, W. M. (1952). Education in Austin before the public schools. Master's thesis, University of Texas at Austin.

Lossing, B. J. (Ed.). *Harper's Encyclopedia of United States History*, vol. 9. New York: Harper and Brothers, 1912.

Maass, M., and González, J. (2005). De memoria y tecnología radio, television e internet en México. *Revistas Estudios Sobre las Culturas Contemporáneas* 11(22): 193–220.

Manaster, J. (1986). The ethnic geography of Austin, Texas, 1875–1910. Master's thesis, University of Texas at Austin.

McDonald, J. J. (1993). Race relations in Austin, Texas, c. 1917–1929. PhD thesis, University of Southampton.

Mears, M. M. (2001). African American settlement patterns in Austin, Texas, 1865–1928. Bachelor of arts thesis, Baylor University.

———. (2009). *And grace will lead me home: African American freedman communities in Austin, Texas, 1865–1928*. Lubbock, TX: Texas Tech University Press.

Myrdal, G. (1944). *An American dilemma: The Negro problem and modern democracy*. New York: Harper & Row.

New libraries held needed. (1951). *Austin Statesman*, December 28.

Orum, A. M. (1987). Power, money and the people: The making of modern Austin. Austin: Texas Monthly Press.

Ross, J. (2003). The aesthetics of gentrification in the Clarksville National Register of Historic Places—Historic District, 1871–2003. Master's thesis, University of Texas at Austin. Retrieved from http://esr.lib.ttu.edu/bitstream/handle/2346/14691/31295018922772.pdf.

School desegregation drive looms. (1954). *Austin American*, July 8.

School hearing concludes. (1970). *Austin Statesman*, January 24.

Schott, R. (2000). Ethnic and race relations in Austin, Texas. Policy Research Project Report 137, Lyndon B. Johnson School of Public Affairs, University of Texas at Austin.

Shapiro, T. M. (2005). *The hidden cost of being African American: How wealth perpetuates inequality*. New York: Oxford University Press.

Shipman, S. S. (1978). Ethnic housing patterns and school desegregation: Austin, Texas. Master's report in community and regional planning, University of Texas at Austin.

3 high schools get 13 Negroes. (1955). *Austin Statesman*, September 2.

University of Texas–BRSS. (1941). Population mobility in Austin, Texas, 1929–1931. Bureau of Research in the Social Sciences, University of Texas publication, no. 4127 (July 15).

Wells, A. S., Holme, J. J., Revilla, A. T., and Atanda, A. K. (2009). *Both sides now: The story of school desegregation's graduates*. Berkeley: University of California Press.

LISA
HARTENBERGER

ZEYNEP TUFEKCI

STUART DAVIS

CHAPTER 3

A HISTORY OF HIGH TECH
AND THE TECHNOPOLIS
IN AUSTIN

In 1623, the writer Campanella described a utopian city of science and technology, the Civitas Solis, or city of sun. It is a mythical place designed and governed by wise scientists where all citizens benefit equally from technology. Campanella's Civitas Solis has a modern equivalent in the technopolis, a city whose economy is based primarily on information management (Smilor, Kozmetsky, and Gibson 1988). While the idea of the technopolis dates back thousands of years, its modern incarnation has been traced to Japan's national and local efforts in the 1970s to convert towns with largely industrial economic bases to an economy based on information processing. Since then, cities and regions around the world have tried to emulate and improve upon the Japanese model.

In the United States, the most well-known technopolis is Silicon Valley. A slew of other areas and cities have sought to imitate the success of Silicon Valley, including Austin, Texas (Florida 2002). The city self-identifies and promotes itself as a technopolis. For example, the local paper, the *Austin-American Statesman*, for several years titled its weekly section on technology "Technopolis." Like many cities, Austin was drawn to the technopolis model by the promise of economic growth, social equality, and environmentally sound technology industries. High-technology industries have led to phenomenal growth in Austin. In some ways, the promises of the Civitas Solis have been fulfilled. Yet some argue that the very success of the model has led to unintended consequences that exacerbate social inequity and environmental destruction. This chapter looks at the historical development of Austin as a technopolis, and examines its changing social dynamics and how issues of social equity have been expressed as a subset of concerns over quality of life.

DEFINING THE TECHNOPOLIS AS MODE OF PRODUCTION AND CULTURAL ENVIRONMENT

In the technopolis model, the driving force behind today's global economy is information management. Robert Preer points out that "a recurrent theme and fundamental assumption of this analysis [of technopolises] is that the world is now experiencing a great technological revolution that is as profound and far-reaching as the industrial revolution or the neolithic revolution" (Preer 1992, 4). Phrases such as "information society" have trickled down from academia to the popular press and become touchstones for discussing and thinking about work and the economy. As Americans perceive themselves more and more as part of the information society, the technopolis has become the ultimate symbol of a progressive city. Although in the information society the upward trajectory of technology is often thought of as inevitable, it is simultaneously perceived as controllable. Thus the modern technopolis is a product of enormous debate, planning, and strategizing in order to properly manage economic growth.

The creation of a technopolis is a deliberate economic development strategy. Preer defines a technopolis as "a region that generates sustained and propulsive economic activity through the creation and commercialization of new knowledge" (1992, 55). Rather than processing goods, technopolises specialize in information management as the primary commodity. Manuel Castells identifies "technopoles" as one type of industrial milieu of innovation. "What defines the specificity of a milieu of innovation is its capacity to generate synergy, that is the added value resulting not from the cumulative effect of the elements present in the milieu from their interaction" (1996, 390). In Castells's definition, the type of commodity—information, goods, or services—is less important than the overarching attitude of innovation and inventiveness that should characterize a technopolis. In their book *Creating the Technopolis*, Raymond Smilor, George Kozmetsky, and David Gibson describe the modern technopolis as "one that interactively links technology commercialization with the public and private sectors to spur economic development and promote technology diversification" (Smilor, Kozmetsky, and Gibson 1988, xiii; see Figure 1.1 for the illustration of their ideal linkage of technology to a wheel of development). All of these definitions emphasize the long-term growth potential of the technopolis as an integrated economic strategy. A key feature of the true technopolis is that high-tech industries engender spin-off development and provide for a diversified economy. In agricultural terms, the technopolis cannot depend on a monoculture. Diversification insulates the technopolis from the vicissitudes of a particular market and ensures a local economy adaptable to global economic forces.

The transformation of Austin into a technopolis along the trajectory Castells defines did not merely occur on the level of economic production: the very fabric of what it means to work and live in the city was fundamentally altered. Put another way, the economic evolution of a technopolis in a region instigates transformations in a much wider set of cultural relations. While the idea of the technopolis was originally coined to delineate the specific modality of economic production, the term also serves to index a host of cultural factors that accompany this process. As Chapter 1 of this volume has already briefly discussed, Richard Florida's *The Rise of the Creative Class* (2002) indexes a wide milieu of cultural factors that arise with the coming of the technopolis. Conducting a nationwide study of over one hundred cities, Florida develops his definition of a "creative city" along three interrelated vectors: technology, talent, and tolerance. In his account, the technology vector falls squarely in line with Castells's definition of the information economy. Talent, also relatively rigidly defined, relates to the level of education of individuals in the city; to qualify for inclusion in the talent category, an individual needs to have received a bachelor's degree from an accredited university (251). The tolerance vector, however, is extremely complicated and is based on a "complex combination of art, music, web design, alternative lifestyles, and sexual preferences" (252–261). Crucially, Florida views all of these practices as indicators of the individual's role in determining his or her cultural experience. Labeling all of these practices or lifestyle choices as "creative," Florida claims that through a process of combination and recombination these cultural assets will produce a "creative class" capable of thinking critically and offering open-minded approaches to the types of information-economy practices central to the growth of a technopolis.

As Toby Miller (2009), John Hartley (2007), and others have emphasized from different sides of the political spectrum, the rise of the technopolis as creative city fundamentally restructures cultural and political life in the locales it inhabits. Miller argues that a technopolis strategy implies a cultural push away from activities associated with "residual business" and "residual politics" (2009, 96). As a city begins to shift more and more toward the vision of an "information economy" implied in the technopolis strategy, other modes of life are transformed. "Residual" businesses such as factories and "residual" political organs such as unions, theories such as traditional class divisions, and policies such as social security are relegated to the status of relics. They are the fossils of a previous generation. The new generation of technopolis workers will be information savvy, computer literate, and able to transform their creative energy in a manner that will add to the accumulated effect of the technopolis.

The rise of the technopolis necessarily results in some being left behind by techno-cultural change. If the technopolis is to be seen as the most advanced form of explicit economic and implicit cultural development, it necessarily creates divisions between the insiders who fit more closely with its values and the outsiders who will inevitably be left behind if no action is taken. Vincent Mosco calls this division the "cyberspace gap":

> Generational divisions are central to the information society's version of end of history myths. On one side lies a generation of well-meaning but old-fashioned people, at best fumbling with the new technology but not quite getting it, at worst acting like curmudgeonly sticks-in-the mud or like Luddites fighting against the technology and clinging desperately to old, dying ways. On the other side are children whose instinctual savvy, willingness to experiment, and youthful exuberance draw them to the new technology and the new age it represents. (2004, 79)

The rise of the technopolis, then, does not merely affect business practice. It stands as a new form of social existence connected to cultural categories of creativity and experimentation.

Theorizing the technopolis as an economic *and cultural* configuration provides a needed rejoinder to earlier formulations. Much of the early information-economy rhetoric emphasized the rise of information technopolises in rural pastures far from traditional industrial areas, implying that these new cities were independent of old structures. Our worn industrial bodies were being discarded for ethereal information centers. Part of the utopic appeal of the technopolis was its "green" image—replacing the smokestacks of yesteryear with inconspicuous electric cables. Rather than looking to old models of industrial development, city planners focused on successful new areas of development such as Silicon Valley or Route 128 near Boston.

Preer finds a remarkable uniformity in technopolis policies, a result of planners visiting exemplar technopolises and copying their strategies: "They [city planners] returned home, and using a formula of reverse engineering, arrived at the same conclusion: The formula for creating a technopolis is a world-class university, an affiliated science park where research has been commercialized, an ample supply of venture capital, a pleasant physical environment, and a stimulating social milieu. Thus a rather superficial analysis was all that preceded the development of many of these policies" (1992, 29).

Yet technology and society develop differently in different times and places. "Technological progress," Preer emphasizes, "is neither predetermined nor inevitable. The interaction of economic, political, and social institutions shapes the pace and direction of technological change" (1992, 8). Rising out of pastureland, the area now known as Silicon Valley was only dubbed as such by the press in the 1970s. By contrast, before adopting high technology as an economic development strategy, Austin was already the state capital, with its own city identity and history. Although the problems that Austin faces are issues that all technopolises must contend with, they take a particular form in Austin that determines how both problems and solutions are framed.

DEVELOPING HIGH TECH IN AUSTIN: THE PRIVATE-PUBLIC PARTNERSHIP MODEL

Austin explicitly planned to become a technology town in order both to replace the oil jobs that it knew were not permanent and to complement and expand upon the only major sources of employment in town, the state government and the University of Texas (UT). The planning goes back to 1957, when, according to David Humphrey, the "Austin Area Economic Development Foundation created a 'blueprint of the future' that set out to recruit industry that built upon Austin's existing economic structure":

> A team of public and private leaders built upon UT's research programs by attracting manufacturers of electrical and scientific equipment. Austin's success in the 1960s and 70s in making the transition from government to high technology manufacturing was built on the traditional factors of relatively low-cost land, a high-skilled workforce at reasonable wages, and a desirable quality of life. (1997, 17)

Austin proceeded steadily and enthusiastically in an effort to remake itself from a sleepy college town. In 1963, IBM moved its Selectric typewriter facility to Austin. This was followed by Texas Instruments in 1967 and by Motorola in 1974.

Austin turned further toward the technopolis development strategy in the 1980s, in the wake of falling oil prices and a general economic slump. The strategy appealed to Austinites for much the same reasons that other government planners have tried to copy Silicon Valley's success. High tech seemed to promise growth and high-paying jobs even in times of economic downturn, it was not dependent on production factors like industrial resources, and it seemed more environmentally friendly than industrial development. Very consciously, Austin increased R&D funding for its universities; provided subsidies, tax breaks, and a variety of incentives to tech companies and consortiums; and made "a visible bid to not only join but lead in the information age" (Williams 1988). In the 1980s and the 1990s, many small and large technology companies located their offices and their plants in Austin, and Austin spawned a homegrown giant of its own, Dell Computers.

However, the city began in earnest to transform itself into a technopolis only after its successful campaign to attract Microelectronics and Computer Technology Corporation (MCC). Austin managed to outbid dozens of competing cities to be chosen as the location of MCC (Browning et al. 1995). The courting of MCC consolidated a varied set of institutional actors and established a method for attracting high-tech firms that Austin would follow and expand on in the next decade. The key feature of Austin's strategy was a strong partnership between the public and private sectors.

MCC itself is a product of private-public partnership. MCC was formed in 1982 by ten U.S. technology corporations in response to Japan's lead in computer-related industries (Browning et al. 1995). It was the first private-sector technology consortium aimed at conducting research and developing technological competitiveness. Mosco (1996) calls the 1980s the "second coming" of Silicon Valley, when Japan's vast lead in semiconductor production, a result of its protected oligopoly industry and cheaper labor, forced the U.S. semiconductor industry to compete aggressively. The ten original MCC firms agreed to pool resources for R&D in microelectronic packaging, advanced computer design, design of very large-scale integrated circuits, and software. The consortium was facilitated by the National Cooperative Research Act of 1984, created to exempt R&D from antitrust laws (Browning et al. 1995).

When MCC was searching for a site for their headquarters, they did not choose to locate in Silicon Valley. They considered fifty-six cities around the nation and, in 1983, decided on Austin (T. Robbins 2003). Originally, San Antonio had also been competing for MCC. However, when it looked as though MCC was seriously considering Austin, San Antonio put their weight behind the Austin bid. In addition, the university, government, and business communities came together to offer MCC $62 million in incentives. For example, UT offered to lease their $23 million Balcones Research Center to MCC for a nominal cost. UT also strengthened their science departments, creating endowed chairs in engineering and natural sciences. The city offered $20 million in subsidized mortgage loans for MCC employees. Austin's aggressive marketing attracted national attention and accusations of buying off MCC. However, other cities had offered MCC even more attractive financial packages. In newspaper interviews, MCC officials cited Austin's low cost of living and high quality of life as key reasons why they chose Austin over other cities. They were also impressed by the united front shown by the university, city officials and the business community, whose leaders came together to show them around Austin—taking them on tours of the city and boat rides on Lake Travis, and generally giving them the red-carpet treatment (T. Robbins 2003).

Also in 1983, George Kozmetsky founded UT's IC^2 Institute (Innovation, Creativity and Capital Institute), which describes itself as "a think tank that actively promotes technology commercialization" (Butler 2003). At IC^2, Kozmetsky pioneered the concept of the technopolis, a city-based framework for technology-driven economic development. The model proffered by IC^2 (a model which would later be exported to cities throughout the United States, Latin America, and other parts of the globe) privileges a triangular relationship between city government, universities, and private firms.

According to a case study of MCC's move to Austin, a strong private-public partnership proved to be the decisive factor: "Based on interviews with key participants on the MCC site selection team . . . one central issue stands above all others as the reason that MCC decided to locate in Austin: the segments of the Technopolis Wheel, especially statewide, were balanced and working" (Smilor, Kozmetsky, and Gibson 1988, 174). Smilor, Kozmetsky, and Gibson create a visual representation of the private-public partnership model with the technopolis wheel (see Figure 1.1). The elements of the technopolis wheel include all of the actors who participated in the courting of MCC: the university, large technology companies, small technology companies, state government, local government, federal government, and support groups. Although the image of the technopolis wheel has not been popularized, most scholars and journalists would agree with Smilor, Kozmetsky, and Gibson's assessment of Austin's private-public partnership in 1983: "The spirit of a team of prominent individuals working together for the common good was so strong that arguments over parochial issues were put aside" (1988, 175).

The Greater Austin Chamber of Commerce had been the leading force in planning and coordinating the MCC offer. Flush with the success of their venture, the chamber of commerce next constructed an economic development strategy to attract more technology companies. In 1984, they hired the Stanford Research Institute's Public Policy Center to develop a long-range plan for Austin. The resulting report, "Creating an Opportunity Economy," was adopted by the chamber of commerce in 1986. The focus of the plan was to attract high-technology companies and provide opportunities for local spin-off development. The plan's numerous programs required considerable cooperation among the university, local government, and business communities. For example, the Target Market Program marketed Austin to designated industries. For each industry a committee of academics, business leaders, and city officials gathered information used to select and market to companies through direct mail and personal contacts. The Target Partner Program paired business people and university professors with an average of fifteen contacts. These individuals personally signed all chamber correspondence to their contacts. The Travel Network kept track of the travel plans of Austin businesspeople and coordinated personal visits to prospective recruits.

Individual businesses also supported particular programs. For example, beginning in 1987, Southwestern Bell underwrote the Business Expansion and Retention Program, a program to research and make recommendations on how to make life easier for businesses in Austin. In 1989, the City of Austin, the chamber of commerce, UT's IC² Institute, and the UT business school created the Austin Technology Incubator to provide start-up technology firms with common administrative, marketing, and other support systems. The state had already encouraged UT faculty to conduct applied research by allowing faculty to be shareholders in private companies that emerge from their research. Faculty profit making was institutionalized with the 1985 creation of the Center for Technology Development and Transfer, which linked investors and inventors. Austin's private-public partnership was formalized in the late 1980s through these and other institutions and programs. With its approach formalized, Austin was poised to repeat the MCC experience.

The second great success of Austin's private-public partnership model came in 1988 with Sematech's decision to locate its headquarters there. Sematech is a consortium of semiconductor manufacturers dedicated to R&D. Until 1996, Sematech was funded through a combination of private and federal monies from the Defense Advanced Research Projects Agency. Like MCC, Sematech arose from concerns over Japanese superiority. It was formed following a 1985 Department of Defense–sponsored conference as a response to a perceived national security threat from the foreign supply of microchips. The Department of Defense justified public spending by reasoning that the United States needed to maintain a steady supply of microchips in case of war. As in the case of MCC, the competition for Sematech headquarters was fierce. Austin was chosen after an exhaustive search of 132 communities. Once again, Austin's selling points were its low cost of living and high quality of life, sweetened by an incentive package of $68 million put together by the private and public sectors. For example, UT constructed a "cleanroom" (necessary for semiconductor manufacturing) for its Montopolis Research Center. Through the chamber of commerce's Advantage Austin Fund, Austin's business community offered $1.5 million, half in cash and half in services (L. Robbins 2003).

Austin's successful bid for Sematech garnered more national press attention and the inevitable comparison with Silicon Valley. Giving the image of the technology corridor a Texas flair, a 1988 *U.S. News and World Report* article called Austin "Silicon Gulch" (Sheets 1988). Austin was viewed as part of a larger technology corridor running along Interstate Highway 35 from Austin to San Antonio, much in the way that Silicon Valley and Route 128 were regions whose group identity depended on a technology-based economy. Austin joined these regions and Seattle in the small group of highly visible cities experiencing a dot-com boom in the 1990s (Miller 2002). This image would later give way to that of Austin as a technopolis in the Greek city-state sense of the term *polis*.

But in the 1980s, Austin was only one link in the regional chain. A 1983 *Inc.* article called Austin the "smart little city" at the center of the "Texas triangle . . . the country's hottest new growth belt" (Kahn 1983). In 1987, UT hosted its first international technopolis conference and produced a book (from which the discussion on the technopolis wheel is quoted above). The directors of UT's IC^2 Institute, Smilor and Gibson (with Kozmetsky, then dean of the School of Business), wrote a chapter on the development of the "Austin–San Antonio Technology Corridor," which includes information on the role of San Antonio—with its universities and high-technology health sector—as well as the Hill Country surrounding Austin. The authors measure the success of the entire region through its population growth: "By 1980 the rate of population growth in the Corridor was 2.5 times that of the United States" (Smilor, Kozmetsky, and Gibson 1988, 148). Although they call Austin a technopolis, the authors define the technopolis as a corridor or technology region.

Given that Austin's technology development plan was modeled on Silicon Valley, the direct parallel to Silicon Valley and regional definition of the technopolis are understandable. Preer (1992) identifies eight strategies pioneered by Silicon Valley and often used to attract high-technology companies. Austin's plan follows each one. They include creating science parks; investing in university research; providing capital assistance; creating small-business incubators; building necessary infrastructure such as roads, airports, housing, and telecommunication networks; playing up quality-of-life factors; investing in education and training programs; and creating private-public partnerships. Yet Austin's private-public partnership, the strength of its development strategy, has always been tenuous and temporal. Although Smilor, Kozmetsky, and Gibson celebrate Austinites' "remarkable spirit of cooperation," they conclude with the warning that "the very success of the development of a technopolis can lead to greed and many dissatisfactions. The result can be a shattering of the consensus that originally made the technopolis possible" (1988, 175, 179). Current articles no longer refer to San Antonio as part of the Texan technology corridor; instead, they focus on Austin as a center for technology. For example, a 2000 cover story in *U.S. News and World Report* focuses on Austin and the unequal distribution of technology within the city (Holstein 2000). The image of the corridor, which requires combined planning efforts in San Antonio, Austin, and other cities in the corridor, has been replaced by a singular image of the Austin technopolis.

The fissures between different groups in Austin are also more visible today. The social problem of unequal access to and use of the Internet, at a time when more and more services are moving online, has drawn national and local attention. The *U.S. News and World Report* article on Austin's digital divide emphasizes how Austin's problems are emblematic of the downside to the nation's technology-based "new economy" (Holstein 2000). A 2000 article in the alternative weekly the *Austin Chronicle* asks whether the price of success has been too high if the result is an ever-widening income and knowledge gap. Although Austin continues to ascribe to a private-public partnership model, the balance of power among groups has shifted. The chamber of commerce is no longer leading the way. Instead, the high-technology business community has begun to take a much more active role, not only in business development but also in civic life—trying to tackle many of the issues of social equity that they feel the city government has inadequately addressed. However, in applying the principles of high-technology business to government, some feel that the high-technology community is bypassing democratic processes (P. Robbins 2003). As Smilor, Kozmetsky, and Gibson predicted in 1988, the success of the technopolis has led to new problems in the private-public partnership model.

QUALITY OF LIFE: AN AUSTIN CRY TO ARMS

Though theorists hoped that the technopolis would eventually reach a point at which the rate of growth of technological innovation and the quality of life would become mutually beneficial, this scenario did not autochthonously materialize (especially in the early phases). Even in the initial heady years of technopolis development, issues of social equity in Austin were present under the banner of quality of life. Preserving Austin's quality of life has always been the rallying cry of Austin groups with varying goals. For example, the Save Our Springs (SOS) Alliance, a powerful local environmental group, was formed in 1989 to protect a local swimming pool called Barton Springs from toxic runoff from construction sites. Today, SOS is a key community group involved in setting environmental policy and "smart growth" initiatives. Neighborhood associations and groups like People in Defense of the Earth and Her Resources (PODER) and the East Austin Strategy Team have been critics of the technopolis tendency to drive up the cost of living for longtime residents of Austin.

The dilemma is apparent—how can Austin maintain a low cost of living and high quality of life in the face of a population boom from new arrivals? The mix of new arrivals, many from Silicon Valley, and longtime residents has created a distinction between technology insiders and outsiders, which have begun to replicate long-standing local divisions between rich and poor neighborhoods.

One of the defining features of the technopolis is that growth becomes less dependent on exogenous forces, such as existing semiconductor industries moving to Austin, and more dependent on the new local firms that arise to create related products such as software or to provide services (Castells 1996). Part of the purpose of Smilor, Kozmetsky, and Gibson's 1988 book was to "prove" that Austin qualified as a technopolis because six homegrown high-technology companies had been formed.[1] They chart the growth of the private sector by relocation of high-tech companies or development of homegrown companies. Later, in a chapter in *The Technopolis Phenomenon*, Kozmetsky emphasized the importance of nurturing homegrown talent over recruiting: "Building indigenous companies on the one hand and retaining and expanding firms on the other hand have become the cornerstone of a competitive strategy for economic development" (Gibson, Kozmetsky, and Smilor 1992, 7).

Later, the city's emphasis has firmly shifted from recruiting firms to encouraging local growth. In 1998, the Greater Austin Chamber of Commerce hired ICF Kaiser Economic Strategy Group to conduct a study of Austin's economy. The study was headed by Ted Lyman, the same person who in 1986, under the aegis of the Stanford Research Institute, presented a similar report that helped direct Austin toward high-technology industries. The *Austin-American Statesman* summarized the main point of the Lyman report: "To maintain Austin's economic success and livability, the region should focus on the businesses it has rather than trying to attract new industry"

(Golz 1998). Although the report found that computers, software, and semiconductors—"the industries most responsible for moving Austin to the big leagues"—still dominate the economic growth of the region, new firms are popping up: "The newer companies tend to be more innovative and homegrown than their predecessors" (Golz 1998).

The emphasis on homegrown business over Silicon Valley imports reflects a certain ambivalence of heritage that Austin has toward its parent technopolis. One the one hand, Austin's technopolis was built using the same development strategies as Silicon Valley. On the other hand, Austin was at pains to differentiate itself from Silicon Valley in order to attract high-technology companies. Austin's "unique" identity as a symbiotic system of cultural creativity and technological innovation was a key selling point and defining feature of the technopolis. As the metropolitan population has risen—doubling from 1990 to 2005—the viewpoints of Austinites critical of technopolis growth have gained prominence.

In 1988, Smilor, Kozmetsky, and Gibson dismissed concerns over quality of life as reactionary:

> With each new economic development activity there was likely to be some community group that felt the loss of some, from their view central, aspect of Austin that made the city unique, desirable, and affordable. Such a list of "losses" might include more days when Barton Springs Pool, the city's best swimming location, is closed because the spring-fed pool is too full of silt from run-off at construction sites; the loss of landmarks, such as the Armadillo World Headquarters, where music greats and yet-to-be greats performed in a casual, intimate setting; and the loss of affordable land and housing. (166)

As the architects of Austin's technopolis, the three professors argued that the technopolis, as an aggregate of creative laborers working in the information society, would ultimately obviate the need of the state to intervene. The efforts of individuals working together in the new economy would alleviate social ills. This emphasis on the creative potential of the individual to solve societal problems deeply reflects what political theorist Wendy Brown calls the "age of the entrepreneur": "As individuals become 'entrepreneurs' in every aspect of life from business to culture to everything in between, subjects become wholly responsible for their well-being and citizenship is reduced to success in entrepreneurship" (2003, 233).

The idea of the technopolis as a self-regulatory composition of entrepreneurially minded individuals clashed with other professors and community leaders who argued the importance of preserving government intervention, especially in environmental matters. In the 1990s, journalists quoted UT professor of urban planning Bob Wilson, who warned that dependency on high technology would lead to an economic bust, as well as a higher cost of living: "If you want to look 20 years down the road, Silicon Valley is where we'll be" (de Marban 1995). Since the early to mid-1990s, Silicon Valley has often been held up as a negative example of the unintended consequences of technology growth.

Longtime residents had cause to be worried about a declining quality of life. As the *U.S. News and World Report* pointed out, only a fraction (20 percent as of February 2000) of the city's population was employed in high-technology jobs, yet all of the residents had to contend with the rising cost of housing (Holstein 2000). Despite the shift toward creative and innovative work described by the early theorists of the "new" Austin, the actual composition of the labor pool has changed quite slowly, as has the economic conditions of many Austinites. The *U.S. News and World Report* article contrasts the opulent wealth of the "Dellionaires"—those who made millions on Dell stock—with the bottom third of the workforce, making about $350 a week.

In particular, East Austin, home mainly to lower-income minority residents, and South Austin, made up of traditionally white working-class neighborhoods with increasing minority populations, was shut out of the economic benefits of the high-technology economy. Whatever income gains they made from providing services to the wealthy technology elite were swallowed by increases in cost of living (Holstein 2000). Over the years, East Austinites joined forces with environmental groups to negotiate common benefits for their respective communities. Many high-technology facilities were located in East and South Austin, but rather than reaping significant economic rewards from the companies, these poorer areas suffered the environmental consequences of industrial toxins. According to the Environmental Protection Agency, in 1994 Motorola and Advanced Micro

Devices released a combined 275,000 pounds of toxic chemicals into the air (de Marban 1995).

Public discourse over environmental policy was evident in the local papers, particularly the *Austin Chronicle*, during the city's periodic renegotiation of tax abatement policies. For example, a 1995 article questioned whether Austin was giving away too much and not getting enough in return with a proposed property-tax abatement for capital-intensive projects (mostly chip plants) that allowed up to 55 percent off for up to ten years. The offer was similar (80 percent abatement for seven years) to the city's policy from 1989 to 1993, which did attract eight new companies. But the author expressed concern as to whether new companies would stay once the attractive offers expired. He quoted county judge Bill Aleshire as saying, "Sematech sold the American Dream to the poor community and nothing came of it. But we're trying to prevent that from happening again" (de Marban 1995).

In order to both prevent environmental destruction and provide East Austin with jobs, PODER successfully negotiated a two-year training program in the late 1990s in semiconductor manufacturing supported by Sematech and conducted through the Austin Community College (ACC). PODER was formed in 1991 to negotiate with Sematech and the city over tax abatement policies. Although Sematech had promised to create almost seven thousand jobs over ten years, after two years only eighty-four workers had been hired. In 1992, PODER's lobbying efforts paid off when the city began requiring companies to hire local workers and follow environmental regulations. At the federal level, Congress also set aside 10 percent of tax subsidies for developing "sustainable manufacturing processes" that are more environmentally friendly. However, despite city efforts to require local hiring, Sematech company jobs were not going to East Austinites because the companies only hired people with two-year degrees. So community activists pushed for job-training programs. The *Austin Chronicle* quoted PODER board member Sylvia Ledesma on the Sematech-ACC training program: "Before, we were getting the toxins and not the jobs; at least now we might get the jobs, too" (de Marban 1995). In this case, the concerns of environmental groups and community activists coincided under the quality-of-life rubric. Quality of life is also the primary motivation for the latest merger of environmentalists, social activists, and the high-technology community.

"ENTER THE DIGITAL CALVARY"

Austin's solution to the problems brought on by rapid growth in technology industries once again borrowed from Silicon Valley strategies but played out within the unique environment of Austin. While the language of the creative technopolis had been conceptualized as a salve for the city's problems, Austin still experienced a degree of unrest at the actual state of affairs. The 1998 Lyman report noted that the benefits of high-technology industries were not being equally distributed among all the residents of Austin. One solution he recommended was to increase philanthropic efforts within the high-technology community: "Some cities are known for traditions of paying back the community by individuals and businesses who have gotten wealthy off of this economy. . . . You are not a successful leader unless you are giving back to the community" (quoted in Golz 1998). For example, Silicon Valley and Seattle venture capitalists and technology entrepreneurs have organized nonprofit organizations to fund social ventures. In Austin, Michael Dell of Dell Computers contributed to digital divide programs in Austin under the Wired for Youth and Connected Youth programs through the Austin Public Library.) But there was no larger forum for the entire technology community to participate in philanthropic efforts until January 1999, when Austin technology entrepreneurs Peter Zandan and Steve Papermaster organized the first annual 360 Summit. The meeting was designed to "connect the emerging technology community and to encourage greater participation in Austin's future" (Clark-Madison 2000).

Most high-technology participants were drawn to the summit by perceived problems with declining quality of life, but other community groups tried to merge their interests and needs with quality-of-life issues. As Brigid Shea, cofounder of SOS, said, although the high-technology community contributes to the problems of the boom, "they also have the biggest financial stake in preserving the quality of life of any industry. So they're the people to partner with on the environment, on transportation, on affordable housing" (quoted in Clark-Madison 2000). Topics at the summit ranged from traffic congestion to live music venues to the digital divide. At the end of the daylong summit, participants voted on a "Declaration of Interdependence" that outlined four areas for continued participation: quality of life, social equity, diversity and entrepreneurship, and assisting government agencies. They also established the Austin Network, headed by former SOS chairperson Robin Rather, to coordinate efforts and link individual entrepreneurs with needy organizations.

The rhetoric of the 360 Summit echoed much of the "united we stand" attitude of Austin's earlier private-public partnership model. In an interview with the *Austin Chronicle*, Rather declared, "I think the most important way for Austin to respond to the boom is to re-dedicate ourselves to working together, across the artificial divisions of income, electoral party, lifestyle, and philosophy, to bear down and find solutions that we can all live with" (quoted in Clark-Madison 2000). But follow-up articles in the *Austin American-Statesman* and *The Austin Chronicle* also pointed to important changes in the private-public model and schisms between groups. The articles stressed that 360 Summit participants were not interested in moving through traditional channels of government, which they perceived as inefficient, unwieldy, and boring. Summit participants prided themselves on their hip, casual approach as opposed to the "old" Rotary Club atmosphere.

According to a reporter for the *Austin American-Statesman*, the new economy needed a new approach to governance, and high-technology entrepreneurs were the model to be followed (Bishop 2002). In 2000, Lee Walker, board chair of Capital Metro, Austin's public transportation system, was quoted as saying, "In high-tech, you need to go from the idea to the marketplace in 90 days or you're chopped liver. In 90 days at Capital Metro, I can't get a resolution to sing a hymn to the Blessed Virgin Mary" (quoted in Clark-Madison 2000). This statement oozes with the ideology of the entrepreneur Brown (2003) describes as central to the new creative economy. Organizations such as the Austin Network, Austin Entrepreneurs Foundation, Austin Social Ventures Project, or GetHeard.org all spun-off from the 360 Summit. Some speculated that traditional business organizations like the Greater Austin Chamber of Commerce, which once led the move to the technopolis development strategy, were becoming obsolete. Newer, nontraditional organizations were likely to attract the business that a decade earlier would have naturally flocked to the chamber. For some, this was good news. Admirers hoped that technology entrepreneurs could apply the same business principles that made for successful private ventures to the public sphere by creating new avenues for action.

However, the good news was not shared by all. The technology community's impatience with established systems of government and the slow pace of change also carries the risk of overlooking or bypassing democratic processes. The 360 Summit, held at the exclusive Four Seasons Hotel, was by invitation only and featured central members of the high-tech literati. While representatives of the university communities, civic organizations, and city government were invited, the various groups did not always share an understanding of the nature of Austin's problems or solutions. *U.S. News and World Report* journalist William Holstein claimed that "just about the only time the high-tech crowd glimpses South or East Austin is on the way to the airport" (2000). He saw signs of the isolation and naïveté of the high-technology community in the party atmosphere of the summit. An *Austin American-Statesman* editorial echoed his sentiment: "Truth be told, the 360.00 Summit had its moments of arrogance, sexism and downright insensitivity to the work of community builders who have pumped money and sweat into worthy projects on behalf of the arts, governance, the environment and disadvantaged citizens here" (January 29, 2000).

These articles reflected a worry that persists today—that the technology mavens, with their autocratic style, will disregard public accountability. Take, for example, the 1999 agreement among SOS, the Real Estate Council of Austin, and the Greater Austin Chamber of Commerce on rules to develop the environmentally sensitive Edwards Aquifer. The seventeen-page agreement was negotiated privately, and only later adopted by the Austin city council (Bishop 2000). If important decisions had been made behind closed doors of office buildings and hotels without providing opportunities for public debate, the privatization of Austin politics could have had disastrous implications for inclusive democratic processes.

There was a sense within the Austin discourse that the technology community must be brought into civic processes in a meaningful way. With memories of the 1970s and early 1980s economic bust still fresh, Austin was not abandoning the technopolis development strategy. Despite some misgivings about the style and substance of the technology community's form of citizenship, there was (and is) a sense of inevitability about technology as the only viable option for Austin. UT public policy professor Gary Chapman noted in 2000 that he saw few alternatives to high-technology development strategies, other than tourism or gambling. He was optimistic about the new mode of private-public partnership: "The high tech community in Austin knows how to get things done, but it doesn't have much experience with the democratic process. Community activists could use some help in getting things done."

CONCLUSION

It remains to be seen whether the goals of social equity can be successfully merged with the goals of improving quality of life in the new civic configuration. To reiterate the critiques of the technopolis launched by Miller and others, the worst possible outcome of this growing presence would be an increasing forfeiture of civic programs to businesses, thereby giving them leading roles in determining the fate of the city. As anthropologist Julia Elyachar (2005) points out, attempts by technological markets to take over the processes of social betterment and improvement of the city's quality of life are becoming a globalized problem that threatens the administrative infrastructures of areas across the world.

Campanella's idea of the Civitas Solis posits an egalitarian society where all citizens benefit from scientific knowledge. Florida's idea of the creative society posits a utopian society where all citizens are able to work, live, and experience culture in a common and equal fashion. But how closely a modern technopolis can approximate these utopian cities will depend on the answer to the question posed at the beginning of this chapter: "Can such regions approach the utopian vision of Companella's Civitas Solis (1623)? Or are such cities of technology more likely to be paralyzed by elite Ph.D.s working in prestigious research institutions and unskilled workers, employed in low value-added, repetitive jobs and services?" (Smilor, Kozmetsky, and Gibson 1988, 231). Preer (1992) saw an ever-increasing digital divide, not only in access to technology but also in the economic benefits of the information society. He claimed that "the decline of the industrial working class has meant a shrinking middle in advanced countries. This 'hour-glass' effect has produced a polarization of society, with a high-paid technical and professional class at one end and unskilled service and unemployed workers at the other." Preer noted a 1987 study by Robert Sheets, Stephen Nord, and John Phelps that concluded that underemployment is associated more with successful economies than stagnant ones. "This polarization has been particularly pronounced in the United States, which does not have redistributional policies effective enough to counter it," argues Preer (1992, 45). Preer's observation points to the paradox of the technopolis—its very success as an economic strategy causes new social problems.

The next chapter (Chapter 4) takes up the story begun here and continues it into the 1990s and early 2000s. It examines some of the questions raised here, about how much the benefit of the new digital and technopolis economies were spread beyond the technology sector itself. It also examines how the structure of work and benefit evolved in Austin after its commitment to become a technopolis.

NOTES

1. They measure three factors: (1) achievement of scientific preeminence, (2) the development and maintenance of new technologies for emerging industries, and (3) the attraction of major technology companies and the creation of homegrown technology companies.

REFERENCES

Austin American-Statesman. (2000). Editorial, January 29.

Bishop, B. (2002). Austin's service class is losing its way out: In high-tech cities, workers finding paths to wealthier, creative jobs are blocked. *Austin-American Statesman*, November 3.

Briseño, V. D. (1999). Does Austin's growth management policy benefit all Austinites? The impact of Austin's smart growth initiative on East Austin: An analysis. University of Texas at Austin.

Brown, W. (2003). Neo-liberalism and the end of liberal democracy. *Theory and Event* 7(1).

Browning, L. D., et al. (1995). Building cooperation in a competitive industry: SEMATECH and the semiconductor industry. *Academy of Management Journal* 38(1): 113–151.

Butler, J. S. (2003). The essential George Kozmetsky. *McCombs School of Business Magazine* (University of Texas at Austin), Spring–Summer.

Castells, M. (1996). *The rise of the network society.* Malden, MA: Blackwell.

Chapman, G. (2000). Austin ahead of the nation on digital divide. *Austin American-Statesman*, April 27.

Clark-Madison, M. Austin at risk. *Austin American-Statesman*, May 12.

de Marban, A. (1995). Let them eat cake. *Austin American-Statesman*, May 5.

Elyachar, J. (2005). *Markets of dispossession: NGOs, economic development, and the state in Cairo.* Durham, NC: Duke University Press.

Florida, R. (2002). *The rise of the creative class: And how it's transforming work, leisure, community and everyday life.* New York: Basic Books.

Golz, E. (1998). Low unemployment creates hiring crunch. *Austin American-Statesman*, December 12.

Hartley, J. (2007). Introduction. In John Hartley (Ed.), *Creative industries.* London: Blackwell.

High-tech access closes digital divide. (1999). *Austin American-Statesman*.

Holstein, W. (2000). A tale of two Austins: How one boomtown is coping with the growing wealth gap. *U.S. News and World Report*, February 21. Retrieved March 21, 2002, from http://www.usnews.com/utils/search.

Humphrey, D. (1997). Austin: A history of the capital city. Texas State Historical Association, Texas.

Gibson, D. V., G. Kozmetsky, and R. W. Smilor. (1992). *The technopolis phenomenon: Smart cities, fast systems, global networks*. Lanham, MD: Rowman & Littlefield.

Miller, J. (2002). *Regional case study: Austin, Texas, or "How to create a knowledge economy."* Washington, DC: European Commission Delegation.

Miller, T. (2009). From creative to cultural industries. *Cultural Studies* 23(1): 88–99.

Mosco, V. (1996). *The political economy of communication*. London, Sage.

———. (2004). *The digital sublime: Myth, power, and cyberspace*. Cambridge, MA: MIT Press.

Preer, R. W. (1992). *The emergence of technopolis: Knowledge-intensive technologies and regional development*. New York: Praeger.

Robbins, P. (2003). Environmental Business—Introduction. Austin, TX, Sierra Club, Lone Star Chapter. Retrieved from www.texas.sierraclub.org.

Robbins, L. (2003). The town that won the pennant. *Environment-Business History*. Austin, TX, Sierra Club, Lone Star Chapter. Retrieved from www.texas.sierraclub.org.

Schott, R. (2000). Ethnic and race relations in Austin, Texas. Policy Research Project Report 137, Lyndon B. Johnson School of Public Affairs, University of Texas at Austin.

Sheets, R. (1988). Welcome to Silicon Gulch. *U.S. News and World Report* 105: 50–53.

Smilor, R. W., G. Kozmetsky, and D. V. Gibson. (1988). *Creating the technopolis: Linking technology, commercialization, and economic development*. Cambridge, MA: Ballinger.

Williams, F. (1988). *Measuring the information society*. London: Sage.

CHAPTER 4

PAST AND FUTURE DIVIDES

SOCIAL MOBILITY,

INEQUALITY, AND THE

DIGITAL DIVIDE IN AUSTIN

DURING THE TECH BOOM

This chapter examines the economic consequences of the technopolis development strategy adopted by Austin, Texas. It concentrates on inequality, the digital divide, and labor-market outcomes for low-income people, with a focus on the tech boom of the late 1990s and early 2000s in Austin, often considered a paradigmatic example of the "new economy" high-tech metropolis and of the (successful) deliberate reinvention of a city. In particular, I will examine the theoretical assumptions that structure the technopolis strategy and proposed remedies to negative economic outcomes caused by the digital divide such as job training, and how these play out within the context of a self-proclaimed technopolis.

Job training in fields such as information technology is a standard policy prescription for low-income workers, especially during economic downturns (including the current Great Recession that began in 2008), which makes the Austin example particularly relevant. However, actual labor-market outcomes for population segments that increase their computer skills have received less attention in scholarly work on the digital divide. The digital divide rubric often conflates two topics: individual outcomes resulting from lack of access to or competence with using the Internet, on the one hand, and the overall changes to the structure of the labor market caused by the increasing prevalence of information technologies, on the other hand. While those two aspects of the divide overlap, they are not identical; a conceptual and analytic distinction must be maintained.

In this chapter, I start by briefly reviewing theories about the labor-market consequences of information technology. Concerns about the workforce effects of computers precede the digital divide discourse, which emerged only in the 1990s. Within the digital divide framework, there are two interrelated issues concerning labor-market outcomes and information technology. The first concerns the overall effect of increasingly powerful information technologies on the structure of the labor market. Which kinds of occupations are growing, and which are shrinking? How does new technology alter power relations between employer and employees? Which occupations gain in prestige and pay, and which lose? What can a locality do to create a better environment for its residents? A commonly proposed answer to these problems has been the technopolis strategy, examined at length in Chapter 3 of this book.

The second major issue concerns feasible strategies for generating upward mobility, or in some cases strategies for stopping or stabilizing downward mobility, for those segments of the labor market that are either already disadvantaged or threatened by technological changes. The commonly proposed remedy is job training. However, the two issues are clearly intertwined: the success of individual strategies will obviously depend on the opportunity structures in the labor market.

INFORMATION TECHNOLOGIES AND LABOR MARKETS: COMPETING THEORIES, NARROW PUBLIC DIALOGUE

While there is significant debate within the academic community about these topics, much of the civic discourse on the economic aspects of information technology policy subscribes implicitly to a viewpoint generally associated with social theorists such as Daniel Bell (1973) or Manuel Castells (1996). While not identical, and generally much more nuanced than their public articulations, these theories essentially propose an economy in which information-technology-related skills are rewarded well and provide social mobility, increased job opportunities, and economic benefit to their holders. This view is often associated with terms such as "information age," "knowledge economy," and "postindustrial society."

In particular, Bell's theory of postindustrial society makes specific predictions about the relationship between work, skill, and reward, following from the key premise that information and the tools for accessing and manipulating information form the critical resource for, and thus the main path to, social mobility (Giddens 1981, 21; Lyon

1988, 2–5; Webster and Robins 1986, 32–48). Postindustrial society theorists all claim to some degree that we have witnessed an epochal shift from industrial society, where the critical resource was capital, to postindustrial society, where the critical resource is technical competence and education.

Bell (1973) underlines three major characteristics (or predictions) of the new information society: (1) a shift in emphasis from manufacturing and material production to a service-oriented economy, (2) the importance of information as a commodity, and (3) an increase in the proportion of the workforce engaged in "knowledge work." Such changes, Bell contends, will fundamentally change the structure of work and the power relations at work, increasing the power of the skilled knowledge worker and thus expanding the base of meritocracy, since social mobility will no longer be limited by access to capital, the critical resource of the industrial society:

> The postindustrial society adds a new criterion to the definitions of base and access. Technical skill becomes a condition of operative power, and higher education means the obtaining of technical skill. As a result, there has been a shift in the slope of power as, in key institutions, technical competence becomes the overriding consideration. . . . The post-industrial society, in this dimension of status and power, is the logical extension of the meritocracy; it is the codification of a new social order based, in principle, on the priority of educated talent. (1973, 426)

Here, Bell joins together multiple assumptions that can be analytically separated. The importance of information as a commodity could increase without necessarily increasing the number of highly paid, skilled jobs. Polarization theory, discussed below, proposes such a scenario. Also, educated talent could be valued without capital becoming less important by comparison. On the contrary, in some settings, the importance of capital could increase at a faster rate since most educated labor requires extensive capital layout to practice. What good are advanced biotechnology skills without a corresponding expensive laboratory?

Following from the Bell-Castells tradition, the "skill-biased technological change" school of thought argues that new technologies require up-skilling from the workforce, and that those who do not fare well in the new economy are those who suffer from lack of education and appropriate high-level skills. The most common data point offered as proof of this theory is the strong positive return on education; on the average, a person with a college degree earns much more than a high school graduate, while a person with an advanced degree earns more than someone with only a college degree (Autor et al. 1997). (PhD holders, however, average less than holders of MAs, MBAs, or other professional graduate degrees.) The reasoning for why higher-educated people are paid more is usually that there is a shortage of them. This explanation is commonly cited by policy makers at all levels—including presidents. For example, President Clinton noted in his State of the Union address in 2000 that "today's income gap is largely a skills gap" (Clinton 2000). Such rhetoric has been echoed by both George W. Bush and Barack Obama, whose administration launched a major effort to promote job training in response to the "Great Recession."

Indeed, while average wages have been mostly stagnant since the 1970s, low-skilled workers have experienced a wage collapse, whereas higher-skilled workers have fared less badly. The disparity between the fates of differently educated segments of the labor market, coupled with the ubiquity of information technology in the workplace, guided many to what seemed like an obvious conclusion: we are moving toward an economy in which skills are rewarded, and those that are left behind could get ahead if they acquired the right skills.

However, the Bell-Castells model also incorporates several leaps in logic. First, it assumes that working with high technology is uniformly a high-skilled endeavor. In fact, many advances in technology have been made with the explicit goal of lowering skill requirements (Noble 1984; Zuboff 1988). Thus, by itself, the prevalence of computers in the workplace does not warrant the assumption that the jobs associated with them have been up-skilled.

Second, many activities related to technology, such as assembling computers, are themselves low-skill jobs. A sector can thus be classified as high tech even though its occupational effects on the economy are mostly confined to the low-skilled, low-paid sector. This confounding of sector and occupational structure bedevils much of the public discourse on the topic.

Third, there are data clearly in conflict with the received wisdom about developed countries in general, and the United States in particular, becoming a predominantly high-skilled economy. In most industrialized nations, the majority of the population is now employed in what is termed the "service" industry—a relatively misleading category that lumps together low-wage corporate positions and McJobs with high-paid, high-skilled professions like doctor and lawyer. Disaggregating the service sector into occupational categories reveals a more exact and sobering conclusion: most service sector jobs are low paid and low skilled. More precisely, these countries have seen the replacement of high-paid, often unionized jobs in capital-intensive manufacturing industries with low-paid jobs, many of which involve providing services rather than producing goods.

By contrast, polarization theorists have argued that information technology may have negative effects on the lower segments of labor markets, either in part or as a whole, even while requiring up-skilling for some segments. Polarization theory, or labor-market-segmentation theory, makes the case that, as a result of advances in technology, jobs requiring medium-level skills are reduced in number or eliminated, with the majority of employees reallocated to low-skilled jobs, while at the same time a relatively small number of new and higher-skilled planning and monitoring jobs is created (Kubicek 1985, 76). Polarization theory dovetails with the work of theorists who have suggested that computers can be used for significantly different purposes at the upper and lower levels of the occupational structure; in the large low-paid, low-skilled job sector, information technology is used to automate, deskill, and control (Braverman 1975) rather than to enhance and "informate" (Zuboff 1988). In fact, a 2006 paper (Autor, Katz, and Kearney) finds that the nature of the existing economic polarization, as well as increases thereof, corresponds closely with differential application of computers in higher and lower segments of the labor market.

In his book *The Work of Nations*, published in 1991, Robert Reich sums up the polarization approach to analyzing the structure of work in an information society and predicts roughly the occupational results depicted above:

> All Americans used to be in the same economic boat. Most rose or fell together, as the corporations in which they were employed, the industries comprising such corporations, and the national economy as a whole became more productive—or languished. But national borders no longer define our economic fates. We are now in different boats, one sinking rapidly, one sinking more slowly, and the third rising steadily. (Reich 1991, 208)

The three boats Reich is referring to are those employed in "symbolic-analytic" services, "in-person" services, and routine production services. According to Reich, members of the first category, symbolic analysts, are highly educated, skilled "mind-workers" who are less and less definable by the old loyalties of nation, corporation, or place. These are the "problem-solving, problem-identifying, and strategic-brokering" jobs. The second category, in-person services, entails "simple and repetitive tasks," and the pay is a function of hours and the amount of work performed. These jobs are defined by necessarily being performed by a person—the wages or the skill level might go down, but the job will still be there. Reich counts waiters, child-care providers, most health-care workers (but not doctors), and taxi drivers, among others, in this category. The third category is the routine producers, who perform repetitive, simple tasks in highly supervised environments. Reich, partially echoing Harry Braverman's earlier analysis of the role of technology in terms of allowing the division of tasks into smaller constituents, contends that information technologies make this kind of job even more possible and prevalent, even in the tech sector. Reich thus asserts a conclusion quite contrary to those of Bell-type theorists:

> Indeed, contrary to prophets of the "information age" who buoyantly predicted an abundance of high-paying jobs even for people with the most basic of skills, the sobering truth is that many information-processing jobs fit easily into this category. The foot soldiers of the information economy are hordes of data processors stationed in "back offices" at computer terminals linked to worldwide information banks. They routinely enter data into computers or take it out again. . . . The "information revolution" may have rendered some of us more productive, but it has also produced huge piles of raw data which must be processed in much the same monotonous way that assembly-line workers, and before them, textile workers processed piles of other raw materials. (1991, 174)

STRUCTURAL AND INDIVIDUAL REMEDIES TO PROBLEMS BOLSTERED BY INFORMATION TECHNOLOGY

Proposed remedies for ameliorating any possible negative fallout from a development in the economy depend on the understanding of the dynamics and mechanics of the question at hand. The theoretical assumptions behind policy decisions matter. It was the Bell-Castells model, stipulating that diffusion of information technologies will create a better labor market overall, and one that especially rewards those who acquire information technology skills, which won the day in popular and policy discourse. This model, whether invoked explicitly or implicitly, ultimately shaped public discussions about technology and labor markets, especially during the high-tech boom of the late 1990s. While polarization theory gained somewhat more of a foothold in popular discourse after the tech bust and also during the Great Recession that began in 2008, during which unemployment soared, it was rarely mentioned in policy decisions in the 1990s.

In the 1990s, for individuals experiencing difficulties in the labor market, job training was the main recommendation (and remains so at the end of 2010). For localities, attracting more high-tech industries and becoming a technopolis was offered as the way to go. These proposed solutions make sense in light of the implicit theories that structured policy and public discourse. If it is assumed that information technology empowers skilled workers and creates an increasing demand for them without differentiating between segments of the labor market, it then makes sense to propose solutions aimed at improving skills of individuals without regard to their class and occupational position. Unsurprisingly, then, a remarkably unified national discourse focused on information technology training as the way to overcome challenges faced by those perceived to have been left behind by a booming high-tech economy. It was within this climate that Austin implemented job-training programs to address the digital divide.

Austin, like many other localities, has been attempting to respond to multiple interrelated economic, technical, political, and financial developments, often referred to as globalization. Over the past several decades, as more and more of the world has been integrated into the global economy, many of the earlier- and more-developed regions have seen the erosion of their industrial production bases, which have largely moved to areas with cheaper labor. Economists and policy makers have generally conceded that the industrial jobs that migrate from the rich countries will never return.

A natural response has been for localities in the rich countries to make efforts to attract high-technology industries to replace those lost jobs. As these efforts have evolved, they have spawned a dialogue about how the regions should proceed in this new economic climate and about how to preserve the American dream of good jobs, a good place to raise a family, and economic rewards at least somewhat commensurate with one's willingness to work hard, learn the right skills, and persevere. It was in this general context that Austin strove to become a high-tech mecca, a technopolis.

AUSTIN: THE SHAPE OF A TECHNOPOLIS

Austin is, by many accounts, a triumphant example of a technopolis. It has successfully attracted many high-tech industries to the region and experienced explosive growth in the high-tech sector (Chapter 3). This section recounts a few key elements of this development as it pertains to high-tech industries in particular before and during the high-tech boom of the 1990s and its aftermath in the early 2000s.

In the late 1980s and early 1990s, Austin witnessed a sizable growth in computer manufacturing and related industries. According to the U.S. Department of Labor, between 1989 and 1995 the manufacture of computers and office equipment grew by 48.1 percent; the manufacture of communications equipment by 43.9 percent; the manufacture of electronic components by 82.2 percent; computer and data processing by 202.7 percent; and engineering, research, and management services by 45.2 percent (Cardella 1999, 34). In the 1990s and during the tech boom, many Internet companies also sprung up in the region, creating a high-tech industry that included both software and hardware production.

Austin regularly places at or near the top of lists of "post-wired cities," "best cities for business," and similar measures. It also ranks just behind San Francisco in the "creativity index" developed by prominent theorist Richard Florida, who argues that distribution of the benefits of the new economy goes primarily to cities characterized by a high proportion of workers in what he calls the "creative class"—including "authors, software writers, top managers, dancers, singers, engineers, lawyers, doctors and scientists" (paraphrased by Bishop and Lisheron 2002). Florida counterposes the success of these creative cities—San Francisco, Austin, Raleigh-Durham, and others—with the lack of success of cities low on his creativity index, like Memphis, New Orleans, or Providence (Florida 2002). With regard to city planning, he focuses on the importance of quality-of-life issues usually associated with liberalism and openness—bike paths, coffee shops, and gay bars—and suggests that the more traditional focus on the highly capital-intensive creation of large, dispiriting office parks and other characteristics associated with "nerdistans" may be misguided.

Technopolis theories, especially with a Florida-type twist, have certainly been very helpful in understanding the economic dynamics of urban areas in the past two decades. It is important to note, however, a major potential caveat to, or limitation of, all such analyses: even in a technopolis, the significant majority of jobs are not in the technology sector. As Ruth Ann Cardella reports in the case of Austin:

> While the majority of area jobs (80 percent) are in the non-technology sectors, such as retail trade, government, construction, finance and real estate, the technology sectors (including manufacturing and services) are growing at a faster rate, which has fueled growth in these producer service and construction sectors. From 1997 to 1998, tech sector employment grew 7 percent while non-tech sector employment grew only 4.1 percent. (1999, 31)

Even if broad technopolis-type conclusions were to hold up in the information technology sector, further ideas about technology-driven development leading to widespread meritocracy and the elimination of divides based on race and class could easily founder on the basic reality that "underclasses" might remain confined to the 80 percent of jobs that are not technology related. However, technology jobs themselves are not necessarily the panacea to economic distress.

In contradistinction to the assumptions of the technopolis strategy, jobs in the technology sector can also be low paid and low skilled. Much of the manufacturing-related jobs and a significant portion of the service-related jobs in the technology sector involve low, even very low, pay. Table 4.1 shows the breakdown of jobs in the technology sector in Austin, which itself only constitutes 20 percent of the area jobs. While software development, which constitutes 21 percent of technology jobs, tends to pay relatively well, much of the manufacturing sector is composed of low-pay factory jobs.

The reality of some of these highly touted tech-industry jobs was highlighted in Austin when high-tech manufacturer Samsung's jobs were revealed to be paying $5.50 an hour (Brunick 2000). When this was reported in local newspapers, it was greeted with outrage, as Samsung had received millions of dollars' worth of tax abatements from

Table 4.1. Breakdown of Jobs in the Technology Sector in Austin, 1999

Computer and electronic manufacturing	31 percent
Semiconductors	22 percent
Software development	21 percent
Computer services	11 percent
Biotech	5 percent
Other	10 percent

Source: Angelou Economic Advisors 1998

the City of Austin in return for locating there (Fullerton 1998). After a sustained campaign by the Interfaith Coalition of Austin, Samsung agreed to raise its wages to $7.50 an hour, which, according to federal standards, still qualified as a poverty-level wage for a family of three.

In addition, I encountered many people in my studies who were casualties of downsizing from the low-paying end of the computer industry. While they had experience assembling state-of-the-art computers, many did not know how to handle a mouse. Such workers appeared to be working in the high-tech industry in sector-based classifications, but in reality they were working in jobs that required relatively low levels of skill and paid very little.

THE DIGITAL DIVIDE AND THE AUSTIN EXPERIENCE

The Internet-fueled boom of the mid- to late 1990s caused an explosion in Austin's economy, as decade-long efforts to attract high-tech industries had already situated the city as a global powerhouse. Austin had both the infrastructure and the quality of life required to attract people, money, and companies to the region. In keeping with Florida's theory, Austin's civic leadership argued that the city's continued economic success depended on maintaining a lifestyle that would remain attractive to the creative classes—postulated to be young, somewhat liberal and socially conscious, fond of the outdoors, and interested in music.

In the case of Austin, the quality-of-life issue was entangled with the question of the digital divide from the beginning. Austin's mayor at the time, Kirk Watson, was a highly visible proponent of improving Austinites' living experiences through engaged social policies. In what was portrayed as a win-win situation, Austin's civic leadership

argued that the tech boom provided both the opportunity and the ob-
ligation to find ways to ease some of the social and economic divides
that Austin had been experiencing. There was not much discussion
of the fact that Austin had consciously engineered the racial segregation that seemed to be at the heart of the income and opportunity
differences between East Austin and the rest of the area (discussed in
Chapter 2). However, for many social activists, it did not matter how
and why Austin had become the way it was. There was money, initiative, and seemingly a theory about how to help Austin's underclass.

This theory was based on the rewards of technology skills. Given
that Austin's newfound riches were coming from technology industries, and the ideas about developing Austin's potential were coming from people who had greatly benefited from the diffusion of computers and the Internet, it seemed natural to argue that including the
less fortunate in the benefits of these new tools would help everyone.
The *Austin-American Statesman* editorialized that the prevalence of
"information have-nots" was bad for economic strength, and invited
tech companies to contribute:

> Although it is not solely responsible for bridging the digital divide,
> the high-tech industry has an important role to play in conjunc-
> tion with the education system in promoting technological skills
> among all groups. . . . Why does this matter? Without basic com-
> puter skills, a growing portion of the work force won't be able to
> fully contribute to the national economy. A class of "information
> have-nots" jeopardizes our standing as a great economic nation.
> ("High-Tech Access" 1999)

Tech companies, awash with cash from IPOs and stocks, responded
to such calls, perhaps viewing them as good public relations through
the demonstration of positive corporate citizenship, and as a means of
ensuring the creation of a larger customer base. Indeed, having more
people using, purchasing, and needing computers was a requirement
for future growth:

> Dell Computer Corporation promotes a three-pronged approach
> to giving, including foundation, corporate, and executive contri-
> butions. . . . Through its diversity programs, Dell Computer Corp.
> funds computer and technology programs in classrooms and neigh-
> borhood centers. Also, executives are frequent contributors to

civic groups and participate in community initiatives. Companies led by IBM Corp. and Powershift Group recently held the second annual AIR Austin competition in which 80 Web designers
built Web sites for local nonprofit groups for free. The recently created Entrepreneur's Foundation encourages startup companies to
contribute small portions of their stock options to trusts. When
the company goes public or is sold, the proceeds go to a nonprofit.
("High-Tech Access"1999)

Even traditional charities like United Way started contributing to
digital divide efforts, as noted in a letter to the editor of the *Austin
American-Statesman* (October 11, 1999):

> In the article titled "High-tech access closes digital divide," you
> made reference to the "uneven use of computers between minori-
> ties and whites." I'm proud to report United Way/Capital Area re-
> cently gave $25,000 through our CHARITech Civic Venture Fund
> to a project that aims to address this very issue.

Reporting and discussion of the question of digital divide was often accompanied in the local press, and in the pronouncements of
elected officials and civic leaders, with an explanation of the theory
that closing the digital divide was important to closing the economic
divide:

> [Austin City] Council Members Daryl Slusher and Gus Garcia
> have agreed the city needs to address this issue. Today's discus-
> sion promises to be the first of many. The pop culture name for
> the wage-gap phenomenon Central Texas is experiencing is the
> "digital divide." The term originally referred to the lack of Inter-
> net connections and computers in poor homes and neighborhoods.
> Economists now say the digital divide includes the failure of large
> numbers of people to tap into the burgeoning high-tech economy.
> Those with skills and training make high wages in the new econ-
> omy. Jobs that demand few skills earn minimum pay. The divide is
> digital in that it is made wider by an economy that rewards people
> with computer or software skills. But it is basically economic, a di-
> vision between rich and poor. And, as Daryl Slusher said, "This is
> not a problem that's peculiar to Austin—it's just exacerbated here
> because of the booming economy." (Bishop 2000)

Although one might have expected the tech boom to close Austin's income divide, it only seemed to exacerbate it. In 2002 the *Austin American-Statesman* (November 3) published the findings of a study it had conducted which concluded that "the gap between the top 10 percent of Austin's private industry workers and the bottom 10 percent doubled in the 1990s," more than was the case for any other Texas city. According to a 2001 report by the Austin Equity Commission (specially formed by the city council to investigate rising inequality), the outlook had become grim for the lower segments of the workforce:

> While the proportion of Austin jobs paying below-poverty wages declined dramatically—from 46 percent in 1990 to 22 percent in 1999—the absolute number of such jobs rose from 85,386 to 99,400 in those years, and the number of people living in poverty increased from 111,412 in 1989 to 122,000 in 1999. In addition, Austin had a higher proportion of workers earning poverty-level wages than any comparison city we looked at. (3)

Even more apposite, and in line with the predictions of polarization theory, the Austin job market developed a heavily two-tiered structure, with a collapsing middle. This structure had clear effects on opportunities for mobility:

> Steven Jackobs directs Capital IDEA, a local group that provides training to low-income people. . . . Austin's job market used to be a pyramid, Jackobs says. Companies encouraged employees to start at the bottom and work their way up. There was a structure to work, provided by unions or large corporate bureaucracies. "Now it's not a pyramid, but an hour glass," Jackobs explains. "And there's just a tight little spot in the middle."
>
> To move from service-class jobs to the creative class isn't a climb, Jackobs says. "Now you have to load yourself into a cannon and shoot yourself into the clouds." (Bishop and Lisheron 2002)

This bottleneck has had obvious effects on the efficacy of any remedial efforts that concentrate on the supply of labor skills rather than the structure of the job market. The job market structured by the technopolis was certainly not a rosy, high-income paradise. Given this reality, remedies for individuals—such as job training—became even more important.

FINDINGS FROM JOB-TRAINING PROGRAMS
AT COMMUNITY TECHNOLOGY CENTERS

In 1999, some members of Austin civil society, including the city government, the chamber of commerce, the University of Texas at Austin, and a collection of nonprofits, obtained funding for a multi-year, multimillion-dollar project aimed at closing the digital divide and providing information technology access and skills to under-privileged communities. Their grant application made specific claims about the nature of the economy and tools of social mobility:

> While there are abundant high tech employment and business op-portunities for those with specific skills and experience, entire segments of the population are being left out. . . . A significant portion of our community is currently excluded from access to the critical tools for success in the global economy of the 21st cen-tury; computers, e-mail, Internet access, and technological liter-acy. (Austin Technology Coalition 1999, 1)

Another belief asserted in the application was that there was a short-age of workers skilled in these technologies, and the groups at whom the project was aimed would be able to step up and meet this need once provided with the right training:

> There is a demand for skilled workers that is unmet by current ef-forts. If barriers to employment can be removed for this segment of workers, [our] businesses will benefit. It is a rare opportunity to meet the needs of employers and the needs of workers simultane-ously. (Austin Technology Coalition 1999, 4)

The rhetoric was strikingly similar to that which could be observed in programs across the country aimed at bridging the digital divide and is an example of the implicit theoretical assumptions discussed in earlier sections. The applicants assume that there are jobs waiting and available *if only* workers had the requisite skills, plausibly ob-tainable through a job-training program.

I conducted research on this program for three years. The program was well run and adequately funded. The staff appeared competent, and participation was enthusiastic and intensive. The program, how-ever, could be seen to be "creaming"—the practice by which a social program accepts only the most qualified, thereby ridding itself of the tougher cases. The attendance requirements, four times a week, three hours at a time, would have made participation very difficult for anyone with unreliable transportation, child-care issues, a difficult home environment, or conditions permitting anything less than total dedication. Indeed, most participants attended every single class—that is, they were a singularly dedicated group with resources that permitted focus and consistency.

My research involved on-site, participatory observation as well as a longitudinal outcome evaluation with multimethod data collection and analysis that followed cohorts of trainees for six months to two years to see their progress in the labor market. I observed all training sessions for multiple cohorts and conducted interviews with participants during training as well as follow-up interviews for six months to two years after the program with participants whose training I had attended.

To the surprise of many of those involved with the project, the program did not provide significant social mobility or job opportunities to any of the twenty-three participants I was able to locate during the next two years, excepting minor career boosts for two of the participants. After initial failure in finding jobs, many participants decided the reason was that they still did not know enough about computers and searched for more training programs. Many were at a loss as to what exactly the next step should be, but remained convinced that they needed more information technology skills.

The general inadequacy many participants felt in the labor market points to alternative mechanisms through which the digital divide can create labor-market polarization and adverse outcomes even among those who are not lacking the skills required to perform the job. These mechanisms include the inability to effectively search for jobs that are listed online and handicaps in applying for jobs for which screening is performed via computer kiosk (now common even in many low-income jobs in the retail sector).

JOB TRAINING AS SAVIOR REDUX: THE GREAT RECESSION AND THE IMPORTANCE OF THEORETICAL ASSUMPTIONS

After the deep recession which began in 2008, a similar discourse concentrating on job training reemerged as well. However, with the effects of the dot-com bust still lingering in recent memory, much of the focus this time around was on "green" jobs rather than on information technology jobs. In an eerily similar replay of the tech boom, I started hearing ads on the radio that promised well-paying green jobs through environmental training. They sounded exactly like the ads I had heard throughout the late 1990s—ads for programs just like the one I studied. Of course, it is possible that this time, because of government-provided stimulus funds, there will be real jobs that are open to unemployed people in the lower end of the labor market.

This repeated focus on job training flows from an inclination to see, and a wish to see, labor-market woes as supply driven—that is, if only one could obtain the requisite skills, one could find work. The problem is identified within the supplier of labor, the worker. That may well be true for some individuals, but it obviously cannot be true for everyone. Labor-market policies must look at the whole picture—anything less can only mislead.

Under what conditions would job training be an appropriate solution? First, there must be a feasible path to the proposed skill set. Whether or not there are lots of jobs for people with biotechnology PhDs is irrelevant to the upward mobility prospects of most unemployed people. "Information technology" is not a single skill set that can be learned through a single linear curriculum. There is a wide range of skills one could acquire, such as using commercial software for clerking in offices, programming to create software, network and system management and administration, digital production, and using social media. Each of these skills corresponds to a different level of training and job market, and some of them may not be attainable through job-training programs, as they may require more than a few months or years of a specific curriculum. High-level programming, for example, or advanced digital media creation fit that category, as most professionals in these fields have a lifetime of immersion in information technology, including a long period of formal and informal learning that often starts at high school and earlier and may include college degrees and beyond. The number of jobs in these categories is all but irrelevant to most of the low-income unemployed that programs such as the one I studied are targeting.

Second, the number of jobs available through the proposed skill set must approximate the number of job seekers. The fact that there might be *some* jobs available to those with computer skills attainable with reasonable effort and within a reasonable time does not make job training a good national or local strategy to recommend to everyone. In fact, such recommendations and policies often end up with credential inflation: if more people are encouraged to obtain a college degree, but the number of jobs requiring a college degree does not change, we end up with many college graduates performing jobs that used to belong to high school graduates. Often, all that changes is the name of various stations in the labor-market queue, rather than who's ahead or who's behind (Lafer 2002).

While a full debate is much beyond the scope of this paper, Table 4.2, from the Bureau of Labor Statistics, provides a snapshot of the economy that workers trying to find jobs in the first decade of the twenty-first century faced. The numbers, reflecting projections for the job market starting from 2006, are sobering. Almost all the jobs with the largest anticipated growth, except registered nurses and postsecondary teachers, require very little education beyond high school, if any. In fact, some of the categories seem to have been made artificially weaker by splitting them up—for example, "Personal and home care aides" is a separate category from "Home health aides." Had they been combined, they would have made up the largest-growing job category by far. Similarly, retail salespeople are ranked second, while customer service representatives, a separate category, are ranked third. These occupational categories are very similar, characterized by their temporary nature, low pay, and unattractive working conditions. Even the market for postsecondary teachers, the only occupational category requiring significant education, is undergoing a heavy polarization, with a shrinking number of tenure-track jobs and a growing segment of underpaid, overworked adjuncts who have no job security and often little hope of a permanent position anywhere.

Among the top ten jobs with the largest anticipated growth, almost all require only short-term on-the-job training. Further, they are concentrated in low-paid service sector jobs such as retail salespeople, customer service representatives, food preparation and service workers, janitors, and nurse's aides. This directly contradicts some of the claims of the Bell-Castells model, as occupations which require high skill, especially in the handling of information through technology, have not become widespread.

Proponents of technopolis strategies often point to the relatively high rate of growth in some well-paid, high-skilled jobs. Such numbers are often misleading and must be interpreted within the context of the absolute and relative *numbers* of jobs, and not just percentage growth. A high percentage growth starting from a small base can indeed look impressive but can also mean very little in terms of the

Table 4.2. Occupations with the Largest Anticipated Job Growth, 2006–2016

Occupation	Employment		Change		Most significant source of postsecondary education or training
	2006	2016	Number	Percentage	
Registered nurses	2,505*	3,092	587	23.5	Associate's degree
Retail salespeople	4,477	5,034	557	12.4	Short-term on-the-job training
Customer service representatives	2,202	2,747	545	24.8	Moderate-term on-the-job training
Food preparation and service workers, including fast food	2,503	2,955	452	18.1	Short-term on-the-job training
Office clerks	3,200	3,604	404	12.6	Short-term on-the-job training
Personal and home care aides	767	1,156	389	50.6	Short-term on-the-job training
Home health aides	787	1,171	384	48.7	Short-term on-the-job training
Postsecondary teachers	1,672	2,054	382	22.9	Doctoral degree
Janitors and cleaners, except maids and housekeepers	2,387	2,732	345	14.5	Short-term on-the-job training
Nursing aides, orderlies, and attendants	1,447	1,711	264	18.2	Short-term on-the-job training

*Numbers in thousands of jobs

Source: Bureau of Labor Statistics 2007

number of jobs that will be available. The Bureau of Labor Statistics highlights percentage growth charts in its news releases regarding employment projections and often buries the numerical growth tables. Digging into the data, however, we find the stark reality: a very significant portion all job creation in the United States is in the form of low-skilled, low-paid labor. This situation cannot be adequately addressed by job training.

THE ROLE OF COMPUTERS IN POLARIZATION AND DESKILLING

I would like to briefly mention a theoretical and analytical viewpoint that these findings and national-level data support and that is often overlooked: that deskilling can also be brought about by technology. I also propose that in certain instances, information technology skills may function as cultural capital rather than as traditional human capital in the sense understood by economists.

The findings summarized in this chapter suggest that more attention should be paid to the deskilling (Webster and Robins 1986; Zuboff 1988) and automating potential of information technologies, ultimately resulting in the disempowering and disadvantaging of employees. This may happen in multiple manners. Jobs that used to require more advanced skills are simplified, automated, and reduced from sophisticated crafts to simple manual and mental labor. Cashiers used to remember prices of many items, and receptionists took into account many business and personal factors when directing calls, such as who was in a meeting and when to interrupt. Automated checkout systems and voice systems are rapidly eliminating or greatly deskilling both jobs. Also, automation allows for breaking up jobs into components and directing each component to the lowest-skilled or lowest-paid employee. Thus, with the development of new medical tools, taking of blood pressure has been passed on from doctors to registered nurses to licensed practical nurses to nursing aides—and with each step, skill requirements have been lowered. Also, an X-ray or an MRI may now be assessed by computerized analysis or passed to a radiologist located in India who charges much less. Without extensive digital communication systems, the breaking up of tasks into constituent parts and dispersing of these parts to maximize profit and employer control would not have been possible. Many middle-level jobs are thus eliminated.

Overall, this process contributes to polarization of the labor market because information technology may have an up-skilling effect for high-income or highly educated employees, while deskilling and disempowering the bottom segment of workers and shrinking the middle. Depending on the ratio of growth between the up-skilled and deskilled job categories, the overall job market may worsen or improve. A secondary but important effect of polarization is that there is no natural way to climb up the ladder. Starting at the bottom of a company's employment structure and working one's way up becomes rarely feasible.

Based on these analyses and the experiences of participants in the job-training program I studied, I propose that, for the lower segments of the labor market, information technology skills may serve as status markers and credentials that employers use to rank and eliminate job applicants, rather than requisite skills that are essential for complicated job tasks and that provide upward mobility (Collins 1979; Lafer 2002). This is not to suggest that in no cases are these skills required. But most of the available positions that use products of high-technology use them in an automating and deskilling fashion, such as cashiers and customer service representatives (Bureau of Labor Statistics 2007).

CULTURAL CAPITAL AND INFORMATION TECHNOLOGY SKILLS

Information technology skills can also act as cultural capital within labor markets. Pierre Bourdieu's concept of cultural capital, with certain modifications so that it can be broadened from its traditional application to cultural tastes and dispositions, is particularly suited to expand a directed, as opposed to a broad, credentialist critique of the labor market, especially with regard to information technology skills as applied to the lower strata, within a context of ideological hegemonic consensus as formulated by Antonio Gramsci (Bourdieu 1986; Collins 1979; Gramsci 1971).

The few participants in the job-training program who reported the training as useful in looking for employment generally mentioned information technology skills as "opening doors" for them by letting them appear informed and up to date, yet they did not see the skills as necessarily being required for the job. Many reported that they were taking the training courses so that they would not feel left behind or "stupid" because they did not know the basics of operating a computer (Tufekci 2003). They asserted that they saw their lack of competence with computers as a sign of not being "with it" and being inadequate in general, and they expected that others would as well. They did not necessarily articulate what part of their potential future job they thought they would be unable to perform; rather, they expressed a general unease about belonging. There was less emphasis on possessing particular skills than on being the right kind of person—one that can use computers. Many participants repeatedly mentioned having been left behind by technology, and they felt their plight would be eased only if they acquired the correct set of skills.

These skills are not mechanisms of economic human capital, but rather of cultural capital. In this conceptualization, information technology skills operate as techno-cultural capital in that people who are not comfortable with technology can be excluded from portions of the labor market even if the particulars of the job do not require technological competence beyond that already held by the person.

The belief in the potential of information technology skills to provide pathways to upward mobility helps legitimize unequal outcomes among those most adversely affected. The national emphasis on job training in general and information technology skills in particular thus serves as a quasi-ideological framework of legitimation in which low-income workers believe that their lack of skills is the root cause of their situation. A cursory examination of the structure of the labor market shows, however, that it is not plausible for most of these people to obtain higher-paid employment—there simply are not enough such jobs.

CONCLUSION

Although the data presented here are partial, if we couple them with a broader look at rising inequality in Austin, disappearance of middle-level jobs in the Austin job market, and similar trends elsewhere, a picture starts to emerge. Results from my three-year longitudinal study of computer-skills training at a Community Technology Center in Austin do not bear out the hypothesis that information technology skills necessarily promote upward job mobility for lower-income people. My research found that recipients of information technology training had little or no differential success in obtaining jobs. With regard, for example, to the recipients of training in the program I observed, the relevant constraint in the area of the job market that these people were being trained for was not a shortage of skills but rather a shortage of jobs. The trainees successfully acquired entry-level information technology skills through an intensive course that required three hours of instruction every day. Most of the participants were dedicated, had near-perfect attendance, and were disappointed when they could find no jobs that matched the skills they acquired or realized that there was no skill shortage in their end of the labor market. Indeed, openings for low-level jobs of the type that require the basic computer and technology skills covered in these courses are generally met with an overabundance of qualified applicants.

These results are small scale but indicative, since they seem to stem from large-scale structural factors. Under the information society paradigm that has dominated public discourse, such a conclusion appears to be heretical, pointing to serious theoretical shortcomings in that entire approach. Also, this study highlights the importance of looking at how information technology skills contribute to the structuring and reproduction of inequality through credentialism and also as exclusionary cultural capital. I propose that information technology skills may be operating in a credentialist manner, and also separately as techno-cultural capital which helps legitimize inequality and shift the focus away from the lack of good jobs.

The training programs I studied did provide important benefits for their recipients. They should be supported, not because they magically compensate for the lack of good jobs, but because they provide civic and personal empowerment. Most important, the participants no longer feel stupid and left behind in an age, as one trainee put it, "where everyone and their mama is computerized." When even Walmart accepts applications at computerized kiosks in its stores, losing one's fear of computers can make a real difference. However, that difference is not enough to provide good jobs and raise living standards for large numbers of people. The problem lies with the job market (Tufekci 2003).

The next chapter (Chapter 5) shifts to a different layer of analysis that extends beyond Austin. It examines the rising policy discourse intended to address some of the issues of preparedness for information work raised in this chapter. It examines how the Clinton administration perceived a digital divide between those who had computer access and knowledge and those who did not, and created a series of programs to address it that had a major impact in Austin. It also examines the subsequent dismantling of many of those programs after 2000.

REFERENCES

Angelou Economic Advisors. (1998). Austin: An economic review and forecast, 1997–1999. Austin.

Austin Equity Commission. (2001). Improving the odds: Increasing opportunities in Austin. Austin.

Austin Technology Coalition. (1999). Community technology training center. Grant application. Austin.

Autor, D. H, L. F. Katz, and M. Kearney. (2006). The polarization of the U.S. labor market. National Bureau of Economic Research, Cambridge, MA. Retrieved August 2, 2009, from http://ideas.repec.org/p/nbr/nberwo/11986.html.

Autor, D. H., L. F. Katz, A. B. Krueger, and National Bureau of Economic Research. (1997). Computing inequality: Have computers changed the labor market? National Bureau of Economic Research, Cambridge, MA.

Bell, D. (1973). *The coming of post-industrial society: A venture in social forecasting*. New York: Basic Books.

Bishop, B. (2000). Austin taking on a tough issue: Income inequality. *Austin-American Statesman*, January 13.

Bishop, B., and M. Lisheron. (2002). Austin's service class is losing its way out: In high-tech cities, workers finding paths to wealthier, creative jobs are blocked. *Austin-American Statesman*, November 3.

Bourdieu, P. (1986). The forms of capital. In John Richardson (Ed.), *Handbook of theory and research for the sociology of education*, pp. 241–258. New York: Greenwood Press.

Braverman, H. (1975). *Labor and monopoly capital: The degradation of work in the twentieth century*. New York: Monthly Review Press.

Brunick, N. J. (2000). Public job creation: Lessons from the past, realities of the present and possibilities for the future. University of Texas at Austin.

Bureau of Labor Statistics. (2007). Occupations with the largest job growth, 2006–16. Retrieved October 10, 2010, from http://www.bls.gov/.

Cardella, R. A. (1999). The Austin computer software industry: An engine for economic development. University of Texas at Austin.

Castells, M. (1996). *The rise of the network society*. Malden, MA: Blackwell.

Clinton, W. (2000). State of the Union. Retrieved October 2002 from http://usinfo.state.gov/usa/infousa/facts/speeches/clinton/1.txt.

Collins, R. (1979). *The credential society: An historical sociology of education and stratification*. New York: Academic Press.

Florida, R. L. (2002). *The rise of the creative class: And how it's transforming work, leisure, community and everyday life*. New York: Basic Books.

Fullerton, K. (1998). Home-grown workers: Is Austin's job boom trickling down to the people? *Austin Chronicle*, March 27. Retrieved October 10, 2010, from http://www.austinchronicle.com/gyrobase/Issue/story?oid=oid:523099.

Giddens, A. (1981). *The class structure of advanced societies.* London: Hutchinson.

Gramsci, A. (1971). *Selection from prison notebooks.* London: Lawrence and Wishart.

High-tech access closes digital divide. (1999). *Austin American-Statesman,* October 3.

Hoffman, D. L., and T. P. Novak. (1998). *Bridging the digital divide: The impact of race on computer access and internet use.* Retrieved July 21, 2006, from http://www.eric.ed.gov/ERICWebPortal/contentdelivery/servlet/ERICServlet?accno=ED421563.

Hotz, R. L. (1998). Blacks get less access to Internet, study finds: When education, income equal, whites still surf Web more. *Austin American-Statesman,* April 17.

Koch & Fowler Consulting Engineers. (1928). *A city plan for Austin, Texas.* Repr., Austin: Department of Planning, 1957.

Kubicek, H. (1985). Information technology and skills: Problem in research politics. In U. Briefs, J. Kjaer, and J.-L. Rigal (Eds.), *Computerization and work: A reader on social aspects of computerization: A collection of articles,* pp. 80–88. Berlin: Springer-Verlag.

Lafer, G. (2002). *The job training charade.* Ithaca: Cornell University Press.

Lyon, D. (1988). *The information society.* Cambridge, UK: Polity Press.

Noble, D. F. (1984). *Forces of production: A social history of industrial automation.* Oxford: Oxford University Press.

Reich, R. B. (1991). *The work of nations: Preparing ourselves for 21st century capitalism.* New York: Knopf.

Schott, R. (2000). Ethnic and race relations in Austin, Texas. Policy Research Project Report 137, Lyndon B. Johnson School of Public Affairs, University of Texas at Austin.

Tufekci, Z. (2003). *In search of lost jobs: The rhetoric and practice of computer skills training.* Dissertation, University of Texas at Austin.

Webster, F., and K. Robins. (1986). *Information technology: A luddite analysis.* Norwood, NJ: Ablex.

Zuboff, S. (1988). *In the age of the smart machine: The future of work and power.* New York: Basic Books.

ED LENERT

MIYASE
CHRISTENSEN

ZEYNEP TUFEKCI

KAREN GUSTAFSON

CHAPTER 5

THE DIGITAL DIVIDE

THE NATIONAL DEBATE AND FEDERAL- AND STATE-LEVEL PROGRAMS

This chapter will recap the digital divide debate at the federal and state levels that arose in the 1990s and will cover both critical and market-based approaches. Understanding the digital divide debate is critical to understanding how technopolis cities like Austin, Texas, as well as the United States as an emerging information society, tried to respond to the crises in the technopolis and information society described in Chapter 4. There was a realization that not all people were advancing in such economies, despite what scholars like Daniel Bell (1973) had predicted. The digital divide debate was one way to understand the new social stratification that was emerging. It also led to a series of policy remedies at national, state, and local levels that affected the attempts of cities like Austin to respond to the perceived problems. There was a sharp reaction to both the analyses and remedies that shaped the policies of the Bush administration (2001–2009) and the evolution of Texas state policy as well, which had the effect of cutting off resources that programs in Austin and elsewhere had depended on. This debate and its associated policies, therefore, were critical to the policy structuring of Austin from above at higher levels of government, although as this chapter and Chapters 6 and 7 will show, the response from below in Austin strained to keep a number of digital inclusion programs alive.

The concept of universal service and its implementation through federal and state policies, especially in the 1996 Telecommunications Act, will provide the backdrop of our scrutiny. We will then review major national programs aimed at ameliorating the digital divide: the E-Rate, the Technologies Opportunities Program (TOP), the Department of Education's Community Technology Centers (CTC) Program, and the state-level program in Texas, Telecommunications Infrastructure Fund (TIF).

THE DIGITAL DIVIDE ISSUE

As a national social and political issue, the digital divide emerged during the Clinton administration, which initially publicized the divide in terms of connectivity through the National Information Infrastructure (NII). Early analyses by the National Telecommunications and Information Administration (NTIA), the Pew Foundation, and other organizations stressed the dangers of an increasingly stratified society divided by inequalities in access, situating the divide as an issue requiring active national policy. They argued that social stratification can be anticipated with the diffusion of new technologies and ideas, in keeping with critiques of diffusion theory in the 1970s (Whiting 1976), and that it was necessary to intervene in the technology diffusion process to lower stratification.

Later studies, however, often reflect the ascendancy of contrarian rhetoric, articulating the digital divide as an issue to be addressed through market logic and what were seen as natural diffusion processes that required no policy intervention. The change in administrations also meant a change in the underlying philosophy and approach to digital inequities. The Bush administration's policy might be termed a kind of market-oriented analysis that assumed that through market mechanisms and the process of technological diffusion, computer and Internet access and use would gradually reach all parts of American society. By contrast, during the Great Recession that began in 2008, the Obama administration included in its initial stimulus plan $7 billion to expand rural broadband access, which was being administered via Rural Utilities Service (RUS) and the NTIA. This can be seen as a clear sign of reversal from Bush-era policies.

EARLY ARTICULATIONS OF THE DIVIDE

As digital information technologies spread in the 1990s, some national policy makers and technology theorists feared that technology adoption and diffusion could increase traditional structural inequalities such as income and education. Policies before 2000 in the United States and before 2004 in Texas reflected a critical approach to diffusion. Starting in the early 1990s, reflecting policy work by Robert

Reich and Larry Irving, among others, there was concern over the likely increased stratification of society that might come with an information society and information economy (Reich 1991). While this body of policy work accepted many of the then-current assumptions of diffusion theories and information society theories, there was an awareness, corresponding to the 1976 critiques of diffusion theory (e.g., Whiting 1976; Shingi and Mody 1976; these critiques were accepted by Rogers 1976), that diffusion of new information media also tended to stratify both access to and benefit from the new media. The critiques clearly noted that to avoid the worst of such stratification, the least advantaged in society, corresponding to what diffusion research would call the late majority or laggards, needed to be specifically targeted by policy solutions that would seek to improve their access to and their ability to use the messages carried in new media (Whiting 1976). In the digital divide policies of the 1990s, this was reflected in an effort to intervene socially to provide public access to and training in information and communication technologies (ICT) to those who would not otherwise receive it. Specific national U.S. policies and programs by NTIA, the Department of Education, the Department of Commerce, and, in Texas, the TIF implemented this general policy.

One initiative that grew out of this concern with information technology is the NII, a plan for a private-public partnership to develop an information superhighway to benefit all Americans. These ambitions were also expressed at a global level as the Clinton administration proposed the establishment of a Global Information Infrastructure (GII) and Global Information Society (GIS). Policy discourse surrounding the NII assumed that the federal government would be actively involved in promoting public access, and ensuring more even diffusion of technology access and services. Secretary of labor Robert Reich emphasized a focus on citizens, rather than corporations, in the development of a new information economy. He suggested that the U.S. government must invest in the education of workers, helping them become technologically sophisticated while discouraging the development of an income gap.

In 1993, Vice President Gore outlined the core principles of the plan for the NII. The plan proposed a need for universal service and open access. Gore stated, "If we allow the information superhighway to bypass the less fortunate sectors of our society—even for an interim period—we will find that the information rich will get richer while the information poor get poorer with no guarantee that everyone will be on the network at some future date." The provision of universal service was positioned as a necessity for the success of the NII and a needed protection against the dangers of unequal technology diffusion. Universal service remains a key concept in federal law. It drives and, as we will cover later in the chapter, sometimes complicates public digital divide programs.

Referring to the societal consequences of this so-called information revolution, Gore and Clinton first used the term *digital divide* as a catchphrase in 1996, borrowing a term coined by journalists and popularized by Clinton's director of the NTIA, Larry Irving. Digital divide as a concept also had global resonance, as the Clinton-Gore administration's proposal for the GII and GIS were both endorsed by the Organisation for Economic Co-operation and Development, which saw these new technologies as potential motors of economic growth (Flew and McElhinney 2002). Both on national and transnational levels, developing countries were struggling to determine how they too could benefit from the emerging digital economy, given other needs and the condition of their electric and telephonic infrastructure (McConnaughey et al. 1999).

Early articulations of the digital divide concentrate primarily on gaps in computer access and ownership. Solutions to information gaps are described in terms of "public safety nets," a phrase used by Gore in his description of the universal service component of the NII. Echoing Reich, Irving framed the need for increased access and education in terms of national economic success. Citing 190,000 unfilled technology-oriented U.S. jobs in 1997, Irving suggested that access and education were critical to maintaining the nation's globally competitive status.

An NTIA report, "Falling through the Net: Defining the Digital Divide" (McConnaughey et al. 1999), described the divide as becoming a "racial ravine." While groups such as the Heritage Foundation were already arguing that advanced ICTs would diffuse naturally to the American public, eventually transcending educational, racial, and economic boundaries, the NTIA report suggested that depending on the market for diffusion was not a wise course of action: "Given the great advantages accruing to those who have access, it is not economically or socially prudent to idly await the day when most, if not all, homes can claim connectivity."

During the 1990s, these concerns with the potentially uneven diffusion of emerging information technology led to a variety of federal programs. Beginning in 1994, the Telecommunications Information and Infrastructure Assistance Program (TIIAP) functioned under the NTIA as a merit-based grant program, providing seed money for projects designed to extend advanced telecommunication resources to underserved Americans. The Community Technology Centers (CTC) Program, administered by the Department of Education, was created to help finance computer activity centers for students as well as adult education. Another grant program, the Technology Opportunities Program (TOP), which replaced TIIAP, was created to provide funds and services to community organizations, such as food banks, needing assistance with their technology development. Finally, the E-Rate, incorporated into the 1996 Telecommunications Act, was promoted by former chairman of the Federal Communications Commission (FCC) Reed Hundt as a way to support the use of advanced telecommunications in schools, libraries, and hospitals. All of these programs were designed to address the increased social and economic stratifications that could accompany the spread of information technology among the general population.

MARKET-BASED DIVIDES: LET THEM BUY BROADBAND

The early 2000s were a turbulent period for federal and state programs designed to address the digital divide. By the early months of 2002, the Bush administration was preparing to cut key programs designed to address digital divide inequalities, including the TOP. It was increasingly assumed that deregulation, a free market, and natural processes of diffusion would ameliorate any residual inequalities in technology and information access.

Contrarian discourses disputing the importance of the digital divide or whether it should be considered public responsibility generally put their trust in the logic of the free market, assuming that the technologies in question will naturally diffuse to different segments of the population over time. Because of this faith in market-led diffusion, contrarians generally oppose direct government involvement—one of the classic targets is the government-mandated universal access cross-subsidy, which contrarians argue inhibits more players from entering the market (Compaine and Weinraub 1997). Other concerns include the unnatural overloading of the information infrastructure, and the argument that those who are on the wrong side of the divide may have deliberately chosen to pass up access to these emerging ICTs. Finally, an increasingly prominent argument concerns the actual existence of a digital divide. Whereas contrarian positions during the 1990s often acknowledged that a divide existed, while arguing against government intervention, more recent contrarian discussions suggest that if any divide did exist, it has now been solved through procompetitive policies and decreasing technology prices.

Recent ICTs were often compared with a variety of other technologies. It was implied, for example, that Internet and computer access would follow a diffusion process similar to that of the television (Powell 1999; Compaine 2001, 318). Adam Thierer (2000), writing for the Heritage Foundation, supported this perspective, suggesting that because television penetration in the United States is now at 99 percent generally, and at 97 percent among poor households, there was no reason to give low-income families tax credits or other incentives to invest in computer and Internet technology. The market was situated in these arguments as a fair arbiter, one that would allow advanced communication technologies to trickle down through the strata of society, given time.

While television was a popular site of comparison in this paradigm, contrarians also pointed to other examples of technological diffusion, generally arguing that it is natural and perhaps even American that technologies diffuse unevenly. The diffusion of new technologies to "Anytown, USA" has never been uniform, but disparities have always existed among different groups' financial and geographic resources—this, however, "does not mean there is a national crisis that requires federal intervention" (Thierer 2000, 2).

Contrarians cite various ways that the private sector has already addressed the digital divide, such as through falling computer prices; free, advertising-supported Internet services; and new Internet appliances that cost much less than traditional computer systems. Commercial ventures were described as solving the digital divide through competition and natural pursuit of profit; at this point, decisions not to purchase a computer or get Internet service have been positioned as voluntary and based on the individual preferences of potential consumers. This conclusion is significant because it frames nonadopters as individuals making independent decisions, rather than as members of traditionally underprivileged groups working within a larger structural framework.

CRITICAL SCHOLARSHIP

The other main source of criticism leveled against those who argue that the digital divide represents a real disadvantage is critical scholarship. According to Hal Berghel (2000), during the first few years of the Clinton administration—against the backdrop of what could be described as a "techno-hype"—the frequency of published articles and reports on the "deficiencies of the U.S. science and technology posture reached a feverish pace." Articles and opinions representing a wide range of perspectives on the issue were to be found in publications from monographs to the popular press. As Berghel puts it, "It appeared for a while that opining about science and technology policy might become a national pastime."

Parallel to this, there was a boom in academic studies that focused on the social, cultural, and political economic impact of these transformations. Many scholars working on the political economic aspects approached the new media more cautiously and have been critical of the industry-pushed visions of information society starting from the 1980s (Robins and Webster 1988, 1999; Garnham 1990; Calabrese and Burgelman 1999; Schiller 1999). Vincent Mosco (1989), for example, criticized the commercialization of communication and the turning of citizens into consumers. Likewise, William Melody contended that technologically advanced economies were altering the form and impact of industrial capitalism by becoming information-based economies. Information economy is a system, he concluded, in which "control is exercised at the market center. Peripheral or hinterland locations are developed primarily to serve the interests of the major centers of power by exploiting natural resources, low labor costs, or other elements of specialized, comparative advantage" (1991, 34). Others, like Manuel Castells (1996, 1997, 1998), have presented arguments over the past two decades as to how new computer and telecommunications technologies will transform countries into "knowledge economies" and "network societies" (Selwyn 2004).

Leah Lievrouw and Sonia Livingstone suggested that, at the beginning, the European tradition of new media research took a rather different direction and emphasized a critical/cultural studies approach to media content and industries on the one hand, and a broadly Marxist political economy of media on the other (2002, 4–5). European scholars drew upon a variety of social theories ranging from Bourdieu's (1972, 1997) conceptualization of human-media relation in terms of cultural capital, which found resonance in U.S. studies (Rojas et al. 2004), to Michel Foucault's linking of technology and power. Jürgen Habermas's theory of the public sphere also influenced extensive research on new media space as providing room for social participation or the lack of it.

Unlike market-based contrarians, most critical scholarship does not deny that the digital divide exists or that it represents a real issue. Rather, attention is drawn to keeping the distinction between corporate interests and policies that encourage and enable civic and social participation of people through information technology. Also, it is important not to treat information technology as an unqualified savior. Lack of access to and competence in using computers may be a real disadvantage; however, that does not mean that most problems will be solved once computers are widely diffused. Technology is entangled with, and transforms and reproduces, power relations within societies.

FEDERAL SERVICES: UNIVERSAL SERVICE AND THE 1996 TELECOMMUNICATIONS ACT

As Internet use spread during the 1990s, one of the basic questions of telecommunications policy makers was whether the Unites States should strive to provide everyone with more than just basic telephone service. In other words, should dial-up or broadband Internet access be included in the definition of universal service? Traditionally, the goal of universal service has been to make sure that everyone, regardless of income and geography, has access to affordable telephone service. In the 1934 Communications Act, Congress instructed the FCC to "make available, so far as possible, to all the people of the United States . . . a rapid, efficient, nationwide, and worldwide wire and communication service with adequate facilities at reasonable charges." The Telecommunications Act of 1996 updated this goal and expanded it beyond the scope of basic telephone service. A 2002 FCC summary states that

> the goals of Universal Service, as mandated by the 1996 Act, are to promote the availability of quality services at just, reasonable, and affordable rates; increase access to advanced telecommunications services throughout the Nation; [and] advance the availability of such services to all consumers, including those in low income, ru-

ral, insular, and high cost areas at rates that are reasonably comparable to those charged in urban areas. (FCC 2002)

However, the 1996 act created a complex and contradictory policy
infrastructure by simultaneously incorporating the adversarial premises of unbridled competition and public service. In the context of
the goals of universal service, free competition in the market acts as
a positive force when the interaction of supply and demand pushes
the prices for telecommunication services as close as possible to their
actual costs, while still allowing the companies that provide such
services to operate at a profit. In this way, an economy provides the
maximum amount of the services to consumers at the lowest prices.
In other words, unlike a pure-market approach, universal service is
concerned with who gets service at what price. In a universal service
model, such as the postal system, a person in a rural area with a high
cost of service, such as rural Nevada, pays the same price to send a
first-class letter as a customer in an urban area with a lower cost of
service, such as Los Angeles. A similar set of issues applies to telecommunication services.

The problem with a market approach in the context of the goals
of universal service is that the efficiency of the market is not concerned with the equity or fairness of the distribution of services. But
the remedy is also a problem: regulatory intervention in the area of
prices to achieve goals of fairness and equity can severely distort the
market, eventually leading to serious inefficiency and ultimately a
decline in the level of service to all customers. In other words, the
imposition of a solution creates its own additional set of complica-
tions and issues. To reconcile the inherent contradictions arising
from this uneasy combination of free markets and regulatory intervention, the FCC has enacted a number of administrative rules and
regulations that, in turn, threaten the effectiveness of universal service with their growing complexity.

This complexity manifests itself in multiple ways. First, as law
professor John C. Roberts (2000) observes, the 1996 act amends the
1934 act but is many times longer. Where the 1934 act was vague and
vested broad discretionary powers in the FCC, the 1996 act is complicated and specific. Because the statute is so long and complicated,
the FCC was left with the daunting task of carrying out a large number of difficult rule-making proceedings within a very short time, an
assignment that has stretched the commission's physical and intel-

lectual resources. Now, for the first time in its history, the FCC administers a long and complex statute, and has much of its regulatory agenda set directly by Congress.

Second, making the FCC's job even more difficult, the 1996 act reflects an important reversal of the principle that the telecommunications industry is an exception to the general rule that government should not intervene in purely economic affairs. The act rejected the notion that government intervention was the only path to the deployment of advanced telecommunications services and economic progress, and instead promoted free-market competition as the best mechanism for ensuring such progress. In summary, while the ultimate policy goal of serving the public interest remained the same, the preferred means for accomplishing it had changed.

In the traditional monopoly environment allowed for by the 1934 act, a monopolist like Southwestern Bell merely had to shift money from one pocket to another to balance its books and provide universal service. The rates that Bell was permitted to charge its customers were based on an overall calculation that allowed it to collect sufficient revenues to make a reasonable profit on its total level of capital investment. In this way, motives of profit and public service were balanced. While regulated firms worked to meet public service obligations, they also maximized their profits.

The policies of the 1934 act required that a telephone company provide service even when there was no hope of breaking even on certain transactions. The rationale underlying this policy was that it is only the service *as a whole* that must be profitable, and even unprofitable customers must be served. This principle was used to extend the telephone system across the United States, even into remote, rural, and low-income areas. As a result of this socioeconomic policy, for many years business users were charged more than residential users. As long as overall profit levels were maintained, it did not really matter whether one part of the system paid below-cost rates and another paid above-cost rates.

In the new competitive environment, after the 1996 act, a system of cross-subsidy is still necessary for universal service, but it has to be administered among competing parties. To generate funds for such subsidies, the FCC requires telecommunications carriers to contribute 6.9 percent of their interstate and international revenues to a pot of money known as the Universal Service Fund. About $5 billion is collected annually for subsidies and used to keep phone connections affordable in low-income and high-cost areas (Hammond 2002). That same fund helps wire schools and libraries for Internet access through the E-Rate program, discussed below.

What this means is that the specific implementation of universal service in the 1996 act concerns more than just social policy; it also directly affects the financial structure of the telecommunications industry. Yet, despite favoring market-driven mechanisms in the 1996 act, Congress still recognized that without government oversight, free competition was likely to result in unequal investment in communications infrastructure and information inequality. Profit-driven companies would invest in areas most likely to yield the highest returns on their investment. They would quickly connect the wealthier suburbs with advanced systems, while leaving poor inner-city neighborhoods or rural areas with existing technologies. However, the mechanisms for balancing out the bias of the marketplace toward serving wealthy segments of the population proved to be more complicated than anyone had hoped.

The present conundrum that surrounds universal service began when the 1996 act ended legal sanction for the former local telephone monopolies and required the incumbent franchisees to take actions that would facilitate the entry of competitors into formerly closed markets. This includes the requirement that a local exchange carrier, at the request of a competitor, share its network facilities. At the same time, Congress decreed that a wider group of telecommunications companies, not just long-distance companies and the former Bell affiliates, would have to pay for the cost of universal service. The duty to help pay for Universal Service was extended to every telecommunications carrier that provides interstate telecommunications services.

However, a new competitor in the telecommunications arena, which provides advanced information services but does not provide ordinary telephone service, is likely to be excused from contributing to the Universal Service Fund. The competitor can thus gain significant advantages that in the long run could damage the dominant firm's market position. As the dominant firm's revenues decline, it too will demand that it be excused from the universal service subsidy payment. In such a situation, it may not be long before the surplus profits that are used for the universal service cross-subsidy, and for funding programs like the E-Rate (discussed below), completely evaporate since competition reduces profit margins for everyone. How this plays out is a matter that depends on many interrelated factors, but from the standpoint of economic theory, this is the essence of the argument of many of those opposed to continuing programs which subsidize Internet access.

To get a sense of the complexity, consider a publication of the Texas Office of Public Utility Counsel (2002) called "Understanding Your Telephone Bill." It takes over six thousand words to answer the question "Why am I being charged for *that*?" The electronic pamphlet details six categories of federal surcharges on a typical consumer telephone bill in Texas including a "universal service charge" and a "federal excise communications tax." In addition, there are no less than eight state surcharges listed, including such diverse items as a "poison control surcharge" and contributions to the Texas infrastructure fund. There are also five different taxing authorities represented, including a "state franchise tax" and a "municipal sales and use tax." As telecommunications professor Harmeet Sawhney (2000) has observed, the complexity of the mechanisms for funding universal service, which is the current social response to the digital divide, can at times seem to overpower the ideal behind the policy. As a result, Sawhney states, it is possible that we will start to lose sight of the goal "and get trapped into a procedural sinkhole."

FEDERAL SERVICES: E-RATE

One aspect of the implementation of universal service in the 1996 Telecommunications Act is the E-Rate program. The E-Rate is officially known as the "Universal Service Fund for Schools and Libraries" (Puma, Chaplin, and Pape 2000). The 1996 act instructed the FCC to establish a support mechanism to ensure that schools and libraries have affordable access to and use of telecommunications services for educational purposes. The FCC is required to ensure that up-to-date telecommunications technology is available in schools—and in classrooms in those schools—around the country on an ongoing basis. To be clear, the E-Rate program is of limited focus. It is about providing access to information technologies and connectivity in centralized locations such as schools and libraries. It is not concerned with increasing the skills of the computer users, for example.

As discussed above, the E-Rate is part of a political compromise that was designed to allow the telecommunications industry to become competitive—that is, to be guided by and respond to technological innovation and market forces—but that also requires adherence to traditional public service goals as exemplified by universal service. By contrast, public service regulation originating with the principles of the 1934 act recognized that there are "important social values that laissez-faire, with its paramount focus on economic efficiency, cannot adequately meet" (Stone 1991, xiii).

Since the E-Rate program began distributing funds in 1998, it has provided more than $15 billion to help schools and libraries acquire Internet and telecommunications services. The E-Rate program currently provides eligible public schools (from kindergarten through grade twelve) and libraries up to $2.25 billion annually for approved telecommunications, Internet access, and internal connections costs. The Schools and Libraries Division of the Universal Service Administrative Company handles the day-to-day operations of the E-Rate program and places schools and libraries into various discount categories, based on indicators of need. In practice, a school or library pays a percentage of the cost for the service and the E-Rate program funds the remainder. E-Rate discounts range from 20 percent to 90 percent, and the discount is based on the number of students eligible for the National School Lunch Program, an indicator of the general level of income in an area. As a result, schools and libraries in low-income urban communities and rural areas qualify for higher discounts than those in wealthier neighborhoods.

Who pays for the E-Rate? The program is structured so that no general tax revenue is used. Instead, consumers of telecommunication services are required to pay an additional charge such as a "federal universal service fee" or "universal connectivity fee" to fund the E-Rate. In terms of its economic structure, the E-Rate follows the path of other universal service policies that require that regulators set rates for certain telecommunications services above their cost to generate a subsidy that then can be used to fund cross-subsidies in other programs, such as the E-Rate discounts. In other words, the E-Rate functions as a redistributive tax on telecommunications. Funds are collected at the federal level and then given to local government institutions such as schools and libraries.

The E-Rate program has its critics. For example, as early as 1999, three Congress members announced their intention to introduce legislation to end the E-Rate, asserting that it is an unnecessary tax because of existing Department of Education funding. Supporters of the elimination of the E-Rate argue that technological innovation and free competition will, without further government intervention, solve the issues of the digital divide. In other words, the magic of the marketplace will take care of the problem all by itself. Scholars such as Adam Thierer (2000) and Benjamin Compaine (2001a) argue that low-cost computers are plentiful and cite statistics that call into question this problem is so significant that it demands a national solution or federal entitlement.

So far, E-Rate supporters have been successful in defending the program. They note that it shows strong signs of addressing disparities in access to information technologies in schools and libraries. In terms of improving equity, a report published in 2000 noted that the program is serving primarily smaller and poorer schools. It also stated that the nation's poorest schools and libraries were requesting 53 percent of the total funds. By contrast, relatively wealthier schools which had applied for discounts accounted for only 3 percent of the total funds requested. In 2002, the fifth year of the program, there were over thirty-six thousand applications for E-Rate discounts, totaling nearly $5.736 billion (Consortium for School Networking 2002).

Unfortunately for the E-Rate, its fate is tied to a larger federal program of universal service, and the entire program of funding threatens to sink under the weight of its own internal contradictions and administrative complexity.

FEDERAL INITIATIVES TO SUPPORT PUBLIC ACCESS: THE TOP AND CTC PROGRAMS

In the United States, two federal programs, the Technology Opportunities Program (TOP) and the Community Technology Centers (CTC) Program, were particularly instrumental in dealing with problems of unequal access.[1] The TOP, initiated in 1994 by the U.S. Department of Commerce as part of NTIA and originally called the Telecommunications and Information Infrastructure Assistance Program (TIIAP), operated in the form of providing grants to nonprofit organizations and public institutions to facilitate the spread of ICTs available to the public. Between 1994 and 2004, the TOP granted funds to state, local, and tribal governments; health-care providers; schools; libraries; police departments; and community-based nonprofit organizations.[2] Within the scope of the TOP, 610 grants totaling $233.5 million were awarded, stimulating the raising of $313.7 million in local matching funds.[3]

As discussed by Norris Dickard (2002) of the Benton Foundation, the TOP was successful in facilitating the partnership of private and public institutions and thereby connecting people to the ICTs in rural areas and underprivileged urban locales. The TOP initiative gave priority to projects which demonstrated a willingness to promote

Table 5.1. Grantees and Amounts Awarded in the State of Texas, 2003–2004

Dallas	City of Dallas	$328,009 (2003)
Irving	Irving Independent School District	$500,000 (2003)
Brownsville	Brownsville Independent School District	$499,963 (2004)
Dallas	Alternative Community Development Services Inc.	$499,387 (2004)
San Antonio	Intercultural Development Research Association	$295,816 (2004)

Source: U.S. Department of Education, Community Technology Centers Program

digital networks to support lifelong learning; help public safety officials protect the public; assist in the delivery of health care and public health services; and foster communication, resource sharing, and economic development within rural and urban communities. Among the twenty-three projects and grantees that were awarded funds in the state of Texas are, to name a few, the County of El Paso, for the creation of a videoconferencing network for use by public safety officials in El Paso; Dallas County Community College District, for the Net on Wheels program to provide low-income communities in Dallas County with job training and employment information services; the Austin Free-Net project, which aimed to provide public access points in a low-income community in East Austin; and the University of Texas at Austin, for a program to provide educational resources to homeless children.

Another pioneering program started by the federal government to bridge the ICT access gap was the Community Technology Centers (CTC) Program, initiated by the Department of Education in 1999 to promote the use of ICTs for educational purposes in less privileged urban and rural areas. Community technology centers provide computer and Internet access to citizens who, generally, do not have access to these technologies at home, work, or school.[4] Within the scope of the CTC Program, learning services to children and adults were also provided. In 2003 and 2004, the last two years in which grants through the CTC Program were awarded, $29 million and $9 million, respectively, were spent toward the creation and expansion of community technology centers nationwide. Both the 2003 and 2004 awards focused on the use of such centers in improving the academic performance of low-achieving high school students, particularly in the areas of reading/language arts and math. Table 5.1 shows the grantees and amounts awarded in the state of Texas in 2003 and 2004.

Similar to other federal digital divide initiatives, these programs were terminated. In 2004, TOP funding was no longer available through the NTIA, and the CTC Program ended in 2006.

STATE-LEVEL ACTION IN TEXAS:
A QUESTION OF PUBLIC ACCESS

Texas was one of the first states to take government-level action to promote private-public partnerships in order to facilitate the use of new communication technologies. The Public Utility Regulatory Act (PURA) of 1995, also known as HB 2128, transformed the telecommunications regulatory environment of Texas, created substantial deregulation and established a new framework to foster higher competition to further the deployment of an advanced telecommunications infrastructure in the state. PURA also established a new agency, the Telecommunications Infrastructure Fund (TIF), "as a catalyst and supporter of public access to an advanced communication technology network" giving priority to rural and underserved populations (TIF 1997).

Although Texas, unlike some other states, did not establish a separate council to deal with the digital divide, the TIF board granted and loaned funds—totaling $1.5 billion for a period of ten years—to public schools, libraries, higher-education institutions, and not-for-profit health-care facilities. To fulfill its mission, the TIF administered grants funded by an assessment—1.25 percent of taxable telecommunications receipts—on wired telecommunications utilities and wireless providers.

TIF grants exclusively targeted "eligible entities" defined by law as public school districts and campuses, colleges and universities, libraries, academic health centers, and public or not-for-profit health-care facilities. From 1996 until 2002, the agency issued almost $1 billion in grants to 6,589 fiscal agents. Priority was given to education, health, and information-sharing projects in public schools, public libraries, higher-education institutions, and health-care agencies.

TIF stressed funding infrastructure instead of services, thereby addressing the "barriers of access" to the technology rather than the "barriers of use" (TIF 1997, 13). The design of TIF programs has been characterized as a "technology-push effort" common to interventions, which assume that by assuring connectivity, communities gain effective access (Strover, Chapman, and Waters 2004). Through the analysis of the discursive structures in TIF's "Master Plan 1998"

(1997), "Strategic Plan 1999–2003" (1999), and "Strategic Plan 2003–2007," Martha Fuentes-Bautista (2004) concludes that the state diagnosed the problem of digital gaps in terms of insufficient and uneven growth of conduits and devices, mainly between rural and urban areas.

Sharon Strover, Gary Chapman, and Jody Waters (2004) evaluate the public access programs of thirty-six Texan communities awarded by the first round of the community networks program. The authors conclude that the intervention did expand public access—80 percent of the sites projected were actually established—but the types of location chosen were not intrinsically attractive or available to all target constituencies (473). Public access was largely equated with expanding computer and Internet access primarily in schools and libraries. The sites chosen were those that represented minimal burdens to participant institutions; new sites and those in areas where poor and minority populations were concentrated were avoided: "The very placement, staffing, and use of public access in these projects largely replicated the power structure and access advantages that already were in place" (484).

Another major issue related to lopsided connectivity patterns in the state of Texas is the geographic boundaries that hinder or limit residential access to the telecommunications networks. As Kyle Nicholas notes, no state has more people living in rural areas than Texas:

> Perhaps no state so startlingly depicts the notion of "digital divide." From "telecom alley" north of Dallas to the Silicon Hills of Austin and south to the international port of Houston, Texas is blessed with a robust network of high-speed communications technologies supporting some of the leading lights in telecommunications and computer industries. Away from this sliver of the state, however, the communications picture is less certain. (2003, 288)

Access to the material basis of information infrastructure in rural Texas remains a major determinant of digital exclusions in this state. Nicholas observes that federal- and state-level policies act to hinder rather than enable access in rural areas. As illustrated by his study, efforts toward providing access through universal service initiatives in rural areas ended up creating local telecommunications monopolies. In the absence of mechanisms to facilitate competition, rural citizens remain dependent on incumbents whose revenues are protected from competition, making the situation even more disadvantageous for users. It remains to be seen whether the $7 billion for rural broadband in the stimulus package by the Obama administration will change this picture.

As case studies indicate, although statewide ICT use in Texas is higher than average at overall levels, a digital divide is still significant along the lines of income, education, race and ethnic origin, place of residence, and age (Strover and Straubhaar 2000; Straubhaar et al. 2005). What is most significant is the fact that although public funding mechanisms were available both for providing public access and for supporting universal access in remote areas in Texas, these efforts seem to have suffered, first, from short-sighted, "techno-push" policy making and, second, from lack of innovative and interpretive approaches that would open the way for flexible implementation.

At the state level, this techno-push attitude—which discounts social factors that influence ICT use, thus hampering innovative approaches—is similar to those found globally, and particularly in newly emerging information societies in countries such as Turkey (Christensen 2006) and Egypt (Warschauer 2003). In the case of Texas, a major factor that influenced the success of TIF-funded public access projects was found to be TIF's own discourse, which discarded spaces such as local shops or malls as eligible locations for ICT access points, although such locations could have better served the public interest (Strover, Chapman, and Waters 2004).

In 2002, TIF released its second strategic plan laying out new directions. "TIF spent the first four years funding infrastructure—the wires and boxes. Now responding to constituent demands, the focus has shifted to funding training and content and giving people the tools to use the infrastructure and make it relevant to their lives," promised the document (2002, 27). This vision did not persuade the legislature. Under growing administrative concerns and budget cuts, TIF came under fire by oversight agencies for its perceived inability to develop satisfactory evaluation mechanisms to demonstrate that in fact target constituencies were served (State Auditor Office 2002, Committee on State Affairs 2003). Finally, the governor of Texas cut the program.

Despite the failings of the TIF program, however, one study (Straubhaar et al. 2005) found that Internet and computer use in Texas had indeed grown between 2000 and 2004, precisely because poor and minority Texans were increasingly gaining access at libraries, community centers, and other public locations. Many of those public access centers had been made possible by TIF funding. A study (Straubhaar et al. 2008) conducted in two poor, largely Latino communities in South Texas in 2004–2008 demonstrated the same thing. Libraries and schools funded initially by TIF and gaining ongoing support from E-Rate were quite heavily used for access, particularly before home broadband access began to be available in 2004–2005 through another program for subsidizing rural access funded through the U.S. Department of Agriculture. So despite the critique of both national- and state-level funding programs as inefficient, they delivered visible results that enabled poor and minority Texans to get Internet and computer access years before the market delivery of services would have reached them.

NEW UNDERSTANDINGS OF THE DIGITAL DIVIDE: LOOKING TO THE FUTURE

Reviewing major trends described by nationwide surveys conducted over the course of nearly a decade by the Center for Communication Policy at the University of California–Los Angeles (UCLA) and the Pew Internet and American Life Project, Lee Rainie and Peter Bell (2004, 47) conclude that the overall percentage of Americans online has stalled somewhere between 60 percent (Pew's findings) and 70 percent (UCLA's findings).[5] Older Americans, those who have only a high school education or less, those who are less well-off, rural residents, and Africans Americans and Hispanics are still less likely to go online. Border states (Arizona, New Mexico, and Texas) stand out as regions of contrast with fairly pervasive wired areas but low Internet penetration rates. The Internet population at the U.S.-Mexico border is mostly young, composed of an interesting mix including the wealthiest residents and those of modest incomes, with significant number of Hispanics users. A recent study of broadband in two Latino border communities (Straubhaar et al. 2008) shows that younger and better-educated residents are increasingly using broadband, while some older residents, particularly those who only speak Spanish, remain unaware of the Internet's existence.

Understanding these trends has demanded a new paradigm that goes beyond old formulations of the divide to look into the emergence of various digital divides and further stratification. A second generation of Internet research has drawn on longitudinal studies tracing different types of use, attitudes among users, and reasons of nonusers for not going online (Wellman 2004). Currently, Internet access and use is better understood as a fluid spectrum that goes from populations that are totally disconnected—approximately a fourth of the total U.S. population (Lenhart et al. 2003, 26)—to groups of "net evaders" and "dropouts" (Katz and Aspden 1998; Katz and Rice 2003), and users with different degrees of sophistication in employing the variety of online applications (NTIA 2002; Madden and Rainie 2003; Digital Future Report 2004).

Users go online from diverse places. The Pew Internet and American Life Project estimates that 23 percent of adult Internet users go online from places other than the home or office (Harwood 2004). Most of these people gain access at schools (27 percent), friends' homes (26 percent) and libraries (26 percent), and only a few have used the Internet at hotels (3 percent), in cybercafés (2 percent), or at other places while traveling (4 percent). A small fraction uses it at community centers and houses of worship. Users of "the third place" (that is, somewhere other than the home or office) represent two very different sets of demographics. The first group consists of heavy users, anxious to go online wherever they are. They are between ages eighteen and twenty-four, and typically are students. The second group is composed of users from households who earn less than $30,000, have lower levels of education, live in rural areas, and have little experience in the online world. Some of them totally depend on the third place for Internet access.

As new layers of connectivity and access add up, and more accentuated differences in use are unveiled, many take these developments as signs that the digital divide is fading. While some assume differential access and use as mere reflection of individual choice, equating the adoption of Internet with the adoption of television (Digital Future Report 2004), others see the phenomenon as a byproduct of inequalities materialized in different levels of techno-competencies (Rojas et al. 2004; Eamon 2004). Building on his work on access to telephones, Jorge Schement (1995) has shown how inequalities in access to information services (telephone, cable) tend to persist in contrast to the rapid diffusion of information goods. Can the potential of the technology be developed through the operation of the Internet as a broadcasting system or as a truly interactive technology? Who will be in better standing to take advantage of the possibilities offered by high-speed connectivity? As these questions wait for a response, we argue that the potential of the technology lies in its uses, and that closer attention has to be placed on the study of Internet use among the less privileged and the disconnected. Only in this way we will be able to articulate new policies to answer the problem of the diversity of divides.

CONCLUSION

The national policy debates that arose over the digital divide and the related federal- and state-level programs are examples of continuing public concern over how to create the fundamental conditions of equal opportunity for all. Initially, the digital divide specifically referred to gaps in ownership or access to computer technology between groups. Later, the concept was expanded to include concerns over more general inequalities in the ability to use information technology and participate fully as a citizen and consumer.

The idea that all Americans will or should have equal opportunity to succeed is deeply rooted in U.S. values. The Internet continues to evolve and create new opportunities and challenges. For example, the growing use of Internet-enabled mobile-devices and the rapid spread of social media has the potential to create new possibilities as well as new divides among the public. But the policy questions and lessons of the digital divide remain relevant: to what extent should government intervene to increase the level of equality of opportunity for all citizens, and by what policy mechanism?

Examination of some of the varied local initiatives taken with federal, state, city, nonprofit, and private support in Austin can help answer that question, by determining what programs were most effective and how they were most efficiently funded. Chapters 6 and 7 do that in some detail. They show that some effective programs, such as local community technology centers, were cut short when federal funding was cut in 2004–2006.

NOTES

1. Originally, the community technology movement was a civil movement initiated and organized by people themselves. CTCNet, a national membership network of community technology centers and other nonprofit organizations with the aim of providing technology access and education to underprivileged

communities, was established in 1990 by Antonia Stone, a public school teacher. However, for the purposes of this chapter, which focuses on federal government initiatives, the discussion of community technology centers will be limited to the Department of Education's funding program.

2. National Telecommunications and Information Administration (NTIA), Technology Opportunities Program (TOP), http://www.ntia.doc.gov/TOP/.

3. Awards were allocated in all fifty states, as well as Puerto Rico, the District of Columbia, and the U.S. Virgin Islands.

4. U.S. Department of Education, CTC Program, http://www.ed.gov/programs/comtechcenters/index.html.

5. University of California–Los Angeles, Center for Communication Policy, http://ccp.ucla.edu/pages/internet-report.asp; Pew Internet and American Life Project, http://www.pewinternet.org/reports.asp.

REFERENCES

Bell, D. (1973). *The coming of post-industrial society: A venture in social forecasting.* New York: Basic Books.

Berghel, H. (2000). U.S. technology policy in the information age. *Information Impacts.* Retrieved from http://www.berghel.net/col-edit/digital_village/jun-96/dv_6-96.php.

Bourdieu, P. (1972). *Outline of a theory of practice.* Trans. Richard Nice. Repr., Cambridge, UK: Cambridge University Press, 1977.

———. (1997). The forms of capital. In A. Halsey, H. Lauder, P. Brown, and A. Stuart-Wells (Eds.), *Education: Culture, economy, society,* pp. 46–58. Oxford: Oxford University Press.

Calabrese, A., and J. C. Burgelman. (1999). Introduction. In A. Calabrese and J. C. Burgelman (Eds.), *Communication, citizenship and social policy.* New York: Rowman & Littlefield.

Castells, M. (1996). *The information age: Economy, society and culture.* Vol. 1, *The rise of the network society.* Oxford: Blackwell.

———. (1997). *The information age: Economy, society and culture.* Vol. 2, *The power of identity.* Oxford: Blackwell.

———. (1998). *The information age: Economy, society and culture.* Vol 3, *End of Millennium.* Oxford: Blackwell.

Christensen, M. (2006). What price the information society? A candidate country perspective within the context of the EU's information society policies. In J. Servaes and N. Carpentier (Eds.), *Towards a sustainable information society,* pp. 129–150. Bristol, UK: Intellect.

Committee on State Affairs. (2003). Report to the Texas House of Representatives 78th Legislature. Austin.

Compaine, B. (Ed.). (2001). *The digital divide: Facing a crisis or creating a myth?* Cambridge, MA: MIT Press.

Compaine, B., and M. Weinraub. (1997). Universal access to online services: An examination of the issue. *Telecommunications Policy* 21 (February): 15–24.

Consortium for School Networking. (2002). Washington update. March. Retrieved October 1, 2004, from http://www.cosn.org/members/washington0302.htm; no longer available.

Dickard, N. (2002). Federal retrenchment on the digital divide: Potential national impact. Policy brief no. 1. Benton Foundation. Retrieved from www.benton.org/publibrary/policybriefs/brief01.pdf; no longer available.

Digital Future Report. (2004). Surveying the digital future: Year four. USC Annenberg School Center for the Digital Future, Los Angeles, September.

Eamon, M. K. (2004). Digital divide and computer access and use between poor and non-poor. *Journal of Sociology and Social Welfare* 31(2), 91–112.

FCC (Federal Communications Commission). (2002). Universal service. Retrieved from http://www.fcc.gov/wcb/universal_service; no longer available.

Flew, T., and S. McElhinney. (2002). Globalization and the structure of new media industries. In L. A. Lievrouw and S. Livingstone (Eds.), *The Handbook of New Media*, pp. 304–319. London: Sage.

Fuentes-Bautista, M. (2004). Muddling through digital inclusion: The construction of state policy promoting community networks in Texas. Paper presented at the first Brazil-U.S. Symposium of Communications, Austin.

Garham, N. (1990). *Capitalism and communication: Global culture and the economics of information*. London: Sage.

Gore, A. (1993). Remarks to the National Press Club, December 21. Retrieved March 20, 2011, from http://www.ibiblio.org/nii/goremarks.htm.

Hammond, A. S. (2002). Digital divide in the new millennium. *Cardozo Arts and Entertainment Law Journal* 20:35.

Harwood, P. (2004). People who use the Internet away from home and work. Data memo, Pew Internet and American Life Project, March. Retrieved October 1, 2004 from http://www.pewinternet.org/pdfs/PIP_Other_Places.pdf.

Katz, J. E., and P. Aspden. (1998). Internet dropouts in the US. *Telecommunications Policy* 22 (4–5): 327–339.

Katz, J. E., and R. E. Rice. (2002). Access, civic involvement, and social interaction on the Net. In B. Wellman and C. Haythornthwaite (Eds.), *The Internet in everyday life*, pp. 114–138. Malden, MA: Blackwell.

Lenhart, A., J. Horrigan, L. Rainie, K. Allen, A. Boyce, M. Madden, and E. O'Grady. (2003). The ever-shifting Internet population: A new look at Internet access and the digital divide. Pew Internet and American Life Project, April 16. Retrieved October 31, 2004, from http://www.pewinternet.org/reports/index.asp.

Lievrouw, L., and S. Livingstone (Eds.). (2002). Handbook of new media: Social shaping and social consequences. London: Sage.

Madden, M., and L. Rainie. (2003). America's online pursuits: The changing picture of who's online and what they do. Pew Internet and American Life Project, December 22. Retrieved July 1, 2004 from http://www.pewinternet.org/reports/index.asp.

McConnaughey, J. (1999). Universal service and the National Information Infrastructure (NII): Making the grade on the information superhighway. In B. A. Cherry, S. S. Wildman, and A. S. Hammond IV (Eds.), *Making universal service policy*, pp. 189–212. Mahwah, NJ: Lawrence Erlbaum.

McConnaughey, J., et al. (1999). Falling through the Net: Defining the digital divide: A report on the telecommunications and information technology gap in America. National Telecommunications and Information Administration. Retrieved October 10, 2010, from http://www.ntia.doc.gov/.

Melody, W. H. (1991). The information society: The transnational economic context and its implications. In G. Sussman and J. Lent (Eds.), *Transnational communications: Wiring the third world.* Newbury Park, CA: Sage.

Mosco, V. (1989). *The pay-per society: Computers and communication in the information age.* Toronto: Garamond Press.

Nicholas, K. (2003). Geo-policy barriers and rural internet access: The regulatory role in constructing the digital divide. *Information Society* 19 (4): 287–296.

NTIA (National Telecommunications and Information Administration). (1999). Falling through the Net: Defining the digital divide. July.

———. (2002). *A nation online: How Americans are expanding their use of the Internet.* February. Retrieved from http://www.ntia.doc.gov/ntiahome/dn/anationonline2.pdf.

Powell, A. C. (1999). Falling for the gap. *Reason Online.*

Puma, M., D. Chaplin, and A. Pape. (2000). E-Rate and the digital divide: A preliminary analysis from the integrated studies of educational technology. Urban Institute. Retrieved October 1, 2004, from http://www.urban.org/education/erate.html.

Rainie, L., and P. Bell. (2004). The numbers that count. *New Media and Society* 6 (1): 44–54.

Reich, R. (1991). *The work of nations: Preparing ourselves for 21st-century capitalism.* New York: Random House.

Roberts, J. C. (2000). Symposium on statutory interpretation: The sources of statutory meaning: An archaeological case study of the 1996 telecommunications act. *SMU Law Review* 53:143.

Robins, K., and F. Webster. (1988). Cybernetic capitalism: Information, technology, everyday life. In V. Mosco and J. Wasko (Eds.), *The political economy of information,* pp. 45–75. Madison: University of Wisconsin Press.

———. (1999). Times of the technoculture: From the information society to the virtual life. New York: Routledge.

Rogers, E. M. (1976). Communication and development: The passing of the dominant paradigm. *Communication Research* 3 (April 2): 213–240.

Rojas, V., et al. (2000). Communities, cultural capital and the digital divide. Paper presented at the 50th International Communication Association Conference, Acapulco, Mexico.

Rojas, V., J. Straubhaar, D. Roychowdhury, and O. Okur, (2004). Communities, cultural capital, and the digital divide. In E. P. Bucy and J. E. Newhagen (Eds.), *Media access: Social and psychological dimensions of new technology use,* pp. 107–127. Mahwah, NJ: Lawrence Erlbaum.

Sawhney, H. (2000). Letter from the guest editor. Special issue, *Universal service. Information society* (Indiana University–Bloomington) 16(2).

Schiller, D. (1999). *Digital capitalism: Networking the global market system.* Cambridge, MA: MIT Press.

Schement, J. R. (1995, August). Beyond universal service: Characteristics of Americans without telephones, 1980–1993. *Telecommunications Policy* 19 (6): 477–485.

Selwyn, N. (2004). Reconsidering political and popular understandings of the digital divide. *New Media and Society* 6(3): 341–362.

Shingi, P., and B. Mody. (1976). The communication effects gap: A field experiment on television and agricultural ignorance in India. *Communication Research* 3 (April 2): 171–190.

State Auditor Office. (2002). An audit report on grant administration at the Telecommunications Infrastructure Fund board. SAO Report no. 03-005, October. Austin.

Stone, A. (1991). *Public service liberalism: Telecommunications and transition in public policy*. Princeton, NJ: Princeton University Press.

Straubhaar, J., S. Strover, M. Fuentes, and N. Inagaki. (2005). Critically evaluating market diffusion policy and the digital divide in Texas, 2000–2004. Paper presented at the International Communication Association Conference, New York, May.

Straubhaar, J., S. Strover, N. Inagaki, R. Larose, and J. Gregg. (2008). Broadband divides of age, immigration and language in two rural Texas communities. Paper presented at the Communication Policy and Technology Section, International Association for Media and Communication Research, Stockholm, Sweden, July 20–25.

Strover, S., G. Chapman, and J. Waters. (2004). Beyond community networking and CTCs: Access, development and public policy. *Telecommunications Policy* 28 (7–8): 465–485.

Strover, S., and J. Straubhaar. (2000). E-government services and computer and Internet use in Texas. Telecommunications and Information Policy Institute, University of Texas at Austin. Retrieved October 1, 2004, from http://www .utexas.edu/research/tipi/reports2/dir_final3.pdf.

Texas Office of Public Utility Counsel. (2002). Understanding your telephone bill. Retrieved October 1, 2004, from http://www.opc.state.tx.us/Phoneb~1.htm.

Thierer, A. (2000). How free computers are filling the digital divide. Heritage Foundation executive summary no. 1361, April 20.

TIF (Telecommunications Infrastructure Fund). (1997). Telecommunications infrastructure master plan 1998. Austin.

———. (1999). Strategic plan 1999–2003. Austin.

———. (2002). Strategic plan 2003–2007. Austin.

Warschauer, M. (2003). Dissecting the digital divide: A case study in Egypt. *Information Society* 19(4): 297–304.

Wellman, B. (2004). The three ages of Internet studies: Ten, five and zero years ago. *New Media and Society* 6(1): 123–129.

Whiting, G. C. (1976). How does communication interface with change? *Communication Research* 3 (April 2): 191–212.

CAROLYN
CUNNINGHAM

HOLLY CUSTARD

JOSEPH
STRAUBHAAR

JEREMIAH SPENCE

DEAN GRABER

BETHANY LETALIEN

CHAPTER 6

CROSSING THE DIGITAL DIVIDE

LOCAL INITIATIVES IN AUSTIN

Since the early 1980s, leaders in Austin, Texas, have made deliberate efforts to strengthen the local economy through developing the high-tech industry, as discussed in Chapter 3.[1] Leadership from the city government and the University of Texas (UT), as well as business leaders in the region, have been particularly dedicated to ensuring Austin's success in this sector. Equally dedicated and powerful efforts have been initiated to address the digital divide in Austin's socially and economically segregated communities, between those who benefit from and have access to computer or Internet technologies and those who do not. During the tech boom there was great optimism, and subsequent funding, for improving computer and Internet access and training, as described in Chapter 5. Much of this early enthusiasm waned, however, as federal, state, and local funding sources and support became scarcer after 2000; as the federal government withdrew funding for several programs and scaled back others; and as state governments and some foundations also reduced their funding.

In this chapter, we look back and analyze federal, state, and local efforts between 1995 and 2009 intended to address the digital divide in Austin, and how they progressed during this half-generation. In 1999, we examined the responses of several kinds of institutions: schools, libraries, community technology centers, workforce training centers, community centers, and churches, as well as larger organizations which provided citywide network support, financial support, training opportunities, webpage design support, and so on for a variety of these institutions. Research in 2003 looked at a larger group of forty-two institutions in East Austin that targeted primarily lower-income and minority communities. Research in 2009 focused on libraries, which had emerged from the resource losses of the early 2000s as a focal point for computer and Internet access and training, since they still had support from the City of Austin and from some local foundations, like the Dell Foundation. By 2010–2011, new federal grant money for broadband development had returned to some key Austin organizations.

For all three of these periods, we address the following research questions. First, what aspects of the digital divide were of concern to which local actors? Second, at whom were these issues and efforts targeted? Third, why did Austin digital divide programs develop an early focus on public access to the Internet? This early-1990s focus on public access was envisioned by several departments at the University of Texas, combined with grassroots activism and city financial support. By 2009–2011, new initiatives had built and expanded on this base. The resulting forces created a very locally specific environment to address the digital divide. In fact, Martha Fuentes-Bautista (2007) observed that fields of study, work, and competition for resources in the sense described by Pierre Bourdieu (1984) had been created in Austin around the interrelated fields of computer and Internet access and computer-skills training. A number of institutions, described below, had cooperated to meet the demand for access and training in these fields, which grew in the 1990s and early 2000s, declined, and then stabilized, although as Chapter 8 recounts, resources in these fields were being drawn away again by 2010, toward a new, somewhat overlapping field of providing wireless access for mobile students and professionals in Austin.

As other chapters in this book have noted, the historical, economic, and political climate in Austin for addressing these issues has placed the city in a unique situation when compared to many other cities and even historically underprivileged regions (Lentz and Oden 2001) attempting to respond to technological inequities. While several studies (Horrigan and Wilson 2001; Servon 1999; Somers 1997) have examined Austin's efforts to "bridge" the digital divide, a deeper historical understanding of individual and institutional factors that facilitated these efforts has been heretofore missing in the literature. This chapter examines the intersection of local, state, and federal initiatives that have contributed to the proliferation of digital divide efforts in Austin since the early 1990s (see also Chapter 5). The findings suggest that the combined leadership and vision of grassroots activists, the city government, and UT have created a unique environment within which solutions to the digital divide have been successfully implemented, which also indicates the importance of institutional responses to technology policy issues. Key local institutions, including UT, local city government, and nonprofit initiatives, helped to conceptualize, implement, and coordinate these efforts. We conclude that Austin's unique approach to creating and maintaining its telecommunications infrastructure, managed through a nonprofit organization, the Austin Free-Net, was in part a result of applying a broader understanding of the importance of social and cultural capital in digital inclusion.

DEFINING DIGITAL DIVIDES NATIONALLY AND LOCALLY

The notion of networking computers in public locations began in the early 1970s. The idea of networking led to the concept of free-nets in the 1980s. Many free-nets in the late 1980s were simply free public dial-up Internet service providers. A nonprofit organization, National Public Telecomputing Network, was founded to promote free-nets. One major goal of free-nets was to provide inexpensive access to the Internet for local residents, based on social demands perceived at the local level. These early efforts eventually led to the development of community networks and community technology centers in the 1980s where people who did not have computers or modems at home could go to use computers and the Internet for free (Schuler 1996). A national organization, the Community Technology Centers' Network (CTCNet), also grew up to promote and coordinate those centers.

Some of the early community networks attempted to use technology to engage communities in civic dialogue and educational pursuits, while community technology centers focused more on providing computer and Internet access to those who could not afford them. Since the 1990s, various efforts and initiatives have provided a number of resources and services to fit the specific needs of the communities in which they operate. Most have offered free or inexpensive access to computers and the Internet, and some provide training. Yet, despite the diversity of policies and programs, there has been no clear policy or academic research consensus on how to define the digital divide, whether it is an issue requiring policy intervention, and, if so, exactly how to intervene (Lentz 2000). Some question whether defining these kinds of inequities as a digital divide is useful (Warschauer 2003). Many now prefer to frame the issue in terms of digital inclusion, while others continue to insist that the problem is largely solved (Compaine 2001). (See Chapter 5 for an in-depth analysis of these debates.)

After 2000, the policy climate shifted decisively at both the federal level and the state level. The Bush administration reduced some programs, such as the National Telecommunications and Information Administration's Technology Opportunities Program, while Congress insisted on maintaining reduced levels of funding for other programs, such as the federal E-Rate program, which helps subsidize telephone service for low-income households. The Texas Telecommunications Infrastructure Fund (TIF) was canceled in 2003, although the funding is still being collected and will likely be applied to other projects to be determined by the state government.

As we explain in this chapter, these national and state events affected what activists in Austin could do to address the city's own digital divide locally. We argue that those digital divide programs that began with local or grassroots movements are better situated to survive reductions in funding than a number of programs that began essentially in response to government funding opportunities. To think of it in terms of the construction and reconstruction of fields of competition for resources (Bourdieu 1984), we argue here that those institutions which were originally most committed to access and training, as compared to those who saw opportunities to obtain resources when they were most easily available, are most likely to stay in the field as resources narrow and become more difficult to get.

As we have begun to describe in earlier chapters of this book, Austin is a unique city that created a striking number and diversity of programs to provide access to and training for people in using computers and the Internet. In 2003, Austin had more than fifty public access Internet sites located in libraries, public housing units, community centers, nonprofit centers, and public schools. Those were noticeably fewer in 2009. As of the 2000 census, Austin's population of just fewer than one million residents was 53 percent white, 10 percent black, and 31 percent Hispanic, and had a median household income of $45,790. The majority of the initiatives for community networks and community technology centers existed in the historically segregated and underserved community on Austin's east side. The infrastructure that presently exists in Austin is due to the efforts of UT, the local city government, and nonprofits, along with donations from some local high-tech companies. Federal grants and the TIF also provided financial support for these efforts. The TIF awarded grants to community networks featuring libraries, community health organizations, community media, and schools.

THE ROLE OF ENGAGED SCHOLARS IN ADDRESSING AUSTIN'S DIGITAL DIVIDE

UT has played a key role in the development of local broadband infrastructure in the city. The combination of professors and students with technical skills and an academic interest in the importance of providing both access to technology and "cultural capital" helped guide the local agenda. This section focuses on three units of UT that pooled their research, teaching, and service capacities to join in a unique multiyear collaboration: the Lyndon B. Johnson School of Public Affairs, the Telecommunications and Information Policy Institute, and the School of Information.

THE LYNDON B. JOHNSON SCHOOL OF PUBLIC AFFAIRS

Even before the notion of a digital divide was introduced into public discourse, academics across the United States were engaged in dialogue with technology professionals about strategies to create equitable access to information technology resources. An early approach was the 21st Century Project, initiated in 1991 by the Computer Professionals for Social Responsibility, an international organization of computer scientists and technology professionals that promotes the responsible use of computer technology. The goal of the 21st Century Project is to bring together both experts and nonexperts to study the Internet, information policy, telecommunications, and the social and political trends of emerging new technologies. The 21st Century Project received its initial seed money from the Rockefeller Foundation. By 1994, the project had found a new home at UT in the Lyndon B. Johnson (LBJ) School of Public Affairs. Gary Chapman, who was involved from the project's early formation, became the director of this nonprofit research and educational initiative.

Relocation of the 21st Century Project to the LBJ School created a natural partnership with professors already working in the area of technology policy. The late professor Susan G. Hadden, whose research focused on telecommunications and environmental issues, was actively involved in helping to set Austin's telecommunications agenda. She was a charter member of the Alliance for Public Technology, a national nonprofit that advocates for affordable access to communication technologies. Additionally, professor Lodis Rhodes has focused his research interests on community development and education policy. Rhodes brought his research interests to East Austin, working with community leaders to form Family Literacy Centers in a number of housing developments. In 1995, this initiative rebranded itself the Austin Learning Academy.

In 1995, the City of Austin was in the process of modernizing its telecommunications infrastructure. Leveraging UT's experience with broadband, faculty from the LBJ School partnered with the city to help develop a citywide infrastructure plan. Hadden, Rhodes, and Chapman were key forces in this partnership. The city plan incorporated their vision of creating neighborhood computer networks for community development. This effort generated the Austin Free-Net. By 1997, the City of Austin had developed a Telecommunity Partnership Initiative, which was largely influenced by Hadden's conceptual framework. Hadden explained the framework as follows:

> Inspired but not controlled by technology, we should adopt a four-fold goal: delivering a network to people's homes, schools, libraries, hospitals, and businesses; ensuring that they can send as well as receive video information and find other people's information easily; ensuring that everyone, regardless of location, disability, or income is connected to and can use the network; and ensuring that health, education, job and community services are available to all. (Hadden 2003)

In 2005 and 2006, the 21st Century Project assisted in the development of the 2006 World Congress on Information Technology, which was held in Austin in May. LBJ School students created web and print materials for the two thousand international delegates who attended, addressing the event's three themes: health care, privacy and security, and the digital divide. All the delegates received a student-produced booklet on privacy and security titled "Secure Your World." A student-produced short documentary film on how Austin was dealing with the digital divide screened continuously in an exhibit hall booth (LBJ School of Public Affairs 2006).

THE TELECOMMUNICATIONS AND INFORMATION POLICY INSTITUTE

The Telecommunications and Information Policy Institute (TIPI), established in May 1996, is an interdisciplinary consortium of UT faculty associates. These faculty associates work toward designing research initiatives and recommending policy solutions for telecommunications policy. Initially, TIPI served as a statewide resource for telecommunications policy issues. TIPI has since grown to be a national and international resource.

TIPI has been actively involved in the local Austin initiatives. Professor Sharon Strover, director of TIPI, partnered with community leaders to apply for a TIF Community Networking Grant in 2000. This grant established a number of public access sites and training programs in Austin. Strover also leveraged TIPI's resources through providing student volunteers to the community network project. Professor Joseph Straubhaar worked with Strover on surveying Internet access in Texas (Strover and Straubhaar 2001; Straubhaar et al. 2005) and mapping and evaluating local community access projects (Strover, Tufekcioglu, and Straubhaar 2001). Over a period of several years, Straubhaar and graduate students worked on libraries as access points (Lentz et al. 2000), which formed the basis for research on cultural barriers to Internet use in East Austin (Rojas, Straubhaar, Roychowdhury, and Okur 2003), and mapping the availability of information and communication technology (ICT) access and training.

In the last years of the TIF (which lasted a total of eight years), Strover and Gary Chapman of the 21st Century Project co-taught a two-semester Policy Research Project at the LBJ School (Fall 2002 and Spring 2003) to evaluate the performance of the communities that had received TIF funding for community networking projects. The analysis involved site visits and interviews in thirty-six communities throughout Texas, data analysis, and consultation with state officials. The goal of the project was to evaluate the strengths and weaknesses in each local project and to present a set of best practices that might be applied to other local networking projects. Straubhaar, Carolyn Cunningham, and Holly Custard adapted the methodology of the TIF project to conduct the 2003 evaluation of Austin access and training sites that formed the initial basis of this chapter.

THE SCHOOL OF INFORMATION

Librarians have been key contributors to the development of the Austin community network infrastructure. Public libraries have worked with the Austin Free-Net to provide a comprehensive city-wide public access network since the early 1990s. In addition, a co-alition of private, public, and academic librarians in 1994 created the Metropolitan Austin Interactive Network (MAIN), which describes itself on its website (www.main.org) as

> a non-profit organization whose mission is to establish and operate efficiently a community-access computer network. The purpose of this network is information sharing and communication among the people and governmental, educational, commercial, cultural, religious, and civic organizations, in order to enhance lives and make the best use of community resources.

Several professors and graduate students from UT's School of Information (then the Graduate School of Library and Information Science) along with librarians from UT's general libraries, the Texas Medical Association, the Texas State Archives Commission, and public libraries in Austin and nearby Round Rock served on the board of directors and participated as founding members of the organization. According to the founding president, Sue Soy of the Austin Public Library (who was also a doctoral student in the School of Information), the creation of MAIN was made possible through the support of private business donations that allowed for the creation and hosting of the MAIN website (Soy 2003). Phillip Doty and other School of Information professors and students have worked on several of the TIPI projects mentioned above, and continue to do a variety of projects connected with the Austin library system and other library systems.

Masters students at the School of Information have the choice of completing "capstone projects" in lieu of a thesis, and many choose to do so. Students became involved in a wide range of activities related to the information professions through these projects, and several took this or other opportunities to get involved in the Austin Free-Net (Rice-Lively 2004). It is also common for students to work with the Austin Public Library's Wired for Youth initiative (Lacy 2004), which is discussed below.

Each of these three academic divisions approached the digital divide in Austin according to the framework of its respective discipline. The LBJ School of Public Affairs worked closely with city policy makers and local nonprofits in the interest of creating innovative policy solutions. TIPI conducted research projects, worked on access projects with nonprofits, and leveraged its resources to attract federal- and state-funded programs. The School of Information's expertise with making information readily and widely available and information professionals' emphasis on service also benefited the city's virtual infrastructure.

CITY OF AUSTIN INITIATIVES

During the tech boom of the early 1990s, the city government in Austin did not have funds allocated for a public infrastructure that would allow open access to computers and the Internet (Jayson 1995). It was not until 1995 that the city created its first informational website. At that time, staff in the Telecommunication and Regulatory Affairs Office discussed the importance of making this information broadly available to the public, realizing access in low-income areas would be especially problematic (Hawkins 2003).

As in many high-tech communities across the country, Austin was experiencing increasing economic and social division due to this new tech-based economy, which tended to shift income toward highly educated information producers and manipulators. In the 2000 article "Austin, We Have a Problem" for the *New York Times Magazine,* writer Helen Thorpe noted:

Austin has always been a city of distinct worlds—a college town, a state capital and a live-music center all in one. But lately the number of worlds that Austin contains has been multiplying, and now, everywhere you look, there is the spectacle of worldviews clashing.

Over the last century, the population of Austin has doubled every 20 years, and in the metropolitan area there are now more than one million residents. Thirty-five thousand people, the equivalent of a fair-sized town, moved here last year alone. And in the last five years, Austin has produced or acquired 17,000 new millionaires. Now an upper class of tech barons lord it over a middle class of state government and university workers; a national Republican campaign machine whirs above a local Democratic power structure; yuppies infiltrate the habitat of punk rockers. It's as if every Austin stereotype has spawned its opposite: easy-going Slackers live beside hard-driving Techies, and old-school liberals drink at the same bars as new-school conservatives.

AUSTIN FREE-NET

No city funding was available for building a network of its own, so the Telecommunication and Regulatory Affairs Office of the City of Austin—along with community activists, private businesspeople, and council-appointed citizens—contributed to the effort of making computers and the Internet more widely available to the public in 1995 by helping to establish the Austin Free-Net (AFN). The city dedicated office space and a full-time professional staff member, Sue Beckwith, to formalize and develop the efforts of AFN into a nonprofit organization that differed from many other free-net models in the United States.[2] The organizational structure of AFN allowed for flexible and diverse service support for the city. Unlike free-net models in other U.S. cities that provided free Internet connections to residents' homes through dial-up connections (Thompson 2007), AFN was created to develop a public infrastructure in sites such as libraries and nonprofits throughout the community and supply them with computers, Internet access, training, and technical support. This initial effort was made possible through cash and equipment donations from local corporations and businesses. After AFN was established, staff continually sought funds in the form of private business donations, government project support, and foundation grants. The city began supporting the effort financially by contracting AFN's services, beginning in 1998, to expand and service the public infrastructure.[3] This action was to be the start of a series of efforts initiated by the city to make technology more accessible to the public.

In 1997, then-councilman Gus Garcia, along with the Telecommunication and Regulatory Affairs staff, began to hold regular meetings to discuss the city's role in addressing issues of the digital divide in Austin (Hawkins 2003). A similar discussion was taking place community-wide. To educate the broader community and to encourage dialogue and collaboration, the city participated in a series of conferences hosted by the Austin public television station, KLRU. These conferences, or "town meetings," facilitated discussion about the digital divide in Austin and drew participation from city officials, non-profits, activists, technology leaders, educational institutions, and others. These discussions were taped and aired on KLRU, followed by a PBS series titled *Digital Divide*. The conferences and production were funded through the MacArthur Foundation and the PBS Television Race Initiative, which was dedicated to promoting discussions in communities around the United States about the digital divide. Not only did these discussions raise important social and economic issues, but they also encouraged the creation of innovative solutions.

As Internet applications began to increase and diversify, many were exploring how the Internet might be used as a tool for increasing civic participation. The city was interested in developing more e-government applications and concerned that not all citizens would have access to these applications. In addition, it recognized the growing economic gap in the community, as well as the need for a more tech-savvy labor force. As such, a funding source was eventually started by the city to support programs that would address issues of technology training and workforce development.

CAPITAL AREA TRAINING FOUNDATION, GRANT FOR TECHNOLOGY OPPORTUNITIES, AND OTHER CITY OF AUSTIN PROGRAMS

In 1998, the City of Austin awarded a $200,000 development grant to the Capital Area Training Foundation, which was started in 1994 and programmatically connected to the Greater Austin Chamber of Commerce, for a new initiative called the Community Technology Training Center (CTTC). It opened training labs in two high schools located in low-income neighborhoods to reinforce technology in the schools, and also opened school facilities for after-hours skills training for lower-income adults. This effort was funded by the city and through grants received from the U.S. Department of Education, as well as private and foundation donations (Chapman 2003; Strover, Tufekcioglu, and Straubhaar 2001). However, the decline in both state and federal funding after 2003 reduced the ability of the Capital Area Training Foundation to conduct major training programs. The Capital Area Training Foundation, which was renamed the Skillpoint Alliance, has maintained the CTTC computer training program (see also Chapter 4), has increased work with K–12 schools to provide career fairs and orientations, provides career training, and participates in broader initiatives like the Community Technology Network and Austin Connects with the City of Austin and Austin Free-Net.

In addition to supporting technology education and workforce development, the city also helped develop a wide-area fiber optic network called the Greater Austin Area Telecommunications Network (GAATN), to connect government and educational organizations in Austin. The GAATN consortium was composed of the City of Austin, the State of Texas General Services Commission, the Austin Independent School District, Travis County, UT, Austin Community College, and the Lower Colorado River Authority. This $12 million effort was to serve as a cost-effective method for supplying high-speed connections to participating members, as well as to ease transmission of data between the entities.

Once these programs and initiatives were established, Rondella Hawkins, an officer with the city Telecommunication and Regulatory Affairs Office, encouraged the creation of an additional funding source, approved by the city council, to expand community-based technology programs that resulted in the Grant for Technology Opportunities (GTOPS) program. The $100,000 GTOPS began awarding several small grants of $5,000–$10,000 in 2001 to organizations that agreed to provide public access to computers and the Internet, but that also created innovative technology-based applications and encouraged community and neighborhood planning and action.

City funding for GTOPS, AFN, and the CTTC continue despite severe city and state budget deficits, and subsequent program cuts in 2003. The city, along with local businesses, technology leaders, and educational institutions, understands the importance of the technology sector to the Austin economy. For now, under current economic conditions, the city hopes to maintain the infrastructure and the programs and services they help to provide to the city. This degree of sustainability shows the importance of local initiative and a local consensus on the need for ICT access and training for local economic and social development.

CITY PUBLIC LIBRARIES

As in many American cities, libraries emerged early in Austin as preferred sites for public access. During the high-tech boom in Austin in the 1990s, many criticized the slow pace at which an infrastructure was being developed for Austin public libraries. The library system's digital infrastructure began through the efforts of two separate aforementioned nonprofit organizations, MAIN and AFN. Both aimed to achieve the same mission—providing people with free or low-cost access to computers and the Internet through public libraries (Chapman 2003). However, after 2005, the city took measures to develop an infrastructure and system of its own in partnership with funding from the Dell Foundation, which earlier produced the Wired for Youth program in Austin libraries.

MAIN was created in 1994, primarily by librarians, Austin technology activists, and members of UT's School of Information. By 1995, the group was also interested in creating a public infrastructure in the Austin library system to provide public access to information via the Internet. MAIN received cash and equipment donations from two high-tech companies located in Austin (Applied Materials and Advanced Micro Devices) to pilot computer and Internet use at two branch libraries, one located in a primarily Latino neighborhood and the other in a primarily African American neighborhood (Kelly 1995). Eventually, the central library was likewise equipped.

The MAIN pilot project was well received by both librarians and residents, so the library system was eager to find additional funding to expand these services to other branches. As no city funding was available for developing the library infrastructure in 1995, branches began actively seeking funding through grants and foundations. Several local businesses donated $10,000 cash and computer equipment to the library system that year, but it was not until the Texas State Library and Archives Commission awarded a $200,000 grant to AFN in 1996 that all public libraries received computers. MAIN was also awarded funding of close to $40,000 to help libraries acquire Internet access. It was at this time that MAIN and AFN decided to focus their efforts in different areas—AFN on developing public access in libraries and MAIN on developing content and hosting for nonprofit organizations (Chapman 2003).

In 1996, AFN also received a federal Technology Opportunities Program (TOP) grant of close to $250,000 to establish computer and Internet access at thirteen public sites ("libraries, schools, community places"). The program was also designed to provide training and to "facilitate information-sharing among parents, students, and teachers through the creation and use of electronic tools" (TOP 2003).

The library system also received financial support for infrastructure, hardware, software, and training through TIF.

Despite all of these efforts, access remained limited at the branch libraries, with two computer stations available on average, until the Michael and Susan Dell Foundation made a $500,000 award to the Austin Public Library in 1999 (with a $325,000 matching grant from the City of Austin) to help Austin teens and preteens bridge the digital divide through a program called Wired for Youth (Jayson 1999). That year, ten branch libraries in low-income and minority neighborhoods each received eight multimedia computer stations, scanners, printers, and other peripherals. The libraries created eleven positions and hired employees to provide activities and assistance to children and teenagers interested in learning about and using technology. The Dell Foundation's support also helped Wired for Youth add part-time "cyber-lifeguard" positions in the summers to allow the centers to be open longer and to serve more children. Many cyber-lifeguards are library school graduate students who work twenty hours a week, helping the Wired for Youth librarians with summer programs and providing one-on-one assistance to the youth. Demand for the centers has been high from the beginning, and they host more than 100,000 visitors a year between ages eight and eighteen (Austin Public Library 2009).

In the first year of the program, Wired for Youth librarians reported that more youth than ever before were visiting the libraries and using the Internet resources for homework, research, and fun. Each Wired for Youth center identified its own target population and developed programs and classes to meet their needs. For example, the Carver Branch Library in East Austin, located in a predominantly African American neighborhood next to a junior high school, focused on youth ages eleven to fourteen and tailored its information literacy programs to that specific age group. Michelle Gorman, the Wired for Youth librarian at the Carver Branch, said her library's Wired for Youth center offered technology-related programming to nine thousand young people in the first year alone.

Carver's Wired for Youth center created a Youth Advisory Committee of more than a dozen young people who represented a cross-section of gender, age, and race of the young patrons of the library. The committee met once a month to plan activities and brainstorm future plans. A girls group, "Sister Soldiers," met once a month for formal activities and informal interaction. The Carver library also held a monthly "Cool Careers" program, inviting guests to talk about their profession and to interact with the young people. Gorman said the placement of technology centers at the neighborhood branch libraries made them accessible to all Austin teenagers, distinguishing the city's initiative from programs in San Antonio, Texas, and Phoenix, Arizona, which started at a single centralized location. The program's decentralized nature allowed librarians to build relationships with young users and helped tailor programs to meet neighborhood needs:

> They come in to use the computers for e-mail, do homework, or read the latest graphic novel or most current issue of Computer Gaming Magazine. Sometimes they come to Carver to socialize, get help with a school project, take a class on web development, or ask questions about anything from how to publish their own poetry to how to find information on the Internet about summer jobs. They feel that they belong here. They know someone is here to help them. They also come to the library because it is a better alternative to hanging around the neighborhood. They have a say in the development of the program, and they are always encouraged to share their ideas on how they envision "their" library. (Gorman 2002)

Over almost a decade, the Dell Foundation awarded four grants to Wired for Youth totaling more than $815,000. More recently in March 2009, the Austin Public Library Foundation announced a new grant to help transform Wired for Youth into the "Connected Youth Project." According to the library's description, Connected Youth would put laptops in libraries and create new programs for teens and young adults throughout Austin. The goal was to inspire creativity, and to empower youth to use the library collection for discovery and to develop a love of reading (Austin Public Library 2009). In the spring of 2009, students ages twelve to sixteen were invited to apply for a Connected Youth "Teen Card" at all branch libraries. The card allows them to check out traditional library materials such as books and DVDs, but with parental permission, they can also check out a laptop computer for two hours a day. Starting March 30, the ten Wired for Youth centers became "Teen Centers," and each branch received in the following months four laptop computers for checkout.

Special programs by teen services librarians were also being planned and piloted. The laptops allowed teen services staff and new interns to create "mobile programs" at branch libraries, including those not having a designated Teen Center. The mobile programs targeted youth ages eight to sixteen, but laptop checkout privileges extended only to those ages twelve to sixteen. Possible program topics included social networking, science programs using 3-D, and creative programs such as Photoshop. The library planned for work from those creative projects to be placed on the "Teen Studio" of the Connected Youth website (www.connectedyouth.com), allowing young people from across the city to participate.

The Wired for Youth program helped public library branches become important public access locations for many residents. In the summer of 2009, when the City of Austin said it needed to cut $30 million to $40 million from the proposed 2010 budget, city officials held a series of public meetings and asked residents to recommend which programs to keep and which to cut. A tally of 530 people who attended the first three meetings ranked preserving evening hours at branch libraries and money for library books among the top ten priorities, along with such services as a twenty-four-hour police line for nonemergency calls, and four senior-level arson investigators. Tim Staley, executive director of the Austin Public Library Foundation, argued at one public meeting, "Especially with the downturn in the economy, people are using libraries more than ever for things like job searches" (quoted in Coppola 2009a). In the $613.3 million budget proposed by city manager Marc Ott, library hours and money for new library materials were ultimately spared budget cuts (Coppola 2009b).

Through corporate, foundation, city, and grant support, the number of computers and the quality of access has improved since 1995. The city continues to contract with AFN to maintain and expand computer and Internet access, the library system itself has been active in seeking funds, and the Wired for Youth program continues—all of which help support the library system's efforts to fulfill its goal of providing free public access to computers and the Internet. Some earlier research in East Austin high schools has shown, however, that parts of the community, particularly minority teenage boys, do not see libraries as a comfortable locale for access (Lentz et al. 2000), so reliance on libraries as primary public access points has to be tempered by other strategies. Libraries in Austin have also had trouble responding quickly enough to demands for more computer access stations, more materials in Spanish and in other languages, more services specifically aimed at immigrants, and more services for immigrants outside the historical immigrant concentration in East Austin. Recommendations made by the Austin Task Force on Immigrant Issues in 1998 led to an expansion of immigrant services to eight Austin public libraries from 1998 to 2004. Still, the historical commitment of Austin city libraries to public access tends to ensure access there when other programs fail for lack of funding.

AUSTIN COMMUNITY BUSINESS SUPPORT

Almost all of the major digital divide initiatives in Austin have been supported in some way by private funding or donations. Local businesses and national corporations aligned themselves with various efforts that provide mutual benefits for the funders as well as the grantees. For example, some technology-based corporations, such as 3M, Southwestern Bell, AMD, and Steck-Vaughn, needed a skilled workforce to support their industries located in Austin, so they promoted and funded adult education and job-training programs like the Capital Area Training Foundation. Dell, on the other hand, focused on developing computer resources for youth by placing computers in public libraries through the Wired for Youth program. Grande, a Texas-based cable and Internet provider that started its business development in primarily low-income minority East Austin neighborhoods, contributed funds to Hispanic Connect, an organization that provided culturally appropriate web content and training for the Austin Latino community, especially youth, working to help them gain admittance to technology-related programs in high school and college. These funds, along with city, state, national, and foundation support were what allowed digital divide efforts to develop and expand, particularly when state and federal funds were reduced.

THE ROLE OF COMMUNITY NETWORKS AND OTHER NONPROFIT ORGANIZATIONS

Austin followed the trend of establishing community networks in order to bring the Internet to the broader community. These community networks followed Hadden's concept of a "telecommunity" locally applied to the Austin Access Model, defined as a "learn and serve" model that brings technology to low-income neighborhoods. The model begins with the notion that information technologies should be woven into existing social networks with other members of the community, and that these should be taken into account when developing a community network. Using this model, AFN received a $246,679 grant in 1996 from the Telecommunications and Information Infrastructure Assistance Program (TIIAP, which later became TOP), a program of the U.S. Department of Commerce's National Telecommunications and Information Administration. AFN's goal was to create a community technology network within low-income community social networks in East Austin. As part of this grant, AFN partnered with the Austin Learning Academy, which was responsible for the training component of the grant, and the LBJ School of Public Affairs, which was responsible for grant and project evaluation.

The East Austin Community Network (EACN) project was envisioned as an application of the Austin Access Model. Upon receiving the TIIAP grant, AFN implemented the EACN's ideas. The primary goal was to bring AFN's services to East Austin as a way to diffuse computer and Internet access, which was previously situated in central Austin libraries. Access in the EACN model focused on addressing economic and educational disparities in low-income neighborhoods and finding more efficient ways to provide information, such as bus schedules, to residents in order to make their lives easier. According to AFN's TIIAP grant application:

> Poor people spend more time than others tending to their most basic economic, education, and health needs. Even then, a lopsided share of their time is lost traveling to get help or waiting to be served. . . . Poor people and poor communities are victimized because no one values their time. If they could recapture the time lost waiting, there would be more time to actually do the work needed to strengthen their families and communities. (Somers 1997)

The EACN focused primarily on 11th and 12th streets in East Austin. In identifying where to place public access sites, project leaders believed that these locations would not be controlled by technology, but rather be inspired by it. EACN became an outgrowth of community development efforts already in place. EACN began as a network of forty-one computers placed in eleven locations throughout East

Austin. These computers were connected to the Internet through a high-speed connection. Additionally, AFN created a community website that became a hub for communication and interactions, with pages for community organizations, churches, and schools. Many of the pages are available in Spanish.

In 2000, community stakeholders realized the need to expand the EACN to other locations in Austin that did not have adequate access. Austin Community College, UT, AFN, Knowbility (a nonprofit that aids organizations in incorporating accessible technologies into their computer centers), and the City of Austin received a Community Networking Grant from TIF. The TIF grant helped establish the Austin Telecommunity Partnership, which added fifteen new computers to the DeWitty Job Training Center, discussed below, and established new public access sites at the University Hills Library, Austin Community College, Bedichek Middle School (in South Austin), and the Lamar Senior Activity Center.

Several other nonprofit organizations helped sustain the community network project by expanding their missions to include public access to computers and the Internet, training and technical support, and job skills. This section highlights some of these efforts. For example, the Austin Learning Academy began as the Family Literacy Centers in 1990, located in seven public housing centers and funded by the Austin Housing Authority and the Department of Education. Each center was placed in established community-based organizations.

The primary focus of the Austin Learning Academy is to provide technology training and skill development. Its partners now include the Housing Authority, the LBJ School of Public Affairs, and the Austin Independent School District. The academy serves residents from East and South Austin. Its family learning centers are located at Garza Independence High School in East Austin; American YouthWorks, a nonprofit in Central Austin that links classroom education with service learning; Foundation Communities Trails at Vintage Creek, a nonprofit in a North Austin affordable housing community with on-site educational programs; and four elementary schools in South Austin.

The Austin Learning Academy also offers classes in parenting, early childhood development, GED (general equivalency diploma) preparation, and English as a second language. FamilyCARE (Computer Assembly, Refurbishment, and Enhancement) is a program that helps families learn to build and maintain personal computers. Additionally, an R&D lab develops curriculum and projects related to technology and the Internet. In 2007, the Austin Learning Academy won the KDK-Harman Foundation's first GED Award of Excellence, receiving $35,000 for its work using innovative strategies to increase the number of students who complete their GEDs and continue into postsecondary education or enter the workforce (Austin Learning Academy 2007).

The DeWitty Job Training Center has become a center for educational and employment programs in East Austin. Three programs are co-located in the DeWitty Center: the City of Austin's Job Training and Employment Center, AFN, and Eastside Story. The Employment Center helps adults with some computer-related skills. AFN's East Austin Community Networking Lab contains over twenty computers for public use. AFN offers free computer classes there, including beginner's open-door computer clinics for adults and seniors. Eastside Story provides after-school programs to nearly eight hundred students from the Austin, Manor, and Del Valle independent school districts, as well as charter and private schools in East and Northeast Austin. Eastside Story's goal is to involve parents in this program. Parents whose children attend the program must volunteer for four hours a month. Eastside Story also hosts a Science, Math, and Technology Summer Camp and a Life Skills field trip. Eastside Story helps sponsor the Digital Workforce Academy, which provides low-cost telecommunications and technology training. Participants in this program collaborate with a social worker in order to monitor progress and identify family needs. With the help of this training, many participants are able to receive jobs in the high-tech sector.

American YouthWorks was chartered as a public high school in August 1996. It is designed to educate youth considered at risk of dropping out of high school or who have already dropped out of the Austin Independent School District and surrounding districts. American YouthWorks uses a methodology based on the concepts of project-based education and service-learning. Students at the charter school work toward attaining their GEDs and can receive high school credit for participating in a number of service programs offered there.

A final example is Computer Corps, which trains participants to teach technology classes throughout Austin and is funded in part by the AmeriCorps program. Computer Corps teaches technology classes, refurbishes donated computers and recycles them back into the community, and designs websites for social service organizations. Members work closely with AFN to ensure sustainability of their programs.

PUBLIC SCHOOLS

A number of the nonprofits discussed above created programs that worked within Austin public schools. These programs were designed to reach both younger students and older people in after-school programs. They focused on access and education about technology and its use. Several nonprofits focused on schools because the challenges faced by Austin schools are significant. While white professionals largely dominate the city economy, the schools reflect a much more diverse, increasingly immigrant population: 59 percent of Austin Independent School District (AISD) students are Hispanic, 26 percent are white, and 9 percent are African American. Many are from poor families: over 63 percent qualify for free school lunches based on low incomes (AISD 2010). The district as a whole has tried a number of strategies for technology access and education. However, overall, AISD's performance in this area was very uneven. The Texas state government's review of AISD in 2000 said, "The district has no comprehensive plan for replacing its outdated information systems or managing its technology projects. AISD has a history of failed technology projects and technology plans" (Texas School Performance Review 2000).

AISD put most of its technology resources into administrative networks rather than actual classroom education. Only 10 percent of AISD funds designated in 2001–2004 for information technology was for instructional technology: $1,670,000 of $16,700,000 (Texas School Performance Review 2000). AISD has received over $1 million from TIF. It has also received training support from UT and Intel (AISD 2001).

AISD has offered a number of teacher training initiatives, both formal and informal. However, the actual level of teacher training for technology use in the classroom is fragmented, and it is mostly left up to the individual teachers to seek out training or learn the needed technical skills and pedagogical techniques on their own. Initially, teachers could get a computer installed in their classroom as a reward for training. Now almost all teachers have a computer in their room, but there are still large gaps in technical skills and knowledge of how to integrate computers (and especially the Internet) into classroom learning experiences. For example, a number of elementary and middle schools in 2003 still taught computers skills for the first time as part of "keyboarding" classes, which were frequently taught essentially as typing classes. A study at Johnston High in 2000 showed that several boys had been turned off by that first exposure to keyboarding since they assumed typing was "for girls" and not pertinent to their personal or working lives (Rojas et al. 2003). Things had improved considerably by 2010, but some schools still lagged behind others.

Schools in AISD have considerable local autonomy, which has helped some schools and stymied others. Those with well-organized Parent-Teacher Associations, particularly with parents in the technology industries, could and did seek partnerships with local industries and dramatically improve access to computers and Internet within their schools. Several schools in middle-class, largely white West Austin neighborhoods benefited from these connections. In other schools, including some with a mixture of upper and lower incomes, particularly enthusiastic teachers and administrators took the initiative to seek out corporate support, even though the parents were not networked into the technology industries. For example, in largely minority and working-class Travis High, teachers, along with supportive administrators, put together a model program to teach computer-based media and design to the students. They also partnered with local industries to obtain resources, resulting in a number of students' getting technology industry jobs straight out of high school. By contrast, in high schools without stable or technology-focused leadership, such as Johnston High, even technology provided by AISD was underused. Late in 2000, computers provided by AISD sat in boxes in the Johnston High gym for months because there was not enough technical support to set them up and network them properly in a lab.

IMPACT OF LOCAL INITIATIVES

In addition to the principal cases described above, our research project also surveyed a total of forty-two individual libraries, community technology centers, training centers, community centers, schools, and so on, many of which were supported by the primary actors described above, such as AFN, the public library system, AISD, and the Capital Area Training Foundation. We noted a striking difference in performance among those projects that were started by neighborhood initiative rather than by the intervention of citywide officials. Locally generated programs tended to be maintained in the face of funding cuts, whereas those that responded to perceived funding opportunities or to suggestions by city activists were more likely to have failed.

There have been several local initiatives in Austin designed to address gender issues associated with the digital divide. Women and girls have a particularly negative relationship to digital technologies, as evidenced by their underrepresentation in information technology fields. Women make up only 25 percent of the information technology industry (Ramsey and McCorduck 2005). Research suggests several cultural and structural barriers that may prevent girls from achieving equality. They include loss of self-esteem during adolescence, limited curriculum and subject matter that appeals to girls' interests, a lack of female role models, and a pervasive masculine culture of technology (American Association of University Women 1998, 2000; Furger 1998; Sadker and Sadker 1995). In Austin, two programs in particular—the Girl Scouts' EDGE and Latinitas—provide all-girl settings to encourage girls' self-esteem and confidence with digital technologies and to engage them in technology-based activities that are relevant to the context of their lives.

The EDGE, designed to give girls a technology edge and launched in 2000 with funding from the Dell Foundation, is the first STEM (science, technology, engineering, and mathematics) program organized by the Girl Scouts in the United States. The EDGE is housed in the Lone Star Program Center, the headquarters of the Lone Star Girl Scout Council. The center, located in the Austin area, has administrative offices and a shop with Girl Scout supplies, and provides spaces for Girl Scout activities. The EDGE has twelve desktop computers, as well as laptop computers that can be used when traveling to rural locations. It also has peripheral equipment for use in program activities, such as digital cameras, digital video cameras, microphones, and color printers. The EDGE follows the primary mission of the Girl Scouts, which is to support girls' social and emotional development, but has a particular goal of encouraging girls in STEM fields.

EDGE classes incorporate best practices intended to address the barriers girls face in achieving equality in technological literacy. Goals include providing a safe learning environment to enable girls to use computers to explore the world; developing girls' comfort level with new technologies, such as cameras, robotics, and programming language; developing girls' self-confidence in their own creative abilities; enabling girls to develop valuable computer knowledge; and teaching girls to become imaginative users of technology. Another goal is to prepare girls to enter STEM fields: "At these workshops [at the EDGE] they solve problems, develop creative solutions, make design decisions, work in teams, visualize the end product—in short, they develop all the skills required to do well in STEM while having fun" (Girl Scouts–Lone Star Council 2001).

Classes include desktop publishing, digital photography, robotics, web design, and word processing. The program offers after-school activities, summer camps, and weekend workshops for both Girl Scout troops and individual members, who can earn merit badges for completing projects. For example, some of the programs at the EDGE fulfill requirements for the Discovering Technology and Communication merit badges. Merit badges denote a level of achievement and are part of the Girl Scout culture. Weekend workshops often last two to three hours and are offered for different age groups. There are groups in public housing to target lower income and minority girls as well.

A second example of targeted assistance to girls is Latinitas, which was formed in 2002 to "empower Latina youth through media and technology" (Latinitas 2008). One of the goals of Latinitas is to address the low level of representation of Latinos in positions of power in newsrooms. As stated on their website, "Despite their growing numbers, statistics show Hispanics make up less than two percent of newsroom staff nationwide. There are important stories that are missing from the current landscape of media" (Latinitas 2008). Latinitas teaches skills in journalism and digital-media production to young Latinas, ages nine to eighteen. It also offers a range of community-based services for Latina girls, including after-school clubs, mentoring, and summer camps. Girls receive training in a range of journalism skills, such as interviewing and writing, and are encouraged to provide content for the group's online magazine, *Latinitas*, which is targeted toward Latina youth and published in both Spanish and English. Since its founding, Latinitas has served over 3,600 young Latinas. The first after-school program, Club Latinitas, was started at Martin Middle School, located in East Austin, in 2003. Since then, Club Latinitas has expanded to high schools and elementary schools in the greater Austin area. In 2008, Latinitas offered eighteen after-school clubs in the Austin area that served about 270 girls per week.

Whereas all girls are subject to a loss of self-esteem during adolescence, Latinitas focuses on the particular struggles that Latina youth face in adolescence. Latina youth are more susceptible than white girls to teenage pregnancy, drug abuse, and dropping out of high school (Ventura, Matthews, and Hamilton 2002). Through creating an online space for Latina youth and providing them with mentors and role models, Latinitas hopes to increase their confidence and abilities. Additionally, Latinitas provides Latina youth with journalism skills and training so they may pursue career opportunities in the future.

Based on the success of Latinitas in Austin, program leaders hope to replicate the program in other parts of the United States. In 2008, Alicia Rascon, co-director, moved to El Paso, Texas, to spearhead a branch of Latinitas in that region. Additionally, Latinitas published the first print version of its online magazine in 2009. A print version of the magazine would help to bridge the digital divide by reaching girls who do not have access to the Internet. Building a national, subscription-based magazine would also expand the reach of the organization and help build sustainability.

CONCLUSION

Digital divide initiatives in Austin show that the issue of digital inequality is more than simply a national agenda initiated by the Clinton administration. A diverse variety of Austin groups took up local initiatives even before the federal discourse of the late 1990s was particularly focused or notable. UT, the City of Austin, local industries, and a number of nonprofit groups like AFN created initiatives before federal or even state funding was available. These initiatives show local articulations of the digital divide focusing on several needs: a qualified workforce for technology industries, training for children in technology use at school, new venues for community communication and participation, and the revitalization of neighborhoods through local training and information resources.

In all of these efforts, sustainability has emerged as a key issue. The Bush administration changed national policy on the digital divide, tending to reduce or even cancel programs. The same is happening in the state of Texas. As funding from national and state sources declines, the prominence of local participants and funding sources may help some of these programs survive. Some specific projects have already failed. Others were in the process of failing when this study surveyed them in spring 2004. For many, there was a loss of optimism because of the slowdown in the economy, which also diminished local sources of support. Future research should focus on how much different sources of funding have influenced their sustainability.

This review of projects in Austin permits an inductive definition of the digital divide focused on concrete local concerns. Organizations like AFN and the Austin Learning Academy—as well as some leaders within AISD—see a digital divide between those students who have access to computers and the Internet at home and those who do not. They see very real outcomes of these differences in access in the prospects of poor, usually minority children compared to those of middle-class, usually white children. As for working adults, a number of Austin organizations, including a variety of companies, the chamber of commerce, the City of Austin, and the Capital Area Training Foundation, see shortages of skilled labor coexisting with numerous recent immigrants who lack skills, notably computer and Internet skills. They also observe major blockages, caused by this lack of skills, in the absorption of those immigrants and their children into the economy beyond entry-level service jobs.

At a less tangible level, many technology activists in East Austin nonprofits and at UT see a challenge in the ability of poorer and less educated residents gaining access to a broad range of cultural and social skills, or social capital. Several local initiatives, such as the Austin Access Model, imagine a blend of access and community organization. Activists continue to be concerned about lower-income and minority residents' ability to participate in the civic life of the city, state, and nation if they do not have access to the online media in which an increasing amount of information circulates. Furthermore, since political organizing is increasingly moving to the Internet, they see these people as having less contact with organized political life. Community radio continues to play an important role in the ability of marginalized groups to communicate with each other and to organize collectively for change. Therefore, we recommend that going forward, digital divide activists, engaged scholars, policy makers, local business leaders, and local officials consider analog as well as digital media as important resources for community and economic development.

NOTES

1. The analysis presented in this paper emerges from research collected by graduate students in a seminar at the University of Texas at Austin in the spring of 2003 and updated by graduate students of another class in the spring of 2009. In 2003, students established a list of more than fifty public access sites and community network programs in the city, whose locations were then mapped geographically as a way to analyze distribution of digital divide initiatives. Students were then assigned to visit the sites to gather baseline data related to hours of operation and number of computer stations, as well as to note special programs, resources, and services made available to the community. The students designed a survey to conduct face-to-face, semistructured interviews with selected site coordinators or managers whose programs represented particularly visible failures or successes. These interviews provided a deeper understanding of what factors led to the development of the sites, including key leaders, funding sources, location, and the mission and vision of the programs. The overall goal was to understand the historical trajectory of the institutions and the key activists or leaders. In 2009, graduate students in a course in ethnographic and qualitative interviewing methods conducted participant observation at the public Internet access sites of branch libraries in several low-income neighborhoods of East Austin, including some that had been studied in 2003. The 2009 researchers studied public Internet usage during two three-hour periods at the library. They recorded the data on a code sheet and wrote field notes based on their observation periods.

2. This was a significant commitment of public resources given that Ms. Beckwith at the time was drawing an annual salary close to $60,000.

3. Item 13, 1998 Austin City Council minutes.

REFERENCES

AISD (Austin Independent School District). (2011). Austin ISD data 2010–2011. Retrieved from www.austinisd.org/inside/factsfigures/.

American Association of University Women. (1998). Separated by sex: A critical look at single-sex education for girls. Washington, DC.

———. (2000). Tech-savvy: Educating girls in the computer age. Washington, DC.

Austin Learning Academy. (2003). Report. Retrieved October 31, 2003, from http://www.alaweb.org/ausmodel/; no longer available.

———. (2007). Report. Retrieved July 27, 2009, from http://www.alaweb.org/news/news.htm; no longer available.

Austin Public Library. (2009). Austin Public Library Foundation recipient of a $185,000 grant from the Michael and Susan Dell Foundation to support the library's young adult initiatives. Press release, March 4. Retrieved July 27, 2009, from http://www.ci.austin.tx.us/library/news/nr20090304a.htm.

Bourdieu, P. (1984). *Distinction: A social critique of the judgement of taste*. Cambridge, MA: Harvard University Press.

Chapman, G. (2000). High-tech leaders, let's step up equity effort. *Austin American-Statesman*, September 21.

———. (2003). Personal communication, September 22.

Compaine, B. M. (Ed.). (2001). *The digital divide: Facing a crisis or creating a myth?* Cambridge, MA: MIT Press.

Coppola, S. (2009a). Public prefers closing nine pools to other budget-cutting options, city says. *Austin American-Statesman*, July 1.

———. (2009b). City budget plan raises taxes, spares public safety. *Austin American-Statesman*, July 23.

Fuentes-Bautista, M. (2007). Reconfiguring public access in the post-convergence era: The social construction of public access to new media in Austin, Texas. PhD dissertation, University of Texas at Austin.

Furger, R. (1998). *Does Jane compute? Preserving our daughters' place in the cyber revolution.* New York: Warner Books.

Girl Scouts–Lone Star Council. (2001). Dell Connected Communities grant report. Unpublished grant report.

Gorman, M. (2002). Wiring teens to the library: Michelle Gorman explains how the Austin Public Library helps teens become information literature. *School Library Journal.*

Hadden, S. (2003). Austin telecommunity. Retrieved October 31, 2003, from http://www.ci.austin.tx.us/telcom/intelecom.htm; no longer available.

Hawkins, R. (2003). Interview with Gunho Lee, Office of Telecommunication and Regulatory Affairs, City of Austin. May 7.

Horrigan, J., and R. H. Wilson. (2001). Telecommunications technologies and urban development: Strategies in U.S. cities. Pew Internet and American Life Project and University of Texas at Austin. Retrieved October 31, 2003, from http://www.pewinternet.org/papers/paper.asp?paper=9.

Jayson, S. (1995). The Austin Public Library's ride on the information superhighway is about to begin. *Austin American-Statesman*, July 28.

———. (1999). Dell gift to library will click with kids. *Austin American-Statesman*, September 16.

Kelly, C. (1995). *Austin American-Statesman*, December 19.

Lacy, L. A. (2004). Personal communication, October.

Latinitas. (2008). Website. http://www.latinitasmagazine.org.

LBJ School of Public Affairs, University of Texas at Austin. (2006). LBJ School class helps welcome the World Congress on Information Technology. Retrieved August 1, 2009, from http://www.utexas.edu/lbj/news/spring2006/wcit.html.

Lentz, B., J. Straubhaar, A. LaPastina, S. Main, and J. Taylor. (2000). Structuring access: The role of public access centers in the "digital divide." Paper presented at the 50th International Communication Association Conference, Acapulco, Mexico.

Lentz, R. G. (2000). The e-volution of the digital divide: A mayhem of competing metrics. *Info* 2(4): 355–377.

Lentz, R. G., and M. D. Oden. (2001). Digital divide or digital opportunity in the Mississippi Delta region of the U.S.? *Telecommunications Policy* 25:291–313.

Ramsey, N., and P. McCorduck. (2005). Where are the women in information technology? University of Colorado, Boulder.

Rice-Lively, M. L. (2004). Personal communication, September.

Rojas, V., J. Straubhaar, D. Roychowdhury, and O. Okur. (2003). Communities, cultural capital, and the digital divide. In E. Bucey and J. Newhagen (Eds.), *Media access: Social and psychological aspects of new media use.* Mahwah, NJ: Lawrence Erlbaum.

Sadker, M., and D. Sadker. (1995). *Failing at fairness: How our schools cheat girls.* New York: Touchstone.

Schuler, D. (1996). *New community networks: Wired for change.* New York: ACM Press.

Servon, L. (1999). Creating an information democracy: The role of community technology programs and their relationship to public policy. Report submitted to the Aspen Institute Nonprofit Sector Research Fund, October 24. Retrieved October 31, 2003, from http://www.ctcnet.org/publics.html.

Somers, L. (1997). Case study report: East Austin Community Network. National Telecommunications and Information Administration, April 26. Retrieved August 23, 2003, from http://www.ntia.doc.gov/otiahome/top/research/Evalu ationReport/case_studies/486096049e.pdf.

Soy, S. (2003). Personal communication, September 15.

Straubhaar, J., S. Strover, M. Fuentes, and N. Inagaki. (2005). Critically evaluating market diffusion policy and the digital divide in Texas, 2000–2004. Paper presented at the Communication and Technology Division, International Communication Association Conference, New York, May.

Strover, S., and J. Straubhaar. (2001). The digital divide in Texas. Paper presented at the 51st International Communication Association Conference, Washington, DC.

Strover, S., Z. Tufekcioglu, and J. Straubhaar. (2001). Final CTTC evaluation: Evaluating the Community Technology Training Program at Reagan and Travis high schools. Report submitted to the Community Technology Training Coalition, Austin, Texas.

Texas School Performance Review. (2000). Austin Independent School District. Texas Comptroller of Public Accounts, Austin, TX.

Thompson, D. (2007). Austin Free-Net: Then and now. Retrieved July 26, 2009, from http://www.austinfree.net/AFNThenandNow.htm.

Thorpe, H. (2000). Austin, we have a problem. *New York Times Magazine,* August 20.

TOP (Technology Opportunities Program). (2003). Who we are. Retrieved October 31, 2003, from http://www.ntia.doc.gov/otiahome/top/whoweare/whowe are.htm.

Ventura, S. J., T. J. Matthews, and B. Hamilton. (2002). Teenage births in the United States: State trends, 1991–2000, an update. *National Vital Statistics Report* 50(4).

Warschauer, M. (2003). Technology and social inclusion: Rethinking the digital divide. Cambridge, MA: MIT Press.

ROBERTA LENTZ

JOSEPH STRAUBHAAR

LAURA DIXON

DEAN GRABER

JEREMIAH SPENCE

BETHANY LETALIEN

ANTONIO LAPASTINA

CHAPTER 7

STRUCTURING ACCESS

THE ROLE OF AUSTIN PUBLIC ACCESS CENTERS IN DIGITAL INCLUSION

 One of the critical policy issues raised both by academic critics of the information society (Herman, McChesney, and Herman 1998; Mosco 1996) and by the Clinton administration (NTIA 1999) in the 1990s was the growth of a digital divide between information haves and have-nots. In the United States, the divide cut between rich and poor, urban and rural, and, particularly, the ethnic Anglo majority and the Latino, Native American, and African American minorities (NTIA 1999). Differential access to computing resources, telephone connectivity, and the Internet was found to be most related to ethnic group affiliation, geographic location, household composition, age, education, and income level, both nationally (NTIA 1999; Hoffman and Novak 1998) and in Texas (Strover et al. 2004).

A number of critics subsequently challenged the idea of a digital divide, however. Some (e.g., Compaine 2001) argued that any such divide would close via natural processes of diffusion, making policy intervention unnecessary. This analysis reflected the Bush administration's policy, which reframed the issue as "digital inclusion" and focused on gains in minority access to information and communication technologies (ICTs) to indicate that government program subsidies introduced by the previous administration could be reduced. Others (e.g., Warschauer 2003) argued that this digital divide concept was too simplistic, focusing too much on recent digital technologies and not enough on how various divides and exclusions have layered over each other, requiring more complex interventions to remedy gaps in access and use of ICTs.

National policy attention in the 1990s and early 2000s focused on divides or gaps regarding Internet access and computer use. Concern about these gaps centered on the likelihood that people without such resources were disadvantaged in terms of achieving educational success, acquiring marketable job skills, and accessing information about jobs and government programs. These gaps were also assumed to limit participation in the forms of political discussion and mobilization that are increasingly being conducted online (Benton Foundation 1998).

Research has identified a number of other aspects of social inequities related to information technology use. Ongoing educational, occupational, and class divides keep many people away from the economic resources and educational skills that are required for effective use of information and communication technology (ICT). People who lack adequate access to education are unlikely to acquire the literacy and numeracy skills required to use computers and the Internet to their best advantage. Those who cannot afford monthly charges for dial-up or broadband access are limited to using computers and the Internet in public settings. A lack of Internet content related to various people's interests and cultural or linguistic backgrounds are other barriers to low-income and ethnic minority groups (Children's Partnership 2000).

This chapter examines the challenges that we observed of gaining access to computer and Internet resources in low-income ethnic communities in Austin, Texas. Our observations suggest that it takes an institutional approach to look at the challenges of providing public access to ICT resources. While economic factors affect the structuring of who does and does not have access to computers and the Internet, a number of other institutional and structural factors are also at play. For example, while socioeconomic factors may limit a household's ability to own a computer or buy Internet access, institutional practices may also limit or constrain that same household from accessing the community resources that public policy initiatives have been created to provide.

This chapter discusses the structuring of access to computers and the Internet in a particular case study of Austin, Texas—a city considered by researchers to be a best-case scenario in terms of public access potential. Austin has had a strongly information-oriented economy, with much new job creation in the high-technology sector during the 1980s and 1990s. It has also had an important, if less tangible, information technology edge to the local culture, at least for the majority of the population. Local institutions have worked to be at the forefront of creating opportunities for public access to computers and the Internet.

These local institutions have taken advantage of federal- and state-level programs that provide funds for public computer and Internet access. The Austin Public Library system, for example, has received three large grants from the Susan and Michael Dell Foundation for equipment, in-library public access centers focused on children, and laptops that can be checked out from libraries. As a result, all city libraries and a number of community centers in Austin now offer free public access to the Internet, and most libraries offer expanded access and supervised use for children.

A case study of such institutional settings in Austin permits an examination of the effectiveness and impact of some of the assumptions in these types of policy initiatives. They include the idea that public libraries should be a primary point of public access to the Internet, a policy now reinforced by private charitable giving. The study reveals some of the strengths and weaknesses of several kinds of local library approaches to supporting public access. It explores who uses public access at these sites to determine how minority communities are being served. Findings suggest that public libraries may not be the most optimal sites of public access. Job training centers, public housing centers, community centers, and churches also are important institutional settings. In sum, the efforts to structure public access in Austin reveal both successes and failures that have implications for other community technology projects.

Given that Austin has offered a relatively advanced level of public ICT access since the late 1990s, public access to the Internet is not a barrier in minority communities. Yet social and cultural structures may continue to constrain certain people from using public access technology. This chapter explores which structural factors at the local level facilitate, and which constrain, residents' use of the Internet. It also examines how public access policies fit in with libraries' other roles and objectives, what aspects of library-based public Internet access work well, what problems arise, and what structural solutions to those problems are possible.

THE ROLE OF COMMUNITY TECHNOLOGY
CENTERS AND LIBRARIES

At the local level, community technology centers have been an important and rapidly growing part of the effort to provide more access to and education about computers and the Internet. Worldwide, the number of community technology centers is still growing, although the momentum in the United States tapered off after federal funding stopped in the early 2000s. There are many types, purposes, and technical configurations of these networks, most of which share one goal: to promote and increase free or low-cost public access to diverse types of information that are available through linked networks, of which the Internet is assumed to be the prototype.

The Community Technology Centers' Network (CTCNet) was a national membership organization with over one thousand affiliated centers across the United States. These centers include libraries, youth organizations, multiservice agencies, stand-alone computing centers, housing development centers, settlement houses, and nonprofit organizations. Center services may also include activities such as adult literacy or after-school programs. In 1998, CTCNet published findings (Chow, Ellis, Mark, and Wise 1998), drawn from Internet users themselves as part of a formal evaluation project, that supported the conclusion that the centers were very important for training and skill development, open or unstructured use, advancing education goals, and building community. Community members' ability to use such centers for interpersonal communication was important for effective technology use. The survey also found that community technology centers were particularly important for access and connectivity for women and ethnic minorities. The number of centers continued to grow, despite federal funding cuts, and CTCNet operated as a redistributor of grants from foundations and other sources until the overall economic recession forced them to stop in 2009.

Libraries have also been an important local component of national policy to reduce the digital divide problem. The Benton Foundation founded a website (www.benton.org) that provided information about the role of libraries in the digital divide—in particular, the programs of the American Library Association (ALA). According to an ALA report, "Public libraries provide access to the Internet more than any other source after schools and work" (Benton Foundation 1999). However, telecommunication policy scholar Jorge Schement (1997) describes many challenges faced by libraries:

> There can be little doubt that we have entered the Information Age. But to understand its course requires thinking beyond libraries or any single institution. There are deeper social forces at work. . . . The Benton Foundation and Libraries for the Future have

spent the last two years seeking answers to these questions. In 1995 the W. K. Kellogg Foundation commissioned Benton to collect and analyze statements from libraries and library organizations concerning their visions for the role of libraries in the Information Age. At the same time, Libraries for the Future began looking closely at how some libraries have started using new technologies to build on their traditional roles both as equal-access gateways to information and as public institutions.

The research in Austin described in this chapter was conducted with the assumption that libraries can play a role in helping resolve problems of the digital divide. By examining the role and use of libraries in providing public access and training in 1999 and in 2009, we can see how libraries adapted to this new role.

RESEARCH QUESTIONS: THEORIZING THE DIGITAL DIVIDE

Researchers of the political economy and policy traditions have noted strong tendencies toward inequality of access to and benefit from new technologies (Schiller 1996; Golding 1998). These scholars focus on the inequities resulting from market economies or capitalist development of new information technologies. Related scholarship has noted the tendency toward deregulation and away from the sorts of government regulation or intervention that might ameliorate the inequalities of access (Hills 1998). Other studies have tended to offer a very broad and economistic view of how this gap or digital divide is produced or reproduced in society.

From the political economy school, Vincent Mosco (1996) makes an interesting innovation by introducing selected elements of Anthony Giddens's structuration theory (1984) to examine stratified access to media and information technologies. This structuration theory helps to guide examination of processes by which connectivity gaps are created and perpetuated in the larger political and economic sphere. Giddens offers several useful concepts that help to explore at macro and micro levels of analysis ways in which specific policies and institutions might unwittingly contribute to structuring aspects of the digital divide. He sees rules as constraints on, and resources as opportunities for, social actors. We drew from this to explore how local institutions such as public libraries constrain or enable access. We examine three issues related to how institutional practices structure the information technology experiences of individuals who cannot afford to pay for access to such resources: (1) how public libraries facilitate access for new computer and Internet users, (2) how content filtering affects public access activities, and (3) how libraries' and other access centers' physical structures affect public technology use.

Another set of questions explored in this study revolves around issues raised by patterns of access use in different disadvantaged communities: (1) Now that public access is available in many low-income areas, who takes advantage of such access? (2) Did the pattern of who used public access change from 1999 to 2009? (3) What helps build local knowledge or cultural capital related to new technologies and their usefulness among economically disadvantaged individuals and households? (4) What social or institutional mechanisms serve to facilitate or limit use of public access facilities?

To address these issues and questions, we explore how the structure of public access in low-income communities meets the disposition of those communities and allows them to take advantage of access opportunities. We find Pierre Bourdieu's (1984) concept of cultural capital useful for understanding how communities might make use of Internet technology. People often have access to information media by virtue of their economic capital—that is, whether they can afford to purchase that access. When individuals cannot afford ICT access on their own, their community, such as Austin, can decide to create public access centers that draw on the collective economic and social capital of the community. However, Bourdieu also notes that even when people have access to sources of information and culture, they do not necessarily use these sources for their intended purposes. Cultural capital, based on education, family socialization patterns, family social networks, peers, and occupational experiences, tends to structure what people choose, enjoy, and understand.[1] These factors are related to economic capital such that a lower economic position may prevent a family from acquiring access to the best education, for example, or from having experiences that expand cultural capital, such as travel or participation in the arts.

METHODOLOGY: A CASE STUDY OF PUBLIC LIBRARIES AND COMMUNITY ACCESS CENTERS

In June and July 1999, twenty-six graduate and undergraduate students in the Radio-Television-Film Department and related departments at the University of Texas conducted participant observation of Internet use while working as Internet assistance volunteers at four libraries and two community centers in East Austin. Over a two-week period, they observed 476 people using the Internet at these sites. In their observation of who used public access, they categorized users by age, ethnicity, and gender, using the form in Appendix 7.1. They used the observation guide in Appendix 7.2 to structure their observations. They interviewed forty-six people (or approximately 10 percent of those observed) about their Internet experience, using the interview guide in Appendix 7.3. Each student completed an analytical report of his or her observations and thoughts as a final project.[2] During a subsequent two-week period in September 1999, in a replication of this participant observation, twenty-five students volunteered in the same libraries and centers, plus one more center. Researchers observed another 354 people to study Internet use at a time when children were back in school. Students also observed the functioning of the libraries and centers to see what limits and rules were placed on users, as well as what resources were offered to them. They observed the immediate, local aspects of how public access to the Internet was structured.

Several years later, in February and March 2009, fourteen graduate students, including some of the authors of this chapter, at the University of Texas revisited this project, attempting to gain information on developments in public access in East Austin in the intervening decade. We observed 887 people at four different public libraries, including two of the libraries which were observed in 1999.[3] Because of the federal funding cuts that closed many alternate kinds of public access centers between 1999 and 2009 (see Chapter 5), the importance of libraries as sites of public access increased. For the 2009 research, we observed all four libraries at different times of day, both weekdays and weekends. We recorded the limits and rules regarding Internet usage as well as the ease of access. We did not conduct interviews, choosing instead to focus more on extended participant observation in order to understand how libraries had adapted to the increased influx of users. In 2011, another group of graduate students also observed two additional centers and one additional library. Since Austin had over a dozen public branch libraries in 1999, with one new one since, we focused on the branches which served disadvantaged populations in Northeast, East, and Southwest Austin.

FINDINGS: HOW LIBRARIES STRUCTURE ACCESS IN DISADVANTAGED COMMUNITIES, 1999 AND 2009

In making decisions regarding Internet access, libraries and library staff must wrestle with varying notions of what services they should provide, while also frequently facing budget shortages, insufficient training, and constraints imposed by their physical environments, including both a lack of space and buildings that were erected before the widespread use of computers in libraries. Furthermore, libraries operate in a political context regarding what kinds of books and online resources, including controversial material like pornography, bomb-making formulas, and content about witchcraft, should be provided to what kinds of people. This topic was hotly debated in the late 1990s and early 2000s, and Austin libraries settled on a formula of providing primarily filtered Internet access, although some libraries provide one or two computers for adult use of any materials. Those computers are usually physically screened so others cannot see what the user is looking at.

Moreover, the role of libraries in providing access to game playing and "surfing," as opposed to directed research, remains questionable. Many librarians that we observed and interviewed in 1999 expressed ambivalence about making public computer access a major part of the library's mission, and we observed a wide range of responses to the introduction of the Internet in the various branches. By 2009, it had become clear that most librarians now accepted computer and Internet access as part of their library's mission. Most of them in 2009 were more comfortable helping people use the computers than the librarians we observed in 1999. The change in mission was visible among library users too. In 2009, visitors to libraries in disadvantaged communities came predominantly to use computers. The libraries observed had, by and large, adjusted to support the presence of technology in the libraries. Newer libraries are clearly being constructed to make computer use more central. The newest libraries now have youth computer centers and specific rooms for computer skills training.

Even in 1999, many libraries in Austin were responding well to the new mandate of providing Internet access in addition to classic library functions. However, public libraries faced challenges in this role. Several sites presented both physical structuring and social structuring constraints. Spatial layouts varied, with newer facilities typically being more Internet friendly, since they had been designed to include computer facilities. Staff dedication to print materials versus Internet resources also varied. Staff attitudes differed in terms of whether they saw public Internet access as an uncomfortable new responsibility or as an opportunity to engage computer-oriented preteens and others in an environment where reading and writing are important.

By 2009, however, the presence of the Internet seemed to be taken for granted by users and staff. Generally, staff seemed comfortable with their role in the libraries, which is not surprising considering that most users were self-sufficient. On occasion, however, staff seemed to begrudge their role as essentially computer lab supervisors—enforcing time limits, helping users register for an account, and so on. Indeed, in our observations, the majority of staff's interactions with users concerned the regulation of computer space and time. Since this role is generally not what librarians are trained for, some remaining tension is understandable.

In terms of the technologies available, each of the libraries in 1999 had three computers devoted to Internet use. The computers and Internet access were provided by the Austin Free-Net (AFN), a local nonprofit promoting public technology access. At most of the libraries, two of the three computers were equipped with the filtering software CyberPatrol, and the third computer was unfiltered. (According to one librarian, however, CyberPatrol blocked only full frontal nudity and sexual acts.)[4] It was the policy of all the libraries to require surrender of picture identification by patrons using the unfiltered computer. By 2009, the number of computers had increased dramatically. In the four libraries observed, there were eighty-five computers available for various types of access. Sixty-nine were available for Internet usage. Adult and youth computers were filtered at the same level, but most libraries had at least one unfiltered adult computer with a private screen.

The Wired for Youth program, instituted in 2000, significantly changed the face of public access in Austin from 1999 to 2009. The partnership between the City of Austin and the Austin Public Library Foundation, funded by the Dell Foundation, equipped ten public libraries with computers in low-income neighborhoods and hired staff to help children and teenagers access the Internet. The staff included professional youth librarians with knowledge of technology to help teach children computer skills, ranging from use of basic applications to web page creation. Some of the Wired for Youth centers held their own special events, such as the "Girls' Night Out with Women Professionals," which invited two women working in technology careers to talk with girls at the Southeast Austin Community Branch about career possibilities and how to prepare for them. The libraries also worked with groups like Latinitas and the Girl Scouts to extend their reach to girls, as described below.

In 2004, the libraries added part-time "cyber-lifeguard" positions to allow the centers to be open longer and to serve more children. Figures from the Dell Foundation report four grants made to Wired for Youth totaling more than $815,000 over almost a decade. In March 2009, the foundation announced a grant of $185,000 to help turn Wired for Youth into the "Connected Youth Project." Connected Youth put laptops into libraries and created new programs for teens and young adults. The project was installed in twenty-three locations across town, mostly teen centers in libraries.

Librarians stated to several of the researchers in 1999 that they were concerned about ensuring users' privacy. Researchers in 1999 also noted that users sometimes turned around to check whether anyone was watching them. Even though the staff made no effort to spy on the users, some users may have altered their activities or chosen not to use the computers for fear of being monitored; the presence of the researchers may also have made the users uneasy.[5] At several sites, the difficulty of turning on and off the filtering program led library staff to leave additional computers unfiltered, which created a logjam of users who were not allowed to use the unfiltered machines because of their age.

By 2009, users had gotten more sophisticated, and privacy had become more of a concern in the eyes of our researchers. While only one of our researchers in 1999 discussed spatial layout in terms of privacy, almost all of our 2009 researchers spontaneously included this as an underlying concern in their analysis. Today, the Internet can be used for a wide range of acts (beyond accessing pornography) which users may want privacy for, including business such as checking bank balances and purchasing items as well as social functions such as e-mail, social networking, viewing photos, and chatting. The difference in use encouraged more of a sensibility for privacy in our observers; moreover, many of them noticed that the computers facing away from the staff desk were more popular than those that the staff had full view of. Increased sensitivity to users' preferences for privacy would be an improvement worth looking into.

In 1999, other constraints included the fact that at all of the libraries, Internet users were allowed to save (download) from and upload material to the Internet using only 1.44 MB floppy disks, which they needed to provide themselves. The libraries' computers all used an outdated web browser. These constraints prevented some users from accessing sites that require the latest plug-ins. In addition, libraries did not seem to have boxes of floppy disks available for users to purchase. By 2009, advances in technology presented other options, such as uploading a file to one's e-mail account, using a flash drive, uploading to web space, and so on.

In 1999, each library's public access computers presented the same initial sign-on screen that included links to sites that offered free e-mail, chatting, searches, and job information. Other links were to the City of Austin site and special sites for children. The initial screen was available only in English, creating a structural difficulty for Spanish-only users. With the exception of the unfiltered machine at the Cepeda Branch Library, which did not permit printing, all the computers had printers. Black-and-white printing was available for ten cents per page. In 2009, the sign-on screens resembled most standard public desktops, displaying an assortment of icons, such as those for Internet Explorer, Microsoft Word, and Microsoft Excel. Youth computers in Wired for Youth rooms featured those icons along with Photoshop and Dreamweaver. Most computers were wired to print. Printing cost twenty cents per page, with the exception of school-related materials in the Wired for Youth rooms, which was free to young users.

In 1999, at all but the Cepeda Branch, placement of the computers was planned only after the building had been built.[6] By contrast, the Cepeda Branch was designed with the computers as a showpiece in the middle of the floor plan. Spatial limitations varied from library to library. In the worst case, one library placed them in the corridor leading to the bathrooms. Nonetheless, there generally was sufficient space to work on the computers comfortably. In 1999 we predicted that some branches would have difficult spatial choices to make as they expanded their Internet capabilities with new grant funds. What it meant to provide access to information—a key aspect in many conceptions of public libraries—was changing, and as libraries continued to collect print materials and equip their buildings with ICTs, they faced conflict over space for the provision of still deeply important print materials and reading rooms on the one hand, and for the provision of ICT access on the other, especially if print and electronic media were viewed as distinct, rather than integrated, concerns.

It appeared by 2009 that libraries had fully considered the placement of their computers as well as prominent collections of audiovisual materials. When Dean Graber, one of the authors, evaluated a recently opened branch library, it was clear that it had been designed in large part for Internet access and other multimedia functions, such as lending DVDs and CDs.

In 1999, AFN (whose role is discussed in Chapter 6) maintained the library's computers, and none of the observers noted serious problems with equipment maintenance, although most noticed problems with screens "freezing." In the event of technical problems, many of the library staff members were uncomfortable doing anything beyond rebooting the computers. More serious problems usually led to a minimum of twenty-four hours of downtime while they awaited help from an AFN technical support employee. By 2009, technology in the libraries had gotten more reliable. Computers in the libraries rarely froze or broke down. In addition, the general public and library staff had ten additional years of practice using the Internet, which most likely translated into an ability to handle basic logistical problems. Plus, the library system had made a point of developing its own infrastructure and technology support, so problems could be answered within their own system.

In 1999, demand for access varied by time and place, but people often had to wait for access. Several branches got about three hundred to five hundred people per day, with about 20 percent coming in just to use a computer, according to observations by several staff members. These numbers grew as awareness of the Internet among minority communities grew and more daily activities and job opportunities required knowledge of and access to the Internet. Conversation with librarians in 2009 confirmed that Internet access accounted for perhaps half or more of library visits, particularly in the late afternoons when use by school children was highest and when use of Wired for Youth centers represented a very high proportion of library patron use.

In 1999, when users accessed a machine, usage was limited to thirty minutes at all of the observed branches. The librarians or their assistants were in charge of monitoring Internet usage. When there was no other person waiting to use a computer, patrons were generally allowed to use the machine for as long as they wished. Researchers observed occasions, however, on which staff members would, apparently arbitrarily, terminate a teen or preteen's session after thirty minutes when no one else was waiting. Our observations suggest that Internet users at public sites often do not have the time and leisure to use computers that people with good Internet connections and computers at home have. Learning how to get the most from the Internet requires large amounts of time to surf and explore possibilities; lack of access time presents a disadvantage to public access Internet users.

By 2009, length of available time on the Internet had increased. Although some libraries still had a thirty-minute limit, users were able to sign up for more than one thirty-minute session. Some libraries had sixty-minute limits or a maximum of two hours per day. In most cases, users found ways around the time limit by "jumping" computers, logging in repeatedly, and waiting for other logged-in users to leave before their time was up. In some cases, this informal system led to conflict, as users who were sneaking on sometimes disrupted those who were waiting for their designated time. In general, the time limit seemed to be the most obvious challenge for libraries in 2009, and the source of most of the frustration we observed for both staff and users. Our observations showed that at each library, certain times of day were more popular than others, and the libraries sometimes had a wait at the busiest times of day. At other times of day, computers were available without a wait time.

Presented with computer resources, libraries have not always been sure whether to dedicate them to their traditional practice of organizing and providing access to print materials or to their new role of providing public Internet access. For example, in 1999 in Austin, Dell Computers had contributed three late-model computers to each observed library branch. These computers were generally not being used for Internet access. One branch, Riverside, used the new computers and three others to equip a room with Internet-accessible computers. This room was used from one to two hours per week for training on how to use the Internet; during the remainder of the week, the computers were unavailable to library patrons. Thus, the choice of use for the new computers reflected some uncertainty among libraries over priorities and necessities. (More computers were about to be donated to the libraries by Dell specifically to expand Internet access [Stafford 1999].)

Another notable change in 2009 was the observation that many people entered the library specifically to use a computer. It is difficult to say whether actual use of books went down between 1999 and 2009, since we have no absolute numbers. Moreover, that question hints at a somewhat arbitrary divide between print and digital media; one can, of course, read books online, look up the definition to words online, look at maps online, and so on. It is very likely that the presence of computers brought people into the libraries who otherwise may not have come through the doors. It was also highly evident that the majority of people who came into the library came with the express intention of using a computer. In fact, most of our researchers observed that the computers that could not access the Internet—the ones devoted to the library database, the card catalog, or printing only—saw little use during the day, often sitting open while users waited for computers with Internet access.

In 1999, all of the libraries provided environments that were good to excellent, with sufficient room for reading and what appeared to be a good selection of print resources. The libraries were generally staffed with two to four librarians and assistants who were friendly and helpful. However, many libraries did not have enough staff to handle the addition of public Internet access to their existing responsibilities, hindering their ability to help patrons with the Internet, so volunteer help was truly appreciated.[7] Most of the children that came to the library to use the Internet were in need of assistance and could have benefited from more help, especially on complicated tasks, such as downloading music and accessing video games that required passwords. Older patrons appeared to need help in general. Staff also had varied levels of training and comfort with computers and the Internet.

By 2009, a very visible increase in the self-sufficiency of users had decreased the burden on staff to provide assistance with Internet literacy, but the regulation of computer use and the enforcement of library policy still proved a prominent activity. Most users who did approach the staff desk asked for help with some aspect of the library's system of computer use, such as logging on or asking other patrons who had overstayed their time limit to leave. Staff members were rarely approached for help with understanding the content of the Internet specifically.

Complicating the picture in 1999 was the perceived conflict between use of library resources for entertainment and for information. At the Carver Branch, some of the assistants were observed taking advantage of a patron's using the Internet for entertainment to demonstrate other uses. However, observed staff seemed mostly to prefer and emphasize resources that the libraries had offered for years. Attitudes varied, but librarians in several of the libraries observed were not as supportive of Internet usage as they were of book reading. Given not only the inexperience and inadequate training regarding Internet resources but also the persistence of questions among both policy makers and information professionals regarding patrons' privacy, the accessibility of pornography, filters, and the proper role of libraries vis-à-vis the Internet, the de facto "you are on your own" policy was not surprising. Yet it had serious implications for effective public access to the Internet. One structural problem was that although users had access to the Internet through the library, they were limited by their own knowledge of what to do with it. The Internet stations usually had signage noting what actions were prohibited, but there was often nothing to help new users know what to do when they found themselves unable to use the resources at their disposal.[8]

In 2009, it remained the case that there were no distinct guides to Internet usage, aside from one sign at the St. Johns Branch that listed popular game sites. Some of our researchers observed peer-to-peer sharing as groups of friends taught one another how to do particular things on the Internet, such as register for an e-mail account or navigate social networking sites like MySpace. Group use, officially prohibited at some libraries yet unevenly enforced, proved popular with many users. Through group use, people can informally share knowledge of the possibilities of the Internet and train one another.

Also in 2009, a variety of technology classes were offered at Austin's central library, both in English and in Spanish. These classes helped users learn how to use reference databases, the Internet, e-mail, Microsoft Excel, and Microsoft Word. While these classes were not available en masse at local branches, they were tailored for new and beginning users. Some skills developed in these classes included setting up one's first e-mail account and learning to save documents.

A separate study (Cunningham 2009) noted that users of one Wired for Youth center at the Southeast Austin Branch stated that they were glad the library let them use MySpace, which was blocked or forbidden at their schools. However, the library was concerned about use of

MySpace by those under the site's stated minimum user age of four-teen. They were also concerned that children be alerted about privacy concerns, so they built that into some of their educational classes for children.

THE ROLE OF COMMUNITY CENTERS
AS POINTS OF INTERNET ACCESS

Researchers observed public access resources and activities at three community centers in 1999: the Montopolis Community Center, the DeWitty Community Technology Center, and the Conley-Guerrero Senior Center. During the summer, the Montopolis Center catered primarily to youth and children, while Conley-Guerrero targeted an elderly population. DeWitty focused on job training for adults but also featured a community computer lab run by AFN.

Although libraries seemed to lack enough staff to provide Internet assistance to patrons, they clearly had more support available and were more suitable for Internet use than two of the three community centers, Montopolis and Conley-Guerrero. The two centers had only one computer each with Internet access for patrons, severely limiting the number of people that could be served. At the Montopolis Center, the computer was in a large playroom/library/television room where distractions and noise were much more common than at the libraries. The computer at Conley-Guerrero shared a room with the janitor's storage space. While both centers appeared to be adequately staffed for their primary functions, volunteers and staff at these centers were not usually well trained in Internet use.

The DeWitty Center was much more adequately equipped and staffed, likely because computer and Internet access was seen as central to its primary mission of job training and career education. With several Internet or network computers in a separate room, DeWitty provided a quiet atmosphere that was conducive to work. In addition, training was available, and access was not limited to half-hour blocks as it was in the public libraries. The DeWitty Center also served a more adult clientele, in contrast to the youth-oriented services provided by the Montopolis Center and several of the public libraries, such as the Carver Branch.

An increase in specialized center facilities, as well as more adequate equipment and staff at some of the existing centers, would likely have helped. National and local government programs, as well as charitable foundations, needed to pay greater attention to such centers. However, as described in Chapter 5, exactly the reverse had happened by 2009. Both federal and state funds had been reduced for all centers other than libraries. The City of Austin and the Dell Foundation expanded their support for public libraries as access points, but most of the other centers lost ground and many stopped offering public access.

WHO USES PUBLIC ACCESS?

Both in 1999 and 2009, students observing at libraries and centers were trained to place users into three sets of categories based on age, ethnicity, and gender. Observations were made from noon to three p.m., three to six p.m., and six to nine p.m. to observe different groups of users, since adults tended to predominate from noon to three and six to nine, while youth and children predominated from three to six.

In 1999, Internet users at the libraries and community centers were predominantly teens and preteens. These two groups made up 55 percent of the Internet users observed. Another 44 percent were classified as adults, and just over 1 percent was elderly. Latinos were the group most frequently observed to be using the Internet at these libraries and centers (44 percent), with African Americans at 36 percent, Anglos at 19 percent, and others at only 1 percent.[9]

For 2009, our data changed, partly because we did not observe the community centers as we had in 1999. Because of community center closures and the growth of facilities such as Wired for Youth, teens and preteens in 2009 primarily accessed the Internet at public libraries in Wired for Youth rooms or alongside adults. We observed that 2 percent of users were elderly, 60 percent were adults, 20 percent were teens, and 17 percent were preteens. (Numbers do not add up to 100 because of rounding.) In terms of race, we estimated that 31 percent of users were African American, 47 percent were Latino, and 21 percent were white. Other races made up less than 1 percent of users.[10]

Of the libraries and community centers observed, Latino users accessed the Internet the most of any distinct racial group, at 46 percent in 1999 and 47 percent in 2009. Use by white users increased from 17 percent to 21 percent, while use by African Americans decreased from 36 percent to 31 percent.

Our 2009 data also showed differences in the ethnic distribution of subgroups of users. White users were virtually only represented as adults; 33 percent of adult users were white. The largest numbers of adult male users in both 1999 and 2009 were Latinos, but both Latino and African American adult male users declined relative to white users. The increase in white users is probably related to the gentrification of the neighborhood, as young white adults, both men and women, moved into new condos constructed near several East Austin libraries.

Adult female use was also heaviest among Latinas in both 1999 and 2009. Use by white women grew somewhat by 2009, probably because of gentrification. Use by African American women continued to be larger than that of white women, but declined relative to 1999.

One of the more striking changes from 1999 to 2009 was the considerable growth in use by Latino teenage boys. By 2009, only 4 percent of teenage users were white, as African American teenage male users also increased somewhat. That last increase is interesting because fieldwork at Johnston High in East Austin in 1999–2000 (discussed in Chapter 9), confirmed by the library observations in 1999 noted here, showed that African American teenage boys were reluctant to use computers at public libraries, perhaps seeing them as overly controlled, overly quiet spaces. We observed fewer of them than would have been expected by their numbers in the population. In the Johnston High interviews, several African American boys confirmed that they found libraries somewhat intimidating.

Use by both African American and Hispanic teenage girls was strong in both 1999 and 2009. By contrast, use among white teenage girls in both years was low.

By 2009, only 5 percent of preteen users were white. Significantly, Hispanics made up 72 percent of preteen users. Moreover, Hispanic preteens formed a sizable chunk of total users. Nearly 13 percent of all library users observed in 2009 were Hispanic preteens. Further research could help determine the impact of the Wired for Youth program on the particular demographic of Hispanic preteens. Some very valuable research has been done (Cunningham 2009) comparing Wired for Youth programs for Latinas with other programs like Latinitas (see Chapter 6 for more on Latinitas).

PREDOMINANT MALE USE OF PUBLIC ACCESS

Both in 1999 and 2009, there was a strong pattern of gender-differentiated usage. In 1999, 60 percent of the people observed using computers were male and 40 percent were female. By 2009, 61 percent of users were male and 39 percent were female. In other words, for every two female users, there were three male users. Men consistently used computers at higher rates than women in every subgroup, which ranged from 57 percent male to 88 percent male, except African American teenagers.

There was notably heavy use at the Austin libraries we visited in 2009 by male and female Latino users, with a total of 425. African American users numbered 253, and white users numbered 189. Our data also reveal that males use outweighed female use in every racial group. Males made up 56 percent of total African American users, 59 percent of total Latino users, and 68 percent of total white users.

In 1999, there was one significant and worrisome exception to the pattern of use by teens and preteens in this study. Recalling that, overall, 36 percent of users observed were African American, while 44 percent were Latino, it is notable that among preteen males, 55 percent were African American, 42 percent were Latino, and only 3 percent were white.[11] That may be due in some part to the observed success of the Carver Branch, in the center of the traditionally African American part of East Austin, in drawing in preteen users and making them feel comfortable, as was observed by Straubhaar and several students at several occasions. It was almost shocking, then, to see that among teenage males observed at the same libraries and centers, 62 percent were Latino, 10 percent were Anglo, and only 28 percent were African American. From follow-up conversations with a small number of users, we gathered that African American teenage males did not feel the Internet was intended for them or of use to them. They were also less likely, it seems, to see the local library as a comfortable place to spend free time, since in interviews they saw these spaces as too quiet and restrictive.

Among girls observed using the Internet in 1999, the ethnic trends were quite different. Among preteen females, Latinas were more often observed as users (61 percent) than African Americans (38 percent). Among teenage females, Latinas were still observed more often (48 percent) than African Americans (41 percent), but African American teenage females were nonetheless present in much larger proportions than African American teenage males. Looked at another way, African American teenage boys made up 6 percent of those observed in public Internet access, while African American teenage girls made up 11 percent. Follow-up conversations with a few African American teenage girls at the libraries revealed that they and their parents saw the library as a safe and desirable place to spend time, especially after school, and that the Internet was seen as an interesting means of expression. (To move beyond these initial indications, this research project is now conducting follow-up research on the social construction of the Internet and access among minority youth.)

In 2009, the demographic pattern of limited use by African American teenage boys reasserted itself. In the case of African American teenagers, females represented 55 percent of users and males represented 45 percent of users, although the absolute number of teenage boys had increased by 2009. This should be considered important in the context of usage patterns in every other demographic category that slants heavily toward male usage. (We are doing a follow-up study to better understand why male users predominate at public access sites.)

HOW PEOPLE ARE USING PUBLIC ACCESS

In 1999, adults tended to use the Internet for information and social purposes. Typical adult usage involved e-mail, chatting, and research. Observed research activities included seeking stock quotes, researching relocation strategies, performing salary calculations, locating genealogical data, and accessing government information or forms. While adult usage tended to be more research oriented with some game playing, teens and preteens tended to focus on game playing and other entertainment activities such as e-mailing, viewing World Wrestling Federation pictures, viewing materials related to other sports, listening to music, reading or watching cartoons, and seeking information on cartoon characters.

In 2009, computer sites accessed by users could be categorized as both entertainment- and information-oriented. In general, the 2009 users demonstrated much higher fluency in the diversity of Internet uses. Social networking sites were observed in an overwhelming number of cases. Watching time-based media online through sites such as YouTube was also a prevalent activity. Other activities observed included chatting, e-mailing, reading online news, editing photos online, attempting to download movies onto portable devices, mapping with Google Maps, browsing Craigslist, filing taxes online, balancing a checkbook online, and printing online coupons.

CONCLUSION

The presence of Internet services at public libraries and community technology centers in Austin expanded considerably from 1999 to 2009. The demand we observed across age, gender, and ethnicity in East Austin is an indication that, with notable exceptions, as public access becomes available in libraries and community centers, people in minority and low-income communities seek it out. Thus, using available resources efficiently should become an even stronger priority for libraries.

The libraries and community centers observed have provided an excellent service to members of their communities that otherwise would not have been available. Many people who were learning about the Internet and its capabilities in 1999 were doing so as a direct result of having the AFN computers available. The challenge for AFN, the libraries, and the community centers was how to help people make better use of the resource, as well as expanding physical access in terms of more computers and connections. Discussions with AFN director Ana Sisnett (now deceased) and others showed that the community was very aware of this need. In 1999, local computing advocates needed more volunteer help for training would-be users and more money to hire people to expand services to meet the community's demand. These needs were at least partially met, starting in 2000, by the Dell Foundation grant that enabled the creation of the Wired for Youth centers and the employment of youth specialists to staff the centers.

Giddens (1984) emphasizes how institutional structuring tends to play out in the enactment of daily routines. In East Austin, we observed some remarkable institutional and structural success stories. By 1999, the Carver Branch, in a predominantly African American neighborhood, attracted children, introduced them to both the Internet and print materials, let them work in groups, and made them feel comfortable and welcome. The library's role had become that of a friendly neighborhood center; the classic routines of the library had evolved but not been broken. People were still expected to behave according to library protocols, and for preteens and teenage girls, that routine was comforting. This kind of community orientation became more widespread by 2009, drawing in a larger number of children into several libraries. However, the space for both preteen and teenage users also seemed to have become more of a male space. By 2009, males outnumbered females among all groups but African American teenagers.

In 1999, a variety of problems existed at the libraries and the community access centers. There were physical structuring and social structuring problems at several of the libraries. Spatial layouts varied, with newer facilities typically being more Internet friendly. Use of computer resources likewise varied. There were state-of-the-art computers in each library that sat unused while patrons waited to log on to the Internet, a situation that appeared inappropriate to outside observers. Finally, staff attitudes varied in terms of whether they saw public Internet access as an uncomfortable new responsibility or an opportunity to attract computer-oriented youth. Like libraries, community centers were good places to get started using the Internet, but to get the full benefit of the Internet's potential, more computers, longer access times, better training, and more help-desk services were needed. Many patrons could have been better served if they had received instruction about how to access information on the Internet. Internet instruction classes were not always promoted and not always widely attended. Librarian training on Internet assistance was an even more important concern. Planning for the future of libraries, community centers, and AFN needed to include someone on-site that could give help when needed. This additional assistance would be of substantial service to the disadvantaged members of the community. Many patrons lacked the needed cultural capital to use the Internet, lacked appropriate Internet access time, and needed increased understanding of how the Internet could be useful in their lives.

By 2009, the libraries had adapted, adjusting to address many of the needs the 1999 study observed. Libraries made many more computers available and increased patrons' access times. Wired for Youth rooms provided access and training to children, as well as a comfortable environment to do homework and play games. Library staff supported, though not without occasional frustration, Internet usage policies and procedures. More reliable technology and increased skill of staff and users enabled more consistently satisfying access. But demand for computer access still outstrips supply at many hours in many libraries, so that librarians have to spend much of their time mediating access to machines, and would-be users are frustrated by the lack of access.

More study is needed about the cultural capital available to many minority community members who do not yet feel comfortable walking into a library and using the Internet, particularly if little help is available. In our observations, preteens were often willing to use the machines and play around until they figured things out, but many teenagers, adults, and elderly people were not so willing to experiment with technology without help. What do people need to know before they can walk up to a computer and imagine a productive or enjoyable use for it? Guidance can be sought from Claude Fischer (1985), who anticipated the following when thinking about the role of technology in our daily lives:

> We cannot assume that people use a technology because "it is there" or because it is "obviously" advantageous, nor because they have been "brainwashed" to buy it, nor because they have been swept along by a cultural ethos. Nor will they necessarily use it as it was designed to be used. We need to ask how and why purposeful actors choose to adopt specific technologies and what they do with them.

Even considering the positive changes libraries in Austin made between 1999 and 2009, more work can be done in helping build cultural capital for users in disadvantaged communities. Reconfiguring library classes, training, signage, and guidance to suit the particular needs of the communities they serve would help libraries move forward with integrating public access into their mission. Wired for Youth rooms and a station that assists new immigrants at Terrazas Branch, for example, stand out as particular measures that are sensitive to the needs of Austin's lower-income communities. Focus on the Internet as a medium, rather than an end in itself, can direct attention to how all members of the community can best be served.

ACKNOWLEDGMENTS

We would like to acknowledge the contributions of the following student researchers who worked on this project in 1999: Monem Adel, Ben Archey, David

Benrey, Forrest Black, Kathy Bolton, K. Bonnicksen, Cara Bradley, John Brending, John Brooks, Theresa Chevas, Karen Cooke, Jon Duffey, Lisa Eisenstein, Chris Hogenson, Orlando Kell, Yangsu Kim, Blake Jones, Molly Lepeska, Corey Lieberman, C. Luncesform, Stan Main, Leean Matson, Jenn Mosley, Molly Norling, Brian Prestwood, Rene Rhi, Hyun Rhim, Griselda Salinas, Chad Schimkowitsch, Michelle Schultz, Evan Scruggs, Bryan Shaw, Ryan Starus, Vanessa Vega, Melanie Villarreal, and Kerstin Wiggins. Graduate students involved included Carol Adams-Means, Loreto Caro, Miyase Christensen, Yinan Estrada, Elissa Fineman, Christine Giraud, Karen Gustafson, Lisa Hartenberger, Roberta Lentz, Ozlem Okur, Viviana Rojas, Debasmita Roychowdhury, and Zeynep Tufekci.

APPENDIX 7.1.

Library/center _____
Date _____
Time period _____

- As you were observing, did you get the feeling that the individuals running the library or center felt comfortable with the public access to the Internet?
- How helpful were the staff to the people who came in to use the computers of Internet?
- What limits to computer/Internet use did you observe: space or layout, number of computers, content filtering, staff ability to help?
- From the log you kept, what kinds of people used the Internet while you were volunteering?
- When you fill out the form below use the following categories:
    Gender: Male/Female
    Ethnicity: Anglo, Latino, African American, Asian, other
    Age: Preteen, teenager, adult, elderly

Gender	Ethnicity	Age

APPENDIX 7.2. OBSERVATION GUIDE

- What kind of institution (library, community center, etc.) did you observe?
- What are the organization's goals for the public computer and Internet access they provide?
- Where does public access to the Internet fit into their overall mission? (You will probably need to go back and talk to the librarian or center director.)
- As you were volunteering and observing, did you get the feeling that the individuals running the library or center felt comfortable with the public access to the Internet?

- Did the staff know enough about the Internet or computers to help people?
- What limits to computer/Internet use did you observe: space or layout, number of computers, location of computers, content filtering, staff ability to help?
- How many people did you observe? How many did you talk to? Were you able to participate effectively as a volunteer or what problems did you find?
- From the log you kept, what kinds of people used the Internet while you were volunteering?
- Were most users who came in already knowledgeable about computers and the Internet? (You can make inferences from who asked questions and who did not.)
- How able were different kinds of users to figure out for themselves how to use computers and the Internet?
- What kinds of questions did people have for you or the librarians/staff?
- From the conversations you had with people, what informed them about the Internet in the first place?
- From the conversations you had with people, what things were those people using the Internet for?

APPENDIX 7.3. INTERVIEW GUIDE

- When and where did you first hear about computers?
- From what person or medium did you first hear about computers?
- What was your first impression of computers? What did you think they were for?
- What was the first use you made of computers?
- What was the first use you made of computers in school?
- Why did you first get a computer at home? Whose idea was it and where did they get the idea?
- When and where did you first hear about the Internet?
- From what person or medium did you first hear about the Internet?
- What was your first impression of the Internet? What did you think it was for?
- What was the first use you made of the Internet?
- What was the first use you made of the Internet in school?
- Why did you first get the Internet at home? Whose idea was it and where did they get the idea?

NOTES

1. Burleson, Delia, and Applegate (1995), studying communication skills, found that parents from more advantaged socioeconomic backgrounds are more likely to transmit to their children complex social thinking skills. They argue that these advantages are transmitted through socialization, perpetuating social imbalances. Their findings seem to support the importance of family socialization in its transmission and maintenance of cultural capital.

2. The libraries observed were the Carver, Cepeda, Riverside, and Terrazas

branches. The community centers observed were Montopolis Community Center, focused on youth, and the Conley-Guerrero Senior Center. Additional fieldwork in September included the DeWitty Job Training Center.

3. The libraries observed were the Carver, Terrazas, St. Johns, and Southeast Austin Community branches. Carver and Terrazas were also observed in 1999.

4. Orlando Kell and Jonathon Duffy, report for class project, observations at an East Austin public library, July 7, 1999.

5. Chad Schimkowitsch, report for class project, observations at an East Austin public library, July 7, 1999.

6. John Brooks, report for class project, observations at an East Austin public library, July 7, 1999.

7. Ben Archey, report for class project, observations at an East Austin public library, July 7, 1999.

8. John Brooks, report for class project, observations at an East Austin public library, July 7, 1999.

9. There was an attempt to sample libraries and centers in both predominantly Latino and predominantly African American sections of East Austin. Many of the users observed (37 percent) were at the Carver Branch, in the center of the traditionally African American part of East Austin on 11th Street. This was balanced by the numbers of users observed at Cepeda (22 percent), Riverside (16 percent) and Terrazas (18 percent), all branches that serve largely Latino or Hispanic neighborhoods.

10. Categorization by ethnic group should be taken as approximate rather than precise, since student observers had to rely on skin color and self-presentation in dress style to categorize people into ethnic groups.

11. The claim of statistical significance is based on the chi-square test at the $P < .05$ level.

REFERENCES

Austin Public Library. (2009). Connected Youth. Press release, March. Retrieved August 3, 2009, from http://www.ci.austin.tx.us/library/news/nr20090304a.htm.

Benton Foundation. (1998). Losing ground bit by bit: Low-income communities in the information age. Retrieved from http://www.benton.org/archive/publibrary/losing-ground/home.html.

Bourdieu, P. (1984). *Distinction: A social critique of the judgement of taste.* Cambridge, MA: Harvard University Press.

Burleson, B., J. Delia, and J. Applegate. (1995). The socialization of person-centered communication: Parental contributions to the socio-cognitive and communication skills of their childen. In M. A. Fitzpatrick and A. Vangelisti (Eds.), *Perspectives in family communication,* pp. 34–76. Thousand Oaks, CA: Sage.

Children's Partnership. (2000). Online content for low-income and underserved Americans: The digital divide's new frontier, a strategic audit of activities and opportunities. Santa Monica, CA.

Chow, C., J. Ellis, J. Mark, and B. Wise. (1998). Impact of CTCNet affiliates: Findings from a national survey of users of community technology centers. CTC-

Net, Education Development Center, Newton, MA, July. Retrieved from http://www.ctcnet.org/impact98.htm.

Compaine, B. (Ed.). (2001). *The digital divide: Facing a crisis or creating a myth?* Cambridge, MA: MIT Press.

Cunningham, Carolyn. (2009). Technological learning after school: A study of the communication dimensions of technological literacy in three informal education programs for female and minority youth. PhD dissertation, University of Texas at Austin.

Fischer, C. (1985). Studying technology and social life. In Manuel Castells (Ed.), *High technology, space, and society*, pp. 284–300. Beverly Hills, CA: Sage.

Giddens, A. (1984). *The constitution of society: Outline of the theory of structuration*. Berkeley: University of California Press.

Golding, P. (1998). Global village or cultural pillage. In R. W. McChesney, E. M. Wood, and J. B. Foster (Eds.), *Capitalism and the information age*. New York: Monthly Review Press.

Herman, E., R. McChesney, and E. S. Herman. (1998). *The global media: The missionaries of global capitalism*. London: Cassell Academic.

Hills, J. (1998). The U.S. rules, OK? Telecommunications since the 1940s. In R. W. McChesney, E. M. Wood, and J. B. Foster (Eds.), *Capitalism and the information age*. New York: Monthly Review Press.

Hoffman, D., and T. Novak. (1998). Bridging the digital divide: The impact of race on computer access and Internet use. February 2. Retrieved from http://ecommerce.vanderbilt.edu/papers/race/science.html.

Mosco, V. (1996). *The political economy of communication: Rethinking and renewal*. London: Sage.

NTIA (National Telecommunications and Information Administration). (1998). Falling through the Net II: New data on the digital divide. U.S. Department of Commerce, Washington, DC. Retrieved from http://www.ntia.doc.gov/ntiahome/net2/.

———. (1999). Falling through the Net: Defining the digital divide. U.S. Department of Commerce, Washington, DC. Retrieved from http://www.ntia.doc.gov/ntiahome/fttn99.

Schement, J. R. (1997). Preface: Of libraries and communities. Benton Foundation, June. Retrieved from http://www.benton.org/Library/Libraries/preface.html.

Schiller, H. (1996). *Information inequality: The deepening social crisis in America*. New York: Routledge.

Stafford, A. (1999). City of Austin, Austin Public Library Foundation, and Susan and Michael Dell to provide 10 community computer centers to South Austin branch libraries. Press release, Austin City Connection, City of Austin, Texas, September 16.

Strover, S., and J. Straubhaar. (2001). The digital divide in Texas. Paper presented at the 51st International Communication Association Conference, Washington, DC.

Strover, S., J. Straubhaar, K. Gustafson, and N. Inagaki. (2004). E-government services and computer and Internet use in Texas. Telecommunications and Information Policy Institute, University of Texas at Austin. Retrieved from http://www.utexas.edu/research/tipi/research/egovernment.htm.

Warschauer, M. (2003). *Technology and social inclusion: Rethinking the digital divide.* Cambridge, MA: MIT Press.

Wilhelm, A. (n.d.). Buying into the computer age: A look at Hispanic families. Tomás Rivera Policy Institute. Retrieved from http://www.cgu.edu/inst/aw1-1.html.

MARTHA
FUENTES-BAUTISTA

NOBUYA INAGAKI

CHAPTER 8

BRIDGING THE BROADBAND GAP OR RECREATING DIGITAL INEQUALITIES?

THE SOCIAL SHAPING OF PUBLIC WI-FI IN AUSTIN

Many recent efforts to close the digital divide have focused on broadband access, as broadband is increasingly seen as a key resource in unleashing the potential of the Internet (Horrigan 2010).[1] The prospects of high-speed connectivity have been with us for more than a decade, but currently the service reaches only two-thirds of the U.S. population. As part of a spectrum reform agenda, the Federal Communications Commission (FCC) has expanded the unlicensed spectrum with a policy goal to foster innovative applications delivering high-speed service to all. Wireless fidelity (Wi-Fi) increasingly serves as the underpinning technology for public Internet access, public safety, and other applications that use the unlicensed spectrum. However, the social impact of such technological innovations is intimately bound to the design, implementation, and uses of technological systems that provide new services to communities around the country.

To examine the factors behind deployment and selective adoption of broadband infrastructure and services, this chapter looks closely at the configuration process of public Wi-Fi networks in one American city: Austin, Texas. A basic assumption of this project is that the quality and extent of access to information and communication technologies (ICTs) are outcomes of the process of design and implementation of technological innovations such as the Internet. Such a process is not random but rather structured by social dynamics such as the values of institutions that produce, distribute, and market technologies. We are particularly concerned with the way in which local communities and civic organizations shape public access to ICTs from below (de Certeau 1984) as they respond to changing policies, market dynamics, technological advances, and issues of social exclusion in a national context that speaks often about the "digital age." We further discuss the implications of how public Wi-Fi networks are configured to address the social and economic geography of urban areas.

Austin serves as our case study because it has become the corporate headquarters for several leading wireless companies in the United States and is seen as a successful example of a technopolis (as discussed in Chapter 3). In addition, public wireless access to the Internet has skyrocketed, placing the city among the most *unwired* in the country. In Texas, as early as 2005, broadband service had reached over 50 percent of computer users in urban areas, well above the national average (Straubhaar et al. 2005). By these accounts, Austin can be seen as the promised land of wireless innovations: a city where wireless is bridging the gap between the availability of high-speed service and its actual use. We examine the way in which wireless innovations are delivering the promise of access for all through the study of the configuration of emerging public Wi-Fi networks in Austin. Through this case study, we attempt to provide answers to the following questions:

- What are the patterns characterizing the growth and configuration of public Wi-Fi infrastructure in Austin?
- What are the factors shaping public Wi-Fi as perceived by the key organizations involved in the provision and support of these networks?
- What are the implications for larger issues of access?

Our research informs the discussion of these topics by examining the directions, challenges, and institutional arrangements shaping the configuration of public Wi-Fi networks in Austin, Texas. By public Wi-Fi networks we mean the provision of broadband Internet service to the public through wireless fidelity platforms (IEEE 802.11x family) in spaces other than the home or office, under nondiscriminatory terms and conditions. This study is also one of the first to assess how communities, local government, and businesses collaborate in promoting public wireless broadband, their reasons for doing so, and the implications of these collaborations for larger issues of access.

Drawing on interviews with stakeholders (at various industries, nonprofits, local government, and research and educational institutions), a survey of managers of public Wi-Fi venues, and sociogeographic information on sites where Wi-Fi is available (known as hotspots) and users of these sites, we examine the adoption process and configuration patterns of public Wi-Fi networks in Austin. We further discuss the implications of our findings for debates on spectrum management and universal access of broadband by calling attention to the possibilities opened for local level interventions, and their impacts in larger issues of access to high-speed service.

THE SOCIAL SHAPING OF TECHNOLOGICAL SYSTEMS

For more than three decades, diffusion of innovation theory has been a major paradigm employed in the studies of adoption of new technologies (see Chapter 5). However, growing awareness about the importance of knowledge and social practices in the domain of ICTs has redirected researchers' attention to what has become known as the social construction of technology approach (SCOT) (Lievrouw 2002). SCOT provides a helpful framework to explore the shaping of tele-access systems (Dutton 1999) and the diffusion of high-speed, advanced communications (Dutton et al. 2004).

SCOT theory is concerned with the ways in which social forces affect the design, adoption, and uses of technology (Williams and Edge 1996). It argues that the primary way in which society is embodied in technological innovations is via the actions of identifiable social groups of individuals or institutions that participate in development of a technology. There are many potentially relevant social groups: scientists, the military, engineers, advertisers, interest groups, citizens, and consumers. An innovation serves different functions for each group, but only few of them prevail to define socially accepted ways of using a new technology (Pinch and Bijker 1987). Choices made by actors in the actual decision-making process significantly influence the trajectory of a technology.

Another aspect of the theory is interpretive flexibility, which refers "not only to how people think of or interpret artifacts but also to the flexibility in the way artifacts are designed" (Pinch and Bijker 1987, 40). Through the concept of interpretive flexibility, SCOT introduces the issue of choice and how decisions are made during the development of technological artifacts and systems. The decisions made by creators, manufacturers, marketers, and users are influenced by the social practices, worldviews, and beliefs of these actors. A corollary to this perspective is that the outcome is not predetermined by the technology as many technological determinists are apt to suggest; instead, an access model may help people overcome social barriers, or it may further reinforce social and economic inequalities.

THE EMERGING BROADBAND DIVIDE AND THE PROMISE OF WIRELESS NETWORKING

Since 2000, the FCC has reported steady advances of broadband deployment in the country. However, the agency recognizes that the service is not yet ubiquitous, the relative costs of deployment remain high, and the adoption is advancing slowly (FCC 2005a, 2005b). The problem is particularly acute in historically underserved areas. Empirical studies have documented the gap in the availability of high-speed service between rural regions and metropolitan zones (Oden et al. 2002) as well as the slow progress of competition in those environments (Strover 2003; Turner 2005). Beyond the issue of availability lies the question of adoption and use. National surveys indicate that only two-thirds of the adult American population use high-speed service, and that it reaches only a fraction of those living in rural areas (Horrigan 2010).

Both the Bush and Obama administrations have made calls for universal broadband access (White House 2004, 2011). Wireless technologies that operate in the unlicensed spectrum—from Wi-Fi to WiMax—are identified as crucial components of this new wave of American innovation that will grant consumers "broadband access in restaurants, airports, and other public places" and in remote and rural areas (White House 2004, 12).

While these issues are being debated, the development of wireless broadband infrastructure proceeds rapidly in the hands of phone companies, cable companies, Internet service providers (ISPs), cooperatives, nonprofits, municipalities, and user groups. Most of the research on Wi-Fi networks has focused on two possible models of wireless deployment: (1) a top-down, planned, centralized strategy carried out by traditional telecommunications operators, cable companies, and specialized wireless service companies; and (2) the implementation of a bottom-up, more organic, and decentralized design attributed to start-up companies, some municipalities, and community-based organizations (Lehr and McKnight 2003; Rao and Parikh 2003; Bar and Galperin 2004). However, results of empirical studies create a picture with more gray areas than the black-and-white map suggested by the top-down versus bottom-up approaches. There is evidence that commercial wireless ISPs are ready to allow their clients (e.g., coffeehouses, apartment buildings, and small communities) to share broadband when perceiving competitive pressures raised by the action of community wireless services (Rao and Parikh 2003).

HISTORICAL BACKGROUND

As noted earlier, Austin is one of the nation's top unwired, or wireless, cities. Experiments in wireless Internet connectivity were already taking place in Austin's public spaces a few years prior to Wi-Fi's debut in the consumer market. One such experiment was carried out in 1997 by a few individuals affiliated with the Austin Free-Net (AFN), local ISP Outernet, the Austin Public Library, and the City of Austin government.[2] The experimenters succeeded in deploying a 3-Mbps wireless network connecting the library's downtown location, city buildings, and the Outernet data center, enabling high-speed connection for public Internet access at the library. However, high prices of wireless broadband equipment in the late 1990s discouraged AFN and the library from pursuing further experiments with the technology.

Despite this experiment, the first public Wi-Fi service in Austin was not an outcome of such private-public collaboration. Wayport, an Austin company pioneering "for-fee" wireless Internet service in public spaces, turned the Austin-Bergstrom International Airport into one of the first airports in the country with wireless Internet connectivity for travelers.[3] This early public Wi-Fi expansion was concentrated in venues that were part of national hotel, coffee shop, and restaurant chains, and the airport. The configuration of public Wi-Fi in Austin in this period was still removed from the everyday experience of the majority of computer users in the city.

A new set of actors became visible in Austin's public Wi-Fi landscape in the 2000–2001 period. These were wireless enthusiasts and tinkerers who individually experimented with Wi-Fi (e.g., devising new antenna technologies to enhance signal coverage) in places such as coffeehouses and restaurants they personally patronized. Their activities gradually become more collective. By the end of 2001, wireless enthusiasts in Austin had organized different Wi-Fi user groups. As these enthusiasts and groups set up more access points in their favorite venues, they engendered the vision of an open, "free-to-end-user" model as an alternative to the then dominant for-fee model. Knowing that the practice of opening closed broadband networks could upset established broadband providers operating in the city, they made a public statement declaring that they had no intentions of taking customers away from these businesses:

> One of the key things the recent media coverage on wireless free-nets has focused on is the concept that those of us putting up free-nets are doing so to provide connections to the masses. . . . The suggestion is that, in doing so, we're taking business from the broadband providers. . . . [However,] in most cases, freenets aren't taking business from the providers, we're just giving their existing subscribers more places from which to connect. (AWCG 2004)

The organized and individual actions of Wi-Fi enthusiasts enabled a number of hotspots in coffeehouses and other venues, but the deployment of these networks was still too haphazard.[4] A strategic vision of network deployment emerged in 2003 with the creation of special-purpose organizations for the provision and advocacy of the free-to-end-user model of access. These initiatives sought to harness "the community-mindedness spirit" of volunteer and user groups with the drive and entrepreneurialism of technology start-ups. The Austin Wireless City Project (AWCP) rapidly became the flagship entity of the so-called free Wi-Fi movement. The organization, composed of members of numerous Wi-Fi groups coexisting in town (user groups, start-ups, nonprofits, and advocacy groups), was created "to self-provision and self-maintain vast community networks of free Wi-Fi hotspots and transform ourselves from consumers of corporate services to co-creators of a technology that better links us to what matters to us" ("Austin Wireless" 2003).

The "free" Wi-Fi services patronized by the AWCP immediately gained followers and popularity in the city. The AWCP's strategy—"Adopt-a-network"—was modeled after AFN's "Adopt-a-site" program, which invited companies and organizations as donors to support public access sites affiliated with AFN. The AWCP's Adopt-a-network encouraged commercial and public venues to become their own sponsors in lighting up public Wi-Fi networks. Within a year, the number of AWCP-supported public Wi-Fi venues outnumbered those of commercial, for-fee venues (Schwartz 2004).

The AWCP's model of public Wi-Fi was unique in several respects. First, it offered free-to-end-user wireless Internet service supported by the venues. Second, the AWCP's activities were carried out entirely by volunteers, occasionally in collaboration with start-ups and broadband providers. Third, the AWCP did not simply add wireless access devices to the wired broadband; rather, it did so in a manner that created managed Wi-Fi networks. This was made possible by networking all AWCP sites via open-source software specifically designed for this application by Less Networks. Such networked design allowed common user interfaces across different Wi-Fi venues, network monitoring for problems and usage statistics, a user verification system for security purposes, and portal sites with contents created by the AWCP and sponsoring venues.

The activities of the AWCP reached beyond commercial venues. The AWCP also formed a partnership with the Austin city government and AFN, and began creating wireless access points in city parks, public buildings, and nonprofit facilities. Through this partnership, the city government has deployed Wi-Fi networks at most of the public library branches, three parks and squares, three public buildings, and a multipurpose building in an economic revitalization zone located in a predominantly minority population area. Public Wi-Fi connectivity operated by the city government is jointly managed by the city and the AWCP.

A different class of wireless Internet providers also emerged in Austin's public Wi-Fi market around 2003. These providers—mostly local start-ups—supported the free-to-end-user model as a means to promote their businesses. They experimented with new business models that sought ways to generate revenues without charging end-user fees. As one of the informants put it, "From a start-up perspective, how would you go against T-Mobile? Wayport got there, T-Mobile is there, but I can't think of anybody really making money in a paid model."[5] As will be discussed in more detail later, some of these commercial Wi-Fi providers offer free public Wi-Fi to end users, while others offer the service for free to both end users and Wi-Fi venues.

In the process of providing Wi-Fi spots, commercial bandwidth providers and the providers and supporters of public Wi-Fi services formed a symbiotic relationship, which can be understood in light of the extensive contact they have had with each other in the past few years. One of the primary venues for such contact was a roundtable discussion on Austin and Central Texas' economic future hosted by the Innovation, Creativity and Capital Institute (IC²) of the University of Texas.

Historically, IC² has been the site for visioning and crafting economic development strategies for Austin and Central Texas. The growth of a thriving high-tech cluster economy in Austin in the past three decades was harnessed under the conceptual framework of the "technopolis wheel" (Figure 1.1; Smilor, Kozmetsky, and Gibson 1988). This strategic vision designed by leadings local entrepreneurs and founders of IC² emphasizes the cooperation between businesses, local and state government, and academic institutions in initiatives that promote technology diversification and economic development. Beyond physical infrastructure, the strategy demands the creation of "smart infrastructure" based on the interactions of intelligent organizations, and people sharing a common purpose and vision: building the technopolis.[6] (See a more extensive analysis in Chapter 3.)

Throughout the course of the IC² roundtable discussion, participants brought attention to the blossoming wireless businesses in Central Texas. The agglomeration of wireless businesses in Central Texas, and the presence of a premier wireless research institute (WNCG), suggested that Austin was ripe for a successful wireless milieu. The roundtable asked IC² to produce a report—*Austin's Wireless Future* (Evans et al. 2004)—on the wireless businesses in the region, and to formulate strategic recommendations for the region's economy. These meetings, and the process leading to the publication of the report, turned into an excellent opportunity for exchanging information among different kinds of organizations about key technologies, markets, and regulatory issues.

An even more tangible venue for contact among local stakeholders in wireless and Wi-Fi businesses came into being during the same period. Some of the participants from the IC² roundtable meetings and other leaders of the wireless industry in Austin formed the Austin Wireless Alliance.[7] The organization's mission is "to develop, sustain, and promote Austin as a global leader in business activity, technical innovation, and community participation within the wireless industry."

A brief review of this history highlights the following dynamics underlying the growth of public Wi-Fi in Austin:

- *Multiplicity of initiatives*: There are a number of initiatives encompassing commercial, nonprofit, and public activities in public Wi-Fi provisioning in Austin. The market is cohabited by diverse actors espousing differing visions of public wireless access.
- *Free Wi-Fi movement*: Organized actions of grassroots groups— in part driven by free-market entrepreneurial spirit—cultivated

the idea of "free," or venue-sponsored, public Wi-Fi access, and presented the idea to the citizens, bandwidth providers, and local government as a viable alternative to a fee-based model of public access.

- *Institutional collaboration*: The growth of public Wi-Fi has been facilitated by collaboration among diverse actors. The know-how for institutional partnerships—gained through the technopolis experiment in the 1980s—served as a backdrop in creating arrangements for mutual benefit.

THE SOCIAL SHAPING OF WI-FI IN AUSTIN

The presence of a sizable number of tech-savvy users who became early adopters of the technology was the most frequently cited factor driving the public Wi-Fi boom in Austin. Our informants characterized users as Wi-Fi enthusiasts and hobbyists, technology and creative professionals, technologically savvy people, students, and "geeks." Being a college town and a high-tech agglomeration economy, Austin has attracted a wide range of creative and technical workers, who are the foundation the newly emerging "creative economy" (Florida 2002). According to our interviewees, these creative workers are very mobile people who tend to use connectivity everywhere. An industry representative emphasized that these users are the first in incorporating the technology into their daily lives, encouraging the development of new applications.[8] However, other informants cast some caution over excessive faith in the natural diffusion of the technology. AFN sees Wi-Fi users as privileged Austin citizens who are not representative of the overall population and are less likely to mingle with users of traditional public Internet access sites such as libraries and community centers in low-income communities.

Strong institutional collaborations and volunteerism combined as another key factor that supported the rapid growth of Wi-Fi in Austin. Partnerships among industry, community-based groups, academic and research institutions, and local government have boosted the growth of Wi-Fi zones in Austin. We identified twenty-nine institutions involved in the public wireless landscape in Austin: nonprofits and user groups (six), commercial providers (ten), business organizations (three), educational and research institutions (seven), and local government agencies (three). Within this network of relationships, there is a core of fourteen organizations with links closely tied to each other, and fifteen isolated actors with one tie to the rest.

The AWCP was credited as the main site of collaboration among different actors engaged in the expansion of public wireless networks in the city. Informants described the organization as a collection of Wi-Fi enthusiasts, industry workers (from large firms to start-up companies), and community leaders. Centrality scores (not shown for purposes of space) confirm that the focal point of the network is composed by the AWCP, the Austin Wireless Alliance (the wireless business association), and research institutions, suggesting the existence of a core network organized around efforts of volunteerism, entrepreneurial initiatives, and research.

Responses to our social network survey revealed that the main forms of collaboration among organizations are visioning and volunteerism. Interviewees praised the AWCP for its demonstrated ability to mobilize and organize volunteers, funneling resources, ideas, and visions from different stakeholders. Our informants found that the leadership of the AWCP is clearly expressed in the popularity of the venue-sponsored, or free-to-end-user, model of access in the city. The AWCP emerged as the most vocal advocate of the idea of free Wi-Fi. In fact, the AWCP actually persuaded Time Warner Cable to allow commercial customers such as coffee shops and bars to open their wireless networks to the public.

Wireless start-ups also see partnership with the AWCP as an effective vehicle to promote their services and to seize business opportunities. Some of these firms have sponsored the installation of wireless access points at venues and catered to them with services such as web hosting, software design, and website development. The city government and the public libraries have also welcomed technical collaboration with the AWCP and start-ups. WiFi-Texas, a young wireless ISP, donated the wireless access points that enabled Wi-Fi connectivity in the city's public libraries.[9] Less Networks, the for-profit arm of the AWCP, made available to the city the software that controls public wireless interface at libraries and all other city facilities. The city benefits from the obvious reduction in the cost of deploying wireless access. Meanwhile, the start-ups and nonprofits believe that these efforts increase their visibility and credibility in the community, potentially opening new doors for their operations.

As a high-tech city, Austin offers a unique milieu that fosters the growth of public wireless Internet. Informants believe that the high broadband penetration in most parts of the city and the availability of state-of-the-art equipment at relatively low cost have facilitated the rapid, ad hoc deployment of Wi-Fi hotspots in Austin. Austin's diverse industrial landscape, consisting of venture capital, chip makers, equipment manufacturers, broadband providers, pioneering wireless firms, and wireless research at the University of Texas, also emerged as a factor stimulating the growth of public wireless networks. Start-up firms reported that Austin offers a particular advantage because operational costs and cost of living in the area still remain relatively low in comparison with other high-tech cities. Finally, Austin's industrial policies encourage technological innovations and promote collaboration. This local tradition has been a factor in stimulating volunteerism as well as entrepreneurial spirit surrounding public Wi-Fi initiatives in the city.

Austin's culture also contributed to this evolution of wireless networks. The city has branded itself as "the city of ideas"—a cutting-edge, hip place in which both technological innovations and live music thrive. As Richard Florida explains it, the mix of technology, talent, and a tolerant culture has proved to be an effective economic development strategy, placing Austin at the top of the fastest growing economies in the nation. We found that user groups and local entrepreneurs see themselves as part of a rising creative class. However, like other creative cities in the United States, Austin registers rising income inequalities between workers of the creative sector and those in manufacturing and other service jobs (Florida 2002, xvi; see also Chapter 4).

Wi-Fi user groups and local entrepreneurs have also been successful at crafting a link between Austin's culture and wireless Internet. Borrowing the popular motto of the town, "Keep Austin Weird," they promoted public Wi-Fi under slogans such as "Keep Austin Wi-Fi" and "Keep Wi-Fi Free." Some informants underscored that over the past twenty years, service businesses in Austin have expanded, catering to the needs of the high-tech industry. This close relationship has made owners of coffeehouses, restaurants, and bars very responsive to the needs of creative workers, increasing awareness and opening the doors of venues to Wi-Fi services. City officials consider public Wi-Fi access at city facilities a natural development of long-standing policies to provide online government services and public Internet access to Austin's 800,000 or more residents. For these goals, the city government sought an aggregated network effect by adding access points to the network maintained by the AWCP.

Another important backdrop to our discussion of the social shaping of Wi-Fi access in Austin is the urban social geography, which is characterized by the economic, ethnic, racial, psychological, and physical boundaries formed by Interstate Highway 35. The neighborhoods east of I-35 are primarily composed of racial and ethnic minority communities with disadvantaged socioeconomic statistics. The western half of the city is composed of predominantly ethnic Anglo neighborhoods. Economic, social, and digital divides mirror this residential segregation.[10] (See Chapter 2 for the history of these divides.)

Experts and providers believe that Austin's geography makes it a suitable place to develop wireless broadband projects. Unlike other Texas cities such as Houston and Dallas, the Austin metropolitan area is fairly compact and concentrated in the central corridor of the city. Although only Verizon has announced a citywide plan for its customers, providers agree that Austin's layout would allow rapid development of wireless broadband networks. The business district, the Capitol, government buildings, and the main academic institutions in town constitute a natural hub of connectivity for adjacent locations. In order to identify the dominant access models prevalent in our case study sites, we inventoried three key dimensions of the public Wi-Fi services available in Austin: access business models, providers, and types of public Wi-Fi venues.[11]

The business models of Austin's public Wi-Fi services can be broadly divided into two groups according to the methods by which the costs of service provision are borne and by whom. The first model is based on the venue-sponsored provision of Wi-Fi service, in which property owners of Wi-Fi facilities pay for the cost of service provision, thereby sponsoring its use. Because there are no direct access fees paid by the end users, we can also call this model a free-to-end-user model. By contrast, the for-fee model relies on the revenues from access usage fees collected from the end users; the end users are thereby responsible for the bulk of service costs.

The dominance of the venue-sponsored model of access in Austin's public Wi-Fi market is clear. In a typical public Wi-Fi venue adopting the venue-sponsored model, any costs incurred in the provision of public Wi-Fi are borne initially by the venue owner but are subsequently recovered through the revenues generated from the sale of merchandise and service to Wi-Fi users. (This does not apply to public Wi-Fi services at noncommercial venues such as public libraries and public parks.) By contrast, the for-fee model operates on a premise that Wi-Fi users are willing to pay extra fees for wireless Internet service in addition to the expenditures they make for buying the core services and merchandise offered by facilities (except at noncommercial Wi-Fi venues).

The geographic distributions of the two models exhibit contrasting patterns. Figures 8.1 and 8.2 compare the locations of public Wi-Fi venues by the two major cost models—venue-sponsored and for-fee. Public Wi-Fi venues offering service free of charge to end users are fairly evenly distributed across Austin's geography, although they still tend to be concentrated in Central and West Austin, areas with average or above average socioeconomic statistics where residents are more likely to have laptops. This laptop disparity between lower-income East Austin and other areas is being addressed by a new cooperative program between the Dell Foundation and the Austin Public Library, which will loan laptops to youth through libraries in the Connected Youth program (see Chapters 6 and 7).

By contrast, for-fee venues are found only in areas west of I-35. For-fee Wi-Fi services are most popular in the city's business districts and upscale commercial areas, but are virtually absent in minority and low-income areas (i.e., east of I-35).[12] This pattern seems to indicate that economic motivations are fundamentally influencing the operation of for-fee Wi-Fi services.

Austin is a surprisingly small market for Wi-Fi services for large telephone and cable companies. As of September 2004, there were only seven public Wi-Fi venues served by the local exchange carriers and cable franchises combined. The low market penetration among this class of providers seems to be primarily influenced by the abundance of free public Wi-Fi sites in Austin, which significantly reduces incentive among venues to choose a for-fee service.[13] Therefore, these telephone and cable companies primarily play the role of bandwidth providers in Austin's public Wi-Fi market. For their bandwidth needs for public Wi-Fi service, 43 percent of the public Wi-Fi venues in our survey sample of fifty-three venues use SBC's DSL service, and 38 percent use Time Warner Cable's cable Internet service.

Figures 8.3 through 8.5 compare the geographic extent of the three most popular types of public Wi-Fi providers in Austin. All three types of providers serve venues that tend to cluster in the downtown area (i.e., the middle of the maps just west of I-35). Beyond this, each group of public Wi-Fi venues has the following distinctive characteristics.

Despite the concentration in the downtown area, the geographic extent of the AWCP-supported sites is fairly large and evenly distributed. The venues in this group spread from the north end of the city to the south end, and have some presence on the east side of I-35.

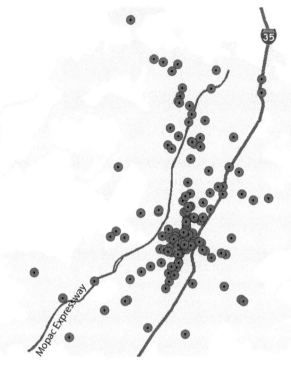

Figure 8.1. Venue-sponsored public Wi-Fi venues

Figure 8.2. For-fee public Wi-Fi venues

Figure 8.3. Public Wi-Fi venues—AWCP only

Figure 8.4. Public Wi-Fi venues supported by commercial WISPS

Figure 8.5. Independent public Wi-Fi venues

The section of the city that has the lowest penetration of AWCP-supported venues is the area west of Mopac Expressway (the north-south highway on the left). This area is composed primarily of affluent residential areas sprinkled with a few upscale shopping centers. Compared to AWCP-supported venues, public Wi-Fi venues served by commercial WISPs (wireless internet service providers) have higher penetration in the more affluent areas west of Mopac Expressway. Commercial providers include not only well-known national companies such as T-Mobile and Wayport but also local wireless ISPs. Also, the hotspots in this group seem to have a greater presence in north and northwest Austin. However, venues served by commercial WISPs are virtually lacking in the poorer area east of I-35. Independent Wi-Fi venues seem to have the smallest geographic coverage among the three major types of providers. This group includes independently operated retail and service outlets that have self-installed wireless access points for their customers. Like commercial WISP venues, independent Wi-Fi venues are mostly absent in East Austin.

The geographic pattern we saw for the public Wi-Fi venues served by the AWCP/Less Networks needs clarification, however. The venues in this group include those operated jointly with the City of Austin government. A different picture emerges when we distinguish AWCP venues from the municipally operated venues. Figure 8.6 maps Wi-Fi venues located at non-city facilities; the AWCP undertakes the entire network operation at these sites. Figure 8.7 maps Wi-Fi venues located at city facilities and jointly operated by units within the city government and the AWCP. The access sites at city facilities, though few in number, spread evenly across the entire city. The geographic pattern of AWCP-only venues, by contrast, appears very similar to those of independent venues and commercial WISP venues. This is not surprising because most of the AWCP-only venues are commercial establishments, a characteristic shared by both independent and commercial WISP venues. Local government sites are much more widely spread across all areas of the city, including poorer areas east of I-35. Thus, public wireless sites in disadvantaged communities are mostly sponsored by the local government.

Public Wi-Fi venues include libraries, coffeehouses, and hotels. There is no evidence of the presence of "Wi-Fi only" access sites in Austin. Therefore, in order to use Wi-Fi, one must enter a space originally designed for other purposes. This a priori access requirement—encompassing physical, social, cultural, and economic access—may privilege or prejudice segments of existing and future users if the types of venues available are biased.

Indeed, there is a strong commercial bias in Austin's public Wi-Fi venues, with 86 percent of the city's public Wi-Fi venues located at sites of goods and service consumption (Table 8.1). Those truly public sites that do not require additional consumption, such as public libraries, constitute only a small minority of Austin's hotspots. While no concrete evidence is available, public Wi-Fi venues in Austin also seem to be biased culturally; Wi-Fi venues tend to be patronized by middle- and upper-middle-class people, creative workers, high-tech employees, intellectuals, or people with professional occupations.[14] Anecdotal evidence also suggests spatial-cultural barriers in the diffusion of public Wi-Fi service. The owners of restaurants and other retail establishments in the underserved areas often express disinterest in the service, are hesitant to explore potential benefits, and cite the lack of demand from customers.[15] Combined with the geographic unevenness of the availability of public Wi-Fi venues, these

Figure 8.6. Public Wi-Fi venues supported by AWCP

Figure 8.7. Public Wi-Fi venues—city government

Table 8.1. Public Wi-Fi Venues in Austin by Type of Venue

	Number	Percentage
Restaurant or bar*	77	35.0
Coffeehouse*	60	27.3
Lodging*	26	11.8
Other retail*	25	11.4
Library	21	9.5
Park or square	5	2.3
Public building	3	1.4
Nonprofit facility	2	0.9
Airport*	1	0.5

Note: Numbers are from September 2004

*Indicates sites of goods and service consumption

spatial biases of public Wi-Fi venues seem to reduce, not enhance, public access opportunities for the poor, less educated, or minority populations.

As expected, public Wi-Fi venues are predominantly located in commercial zones. We observed a positive correlation between public Wi-Fi availability and the density of commercial activities; a higher percentage of commercial zones in a given zip code area is associated with a greater number of public Wi-Fi venues. An even stronger predictor of public Wi-Fi availability is the distance of a given area from the geographic center point of Austin's central business district (CBD). We found that the closer an area is to the CBD center point, the greater the number of public Wi-Fi venues in the area.[16]

However, access to public Wi-Fi in the poorest section of the city defies these statistics. The zip code area 78702, located just east of downtown across I-35, is an area with the city's least educated and poorest populations, and has the second smallest population of ethnic Anglos. Nevertheless, the 78702 area is not an urban ghetto as is found in other large cities, and it has numerous restaurants, coffee shops, and other small retailers—the types of establishments that seem conducive to public Wi-Fi. In the 78702 area, however, its proximity to the CBD and the large presence of commercial zones do not translate into more public Wi-Fi venues. In comparison to three other zip code areas near the CBD, public Wi-Fi hotspots are visibly sparse in 78702. The 78702 area also displays a much weaker locational correspondence between commercial zones and public Wi-Fi.

Testimonies of participants underscored the importance of free public Wi-Fi in their daily work routines. These Austinites highly appreciate the ability to do work outside the office for different reasons. Working at a public space translates into the possibility of "getting the job done" while reading news, surfing the Internet, or doing other online activities. Public wireless Internet also allows users to combat feelings of isolation by working in public spaces surrounded by other people. This style of working is associated with "higher quality of life" and a "better work environment." For example, one interviewee reported,

> I enjoy getting out of the house and being with other folks. I'm self-employed. This way I get to work around people. I don't have to be isolated. Free public wireless access is a fantastic quality-of-life increaser in Austin and really sets Austin apart from many cities in the U.S. (or world). I have largely restructured my working life due to free wireless—I now spend many weekday mornings at a local coffee shop that offers free wireless where I can work quietly and effectively away from distractions. I support the coffee shop extensively (buying coffee and food) so that this remains profitable for them.[17]

Nonetheless, although Wi-Fi is increasing the quality of life of mobile Internet users, and reinvigorating the function of public spaces in the local economy, these benefits remain confined to privileged areas and can further reinforce historical divides in the city.

THE SOCIAL SHAPING OF UNEQUAL WI-FI ACCESS IN AUSTIN

The public Wi-Fi sites operated by the City of Austin government (jointly with the AWCP) have helped reduce the gap in public Wi-Fi opportunities between disadvantaged neighborhoods and the rest of the city, and between commercial and noncommercial access sites. However, the city government has deployed public Wi-Fi in a rather restricted way.

During the 1990s the City of Austin attempted to build a citywide advanced telecommunications network serving the citizens, businesses, and institutions using installed capabilities and the municipal fiber rings surrounding the city (Berquist and Grant 1999). However, the passage of a state bill prohibiting the provision of telecommunications services by municipal entities in 1995, and the opposition from incumbent telecommunications providers, effectively derailed that initiative. This early experience has shaped the understanding of the City of Austin government about possible opportunities to operate public Wi-Fi networks. As the city government "lit" Wi-Fi access points at different locations, it also imposed restrictions on itself in order to avoid friction with private telecommunications companies. This essentially meant that the city would not deploy public Wi-Fi networks in competition with private broadband services.[18] The city defines the restriction on private-public competition in terms of types of facilities: any residential units and commercial establishments fall outside the scope of the city's public Wi-Fi offering. As a result, it eliminated the possibility of leveraging wireless Internet to expand broadband, using it for last-mile connectivity in underserved areas beyond city facilities.

Another factor restricting the expansion of public Wi-Fi to underserved communities is the commercial model of access driving the deployment of Austin's public Wi-Fi. Here we can define commercial public Wi-Fi as a service through which public Wi-Fi users engage in economic exchanges with the venues or providers. Most of the "free" public Wi-Fi services in Austin are commercial in this regard.

There is also a supply-side issue. The example of the 78702 zip code noted earlier raises questions about the ability of the commercial model of access to make broadband access more equitable. In theory the 78702 area's proximity to the downtown core and the substantial presence of commercial zones within the area are factors conducive to prolific public Wi-Fi connectivity. Yet the area remains severely underserved, symbolizing the social barriers preventing it from being considered as a potential market of public Wi-Fi services. We found anecdotal evidence pointing to the relative lack of interest in public Wi-Fi among businesses east of I-35. The commercial model, which has facilitated the proliferation of public Wi-Fi service in many parts of Austin, appears to be an ineffective framework in socioeconomically challenged communities.

Perhaps the most formidable challenge for a more socioeconomically balanced expansion of public Wi-Fi service in Austin is the relative lack of a publicly oriented social vision among the main actors in Austin's public Wi-Fi initiatives. Our interviews with the key stakeholders revealed that their strategies for wireless service and users

Table 8.2. Who Do Stakeholders See as Their Primary Wi-Fi Customers?

Organizations	Wi-Fi venues	Business-people	Owners of wireless devices	Citizens in general
AWCP	X		X	
AFN			X	X
Commercial WISP 1	X			
Commercial WISP 2	X			
Bandwidth provider 1	X			
Bandwidth provider 2	X			
City government unit 1		X	X	X
City government unit 2			X	
Public library			X	
IC²			X	

Note: The table lists only those organizations whose representatives answered the interview question pertaining to the perceived Wi-Fi users.

generally did not address making public Wi-Fi available to all, including the groups of Austin populations that do not have access to high-speed Internet.

We observed two patterns in the perceptions of primary customers and users among the key stakeholders (Table 8.2). First, the majority of stakeholders agree that the primary customers of public Wi-Fi services are owners of wireless-enabled devices who already enjoy some form of connectivity. However, only two entities (a city government unit and AFN) recognize public Wi-Fi as a resource for all citizens. Second, many providers identify commercial venues as the main customers of their services, indicating contractual relationships between providers and venues. Beyond these perceptions, however, stakeholders did not express visions of future users of public Wi-Fi. Specifically, stakeholders have not envisioned broadening the user base to include lower socioeconomic residents of Austin. The lack of a solid social vision for the benefits of the technology for all is illustrated by the responses of stakeholders to our question regarding their plans for deploying or facilitating public Wi-Fi in East Austin.

Issues of sustainability of public Wi-Fi networks, perceived lack of familiarity with the technology, and socioeconomic factors were cited as main reasons for not attempting deployment of public Wi-

Fi in poorer areas. However, these views among the stakeholders do not necessarily suggest a lack of awareness about the new inequalities created around Wi-Fi connectivity. Indeed, the deployment of a few public Wi-Fi access sites by the city government in libraries and parks in East Austin was a conscious decision to close the Wi-Fi access gap. Yet, other institutions and organizations—individually or collectively—have so far failed to formulate a clear strategy for making the benefits of public Wi-Fi available to all.

CONCLUSION

Our assessment of Austin's public Wi-Fi landscape reveals that the opportunities created by the unlicensed spectrum are materializing in two different directions. On the one hand, we found evidence of the proliferation of new spaces for high-speed connectivity in the city, leading to more commercial activities and innovations benefiting the local economy. On the other hand, public Wi-Fi networks are growing in an uneven fashion, further enhancing connectivity in commercial areas and more affluent areas while leaving behind underserved populations in less affluent neighborhoods of the city.

Swift growth and a multiplicity of public Wi-Fi initiatives in Austin have primarily been supported by the existence of a strong demand for wireless broadband services. Workers of the creative economy in Central Texas serve as a well-established market for these services. But these users have not acted as mere consumers of innovations. Employing their technical expertise and entrepreneurial interest, Wi-Fi user groups and start-ups organized multipurpose organizations that have promoted, installed, and maintained open Wi-Fi networks throughout the city. In reality, the organized actions of these groups have promoted the adoption of the technology most heavily in commercial venues. The AWCP, the principal institutional body behind the so-called free Wi-Fi movement in town, has transformed into the single largest provider of public Wi-Fi service in the city.

The multiplicity of initiatives has also been facilitated by a strong network of collaboration and partnerships among stakeholders. Relying on the technical expertise among members, and acting as demand aggregator of Wi-Fi services, the AWCP has played the role of intermediary between broadband providers and Wi-Fi venues. The AWCP has also formed a partnership with the local government, providing support to open Wi-Fi networks in city facilities. These examples show

how private-nonprofit or private-public partnerships actually facilitate the provisioning of a new public Internet access service.

Institutional arrangements have contributed to shaping the access models available in the city. Our survey of venues found that venue-sponsored, or free-to-end-user, access is the prevailing model of public Wi-Fi access in the city. Under this model, the venue bears the cost of bandwidth and, in many cases, the cost of the wireless access point equipment needed for the delivery of Wi-Fi service to their customers. Users perceive this service as free. The popularity of this model is the byproduct of the articulation of diverse interests among providers, user groups, commercial establishments, research institutions, nonprofits, and the local government. The motives for embracing this model are diverse and reflect the unique visions of individual actors.

It is undeniable that the venue-sponsored model has become the hallmark of the AWCP, promoter of the free Wi-Fi movement in Austin. Through the formation and the activities of the AWCP, the visions of the user groups evolved from the original, self-serving idea of wireless enthusiasts seeking the convenience of connectivity into a wider conception of public Wi-Fi as a service for everyone.

The city government has sponsored free hotspots to fulfill three different goals. First, it extends and enhances broadband access at existing facilities where the city already offers public Internet access (e.g., libraries). Second, it enhances access to e-government services for citizens and for groups who use city facilities for gatherings and conferences (e.g., convention center events). Third, the city has installed Wi-Fi for its own operations and use (e.g., health services).

AFN espouses free-to-end-user connectivity in some of its public Internet access sites as a cost-effective solution to enhance connectivity at these locations. However, the inherent limitation of existing nonprofit Wi-Fi initiatives is the lack of access to the necessary equipment (i.e., laptops and other wireless devices) among the very segments of the population they intend to serve. Groups working to enhance access to and use of high-speed services identified the relative cost of the equipment and issues of mobility as factors preventing them from developing a more effective strategy to bring the benefits to all.

Despite the abundance of local talent and technological expertise, and a dense network of collaboration among the public and private institutions, we observed an uneven growth of public Wi-Fi infrastructure. Wi-Fi initiatives are mostly serving the best-connected and technologically savvy users of the Internet in the city. Public access of high-speed wireless services is virtually absent in the city's ethnic minority and low-income areas. We identified three main factors preventing a more aggressive employment of Wi-Fi networks for furthering access to high-speed services in low-income Austin communities.

First, although the geographic unevenness has been remedied to a certain extent by the deployment of public Wi-Fi in city facilities (e.g., public libraries and parks), the local government currently expresses no intention of entering the provision of public Wi-Fi service beyond its facilities. Neither does it have plans to circumvent the barrier of access imposed by the high cost of wireless devices. One informant described these decisions as a "common sense" choice based on the understanding that public and private sectors have clearly demarcated territories for their services. The course of action taken by the city government with respect to public Wi-Fi deployment can be interpreted as the legacy of legislation passed in 1995 restricting municipal telecommunications provision in the state of Texas in order to reserve telecommunications services for private business. This historical lesson has prevented the city from developing local expertise or different types of local interventions to promote digital inclusion of underserved populations.

Second, we found that the proliferation of public Wi-Fi sites is mostly confined to commercial, more affluent areas of the city, and that the majority of hotspots (for-fee and venue-sponsored) are strongly associated with sites of consumption. Arguably, the implicit commercial transaction between these Wi-Fi venues and their customers may restrict access for those with less financial means.

Third, although stakeholders manifested awareness about the new inequalities created around Wi-Fi connectivity in the city, the majority of them have not formulated clear solutions to extend connectivity to the underserved population. Furthermore, most of the key stakeholders do not see themselves as having a role in fulfilling this task. The situation begs for a more proactive framework—whether in the form of specific regulations or a new political discourse—to guide and inform local initiatives about ways in which technology can be distributed and used more equitably. The main redress to this problem so far has come in the form of the Dell Foundation and Austin Public Library program to loan laptops to youth who don't otherwise have access to them. The public libraries also function as public Wi-Fi hotspots that the youth can use. However, their homes and nearby commercial venues still will not have the dense wireless networks that have grown up in more affluent areas.

Wireless platforms have become a strategic component of local-level initiatives for fostering universal broadband access, innovation, and economic development. The case of public Wi-Fi in Austin illustrates how the unlicensed spectrum can be transformed into a valuable resource for new businesses, public services, civic interactions, and local economic development. Austin's experience also shows that the unlicensed spectrum as a resource bears different meanings for stakeholders. The unlicensed spectrum has been transformed into services for citizens, a means of communication for nonprofit groups, a valuable commodity for trade, and an amenity in commercial venues. The coexistence of this multiplicity of uses has been enabled through institutional arrangements between stakeholders. Such arrangements can take the form of commercial relations, volunteer actions, information sharing, or visioning. It is precisely these shared visions and institutional collaborations that prevented even greater disparities in wireless access from materializing in Austin. The active involvement of local stakeholders in the comanagement of the resource has been a crucial factor in creating an environment in which multiple users are sustained.

However, entrepreneurial drive and local management do not ensure that broader societal needs will be met. The uneven growth of public Wi-Fi in Austin poses questions about the ability of local actors to address these problems. More thinking and efforts are required to deliver the promise of universal broadband access using the unlicensed spectrum. We contend that enhanced access through public wireless broadband networks will become a crucial component in these efforts.

The history of Austin, discussed elsewhere in this book, has resulted in a city that has inequality woven into its spatial fabric. We find that efforts to shape the distribution of public Wi-Fi from above and below (de Certeau 1984) largely remain within a commercial framework that privileges those who are already connected. So far, these efforts have been unable to overcome the historical and spatial layers of unequal geographies in Austin.

For more than a decade, telecommunications policy scholars have called attention to the need to expand traditional definitions of universal service to account for different layers of access, including devices that support connectivity to advanced services, as well as software and content requiring specialized skills. Wireless Internet brings new arguments to the table, calling for reconsideration of old notions of access, as well as new solutions that use the sum total of networks' capabilities to extend connectivity to all. Wireless broadband has created new possibilities to turn the old problem of building the last-mile connection into users' first-mile access to the online world. The potential of this technology lies in its uses (Dutton et al. 2004), and its promise will not be fulfilled until stakeholders make a political decision to work on more balanced forms of public access. This effort will require intervention in underserved areas, higher level of coordination, and strategic thinking to renew concerns for activities that promote digital inclusion.

NOTES

1. We would like to express our thanks to the Telecommunications and Information Policy Institute at the University of Texas for funding this research. Some of the results in this paper also appear in the article "Reconfiguring Public Internet Access in Austin, TX: Wi-Fi's Promise and Broadband Divides," to be published in the journal *Government Information Quarterly*.

2. Interview with an Austin Free-Net representative, August 11, 2004.

3. Interview with a City of Austin Airport Authority representative, August 6, 2004.

4. Interview with an Austin Wireless Project representative, May 11, 2004.

5. Interview with an Austin Unleashed executive, July 27, 2004.

6. "Technopolis" or "technopole" is commonly used to refer to initiatives that foster technology-based economic development.

7. Founding members included two University of Texas institutes (IC² and the WNCG), the Greater Austin Chamber of Commerce, and companies such as SBC, Tuanis Technologies, and Metrowerks.

8. Interview with an Austin Wireless Alliance representative, August 14, 2004.

9. Interview with an Austin Public Library representative, July 28, 2004.

10. For example, the 78702 zip code area, which corresponds to a historically disadvantaged area just east of the downtown, on the other side of the interstate, has the city's highest rate of households under the poverty level (25.5 percent). The figure is vastly worse than Austin's average (9.2 percent). Only 36 percent of the population on the east side of the city is non-Hispanic white, well below the city average of 53 percent.

11. We identified a total of 220 public Wi-Fi access points within Austin's city limits as of the end of September 2004. We base our analyses in this section on these venues.

12. The few access points visible on the map in east and southeast Austin are special cases; they are located at the Austin-Bergstrom International Airport and some of the hotels adjacent catering to airport users.

13. Interview with an SBC Lab executive, October 13, 2004.

14. Based on authors' casual observation during numerous visits to public Wi-Fi sites during research.

15. Based on various interviews cited throughout this paper.

16. The area within Austin's jurisdictional boundary was divided into forty-six concentric bands of circles with a 0.5 km increment. $r = -.730$, $N = 46$, $p < .01$, two tails.

17. Interview with an anonymous user, July 18, 2004.

18. Interview with a senior administrator of the City of Austin, Communications and Technology Management Department, August 9, 2004.

REFERENCES

Austin Wireless City Project lights up community network: Making cool places hot and hot places hotter. (2003). *Business Wire*, October 23. Retrieved November 21, 2004, from LexisNexis Academic.

AWCG (Austin Wireless City Group). (2004). Retrieved April 3, 2004, from http://www.austinwireless.net/cgi-bin/index.cgi; no longer available.

Bar, F., and H. Galperin. (2004). Building the wireless Internet infrastructure: From cordless Ethernet archipelagos to wireless grids. Paper presented at the European Communications Policy Research Conference, Barcelona, Spain, March.

Berquist, L., and A. E. Grant. (1999). The emerging municipal information infrastructure: The Austin experience. In D. Hurley and J. H. Keller (Eds.), *The first 100 feet*, pp. 173–193. Cambridge, MA: MIT Press.

Callon, M. (1987). Society in the making: The study of technology as a tool for sociological analysis. In W. Bijker, T. Hughes, and T. Pinch (Eds.), *The social construction of technology*, pp. 83–103. Cambridge, MA: MIT Press.

Cooper, M. (2004). The public interest in open communication networks. White paper of the Consumer Federation of America, July. Retrieved March 10, 2005, from http://www.consumerfed.org/Public_Interest_in_Open_Communications_Networks_White_Paper.pdf.

de Certeau, M. (1984). *The practices of everyday life*. Berkeley: University of California Press.

Dutton, W. H. (1999). Society on the line: Information politics in the digital age. Oxford: Oxford University Press.

Dutton, W. H., S. E. Gillett, L. W. McKnight, and M. Peltu. (2004). Bridging broadband Internet divides: Reconfiguring access to enhance communicative power. *Journal of Information Technologies* 19:28–38.

Evans, E., J. Lebkowsky, L. Welter, G. Hung, D. Mayfield, and H. Gangadharbatla. (2004). Austin's wireless future. IC² Institute, University of Texas at Austin, January. Retrieved January 25, 2004, from http://www.ic2.org/publications/AustinsWirelessFuture.pdf.

FCC (Federal Communications Commission). 2010. Connecting America: Na-

tional broadband plan. Retrieved May 4, 2010, from http://www.broadband
.gov/plan/broadband-action-agenda.html.

———. 2005a. Reports on the availability of high-speed and advanced telecommunications services. Retrieved April 10, 2005, from http://www.fcc.gov/broad
band/706.html.

———. 2005b. FCC: Strategic goals: Broadband. Retrieved March 19, 2005, from
http://www.fcc.gov/broadband/Welcome.html.

Florida, R. (2002). *The rise of the creative class: And how it's transforming work,
leisure, community and everyday life.* New York: Basic Books.

Guthrie, K., and W. Dutton. (1992). The politics of citizen access technology. *Policy Studies Journal* 20(4): 574–597.

Horrigan, J. (2010). Broadband adoption and use in America. OBI Working Paper
Series I, Federal Communications Commission.

Law, J., and J. Hassard (Eds.). (1999). *Actor-network theory and after.* London:
Routledge.

Lehr, W., and L. W. McKnight. (2003). Wireless Internet access: 3G vs. Wi-Fi. *Telecommunications Policy* 27:351–370.

Lievrouw, L. (2002). Determination and contingency in new media development:
Diffusion of innovations and social shaping of technology perspectives. In
Leah Lievrouw and Sonia Livingstone (Eds.), *Handbook of new media: Social
shaping and consequences of ICTs,* pp. 183–200. London: Sage.

MacKinnon, R. (2004.) Richard MacKinnon on building a community wireless
organization. *Muniwireless.* Retrieved August 3, 2004, from http://muniwire
less.com/community/guests/396; no longer available.

Oden, M., S. Strover, N. Inagaki, G. Arosemena, and C. Lucas, (2002). Links to
the future: Information and telecommunications technology and economic
development in the Appalachian region. Report to the Appalachian Regional
Commission.

Pinch, T. J., and W. E. Bijker. (1987). The social construction of facts and artifacts:
Or how the sociology of science and the sociology of technology might benefit each other. In W. E. Bijker, T. P. Hughes, and T. Pinch (Eds.), *The social construction of technological systems: New directions in the sociology and history of technology,* pp. 17–50. Cambridge, MA: MIT Press.

Rao, B., and M. A. Parikh. (2003). Wireless broadband drivers and their social implications. *Technology and Society* 25:477–489.

Schwartz, J. (2004). In Austin, paving a way past invisible tollbooths. *New York
Times,* May 12.

Slam, R. (2004). Wi-Fi clouds and zones: A survey of municipal wireless initiatives.
A report of the Mobile Media Consortium, University of Georgia, August.

Smilor, R. W., G. Kozmetsky, and D. V. Gibson. (1988). *Creating the technopolis: Linking technology commercialization and economic development.* Cambridge, MA: Ballinger.

Snider, J. H., and F. Harold. (2004). FCC comments: Unlicensed sharing of TV
band. New America Foundation, November 30. Retrieved May 4, 2005, from
http://www.newamerica.net/Download_Docs/pdfs/Doc_File_2076_1.pdf; no
longer available.

Straubhaar, J. D., S. Strover, K. E. Gustafson, N. Inagaki, and M. Fuentes-Bautista.

(2005). Critically evaluating market diffusion policy and the digital divide in Texas, 2000–2004. Paper presented at the 55th International Communication Association Conference, New York.

Strover, S. (2003). Remapping the digital divide. *Information Society* 19(4): 275–278.

Strover, S., J. Straubhaar, N. Inagaki, K. Gustafson, and A. Boa-Ventura. (2004). E-government services in Texas: results of public survey. Report submitted to the Department of Information Resources, Texas, July.

Turner, S. D. (2005). Broadband reality check: The FCC ignores America's digital divide. Free Press. Retrieved April 30, 2005, from http://www.freepress.net/docs/broadband_report.pdf.

Wasserman, S., and K. Faust. (1994). *Social network analysis: Methods and applications*. Cambridge, UK: Cambridge University Press.

White House. (2004). A new generation of American innovation. April. Retrieved April 30, 2005, from http://www.whitehouse.gov/infocus/technology/economic_policy200404/chap4.html.

———. (2011). President Obama details plan to win the future through expanded wireless access. Press release, February 10. Retrieved February 25, 2011, from http://whitehouse.gov/the-press-office/2011/02/10/president-obama-details-plan-win-future-through-expanded-wireless-access.

Williams, R., and Edge, D. (1996). The social shaping of technology. *Research Policy* 25:856–899.

VIVIANA ROJAS

JOSEPH STRAUBHAAR

JEREMIAH SPENCE

DEBASMITA
ROYCHOWDHURY

OZLEM OKUR

JUAN PIÑON

MARTHA
FUENTES-BAUTISTA

CHAPTER 9

COMMUNITIES, CULTURAL CAPITAL, AND DIGITAL INCLUSION

TEN YEARS OF TRACKING TECHNO-DISPOSITIONS AND TECHNO-CAPITAL

Much of the debate about the digital divide has centered on the question of who has access to computers and the Internet, as described in Chapter 5. However, as we and others (e.g., Warschauer 2004) have called for, we need to rethink the idea beyond mere access to the capabilities required to be interested in such tools and to use them. In this chapter we document our research efforts to understand the social and cultural barriers that remain in place when most conventional remedies, such as public access centers, Internet-connected schools and libraries, and computer-skills training, became fairly widely available. We wanted to see which groups, including minorities, did or did not use information and communication technologies (ICTs), and why.

Here, we examine comparatively the purpose, design, and findings of two related studies conducted over a ten-year period during the fall of 1999 and spring of 2000, and the spring of 2009. A total of fifty interviews obtained during these years (thirty-six from 1999–2000, and fourteen from 2009) are included in the analysis. Theoretical and methodological challenges are discussed in this longitudinal comparison of case studies drawn from Austin over a period of a decade. Austin is a highly wired city, as indicated in Chapter 8, but with high contrast in terms of digital inclusion, as Chapters 6 and 7 indicate.

The second study used a slightly modified version of two 1999 interview guides. (See Appendix 9.1 for the 1999 interview guide.) We sought to understand the social construction of information technology in the lives of working-class and poor Hispanics and African Americans in East Austin. We examined the economic and social causes for why many individuals and families in disadvantaged communities did not have, did not use, or did not seek access to new technologies. Among other factors, these causes included class, ethnicity, age, geographic location, and gender-role constraints. Our analyses focused on the sources of cultural capital these individuals and families employed as they decided whether and how to make use of technology in their lives. These forms of cultural capital contributed to "techno-dispositions" regarding ICTs.

A central question in 1999–2000 was whether lower-class, minority youth and their parents were forming a more durable and consistent class pattern, or *habitus* (Bourdieu 1984), of not using ICTs than was commonly understood. Interviews with teenagers, college students, their parents, and sometimes their siblings were structured to answer this question. Their responses to questions about their life history and family trajectories as well as a specific questionnaire on information technology access and use were discussed in the first study (see Rojas, Straubhaar, Roychowdhury, and Okur 2004).

The same inquiry remained central in 2009, because we wanted to see whether that same habitus—the seemingly durable pattern among Latinos and African Americans that leaned away from very extensive ICT use—was still evident. In 2009, we developed a more sophisticated theoretical and methodological framework that focused on family trajectories, the transmission of cultural capital and dispositions, and generational differences (Bertaux 1981; Bertaux and Bertaux-Wiame 1997; Bertaux and Thompson 1997; González 1986; Spence 2007). We had begun to see changes in the way minority youth were using media, in that more of them seemed to become involved with ICTs as they diffused into society, but we wondered what generational trajectories or continuities existed between them and other generations within their families. We also wondered whether youth were beginning to influence their parents and others toward greater ICT use. Since in our first study we noticed that some minority youth and adults continued to use ICTs less, we wanted to look more deeply at why. We noticed in 2000 that among Latinos, recent immigrants were particularly less likely to use ICTs, so in 2009 we examined more closely the impacts of generations of migration and the transference of cultural capital among generations.

MINORITIES AND TECHNOLOGICAL CAPITALS AND USES

The studies by the National Telecommunications and Information Administration reviewed in Chapter 5 found that several demographic variables, including income, education level, race, age, and household makeup, were associated with gaps in access to and use of new ICTs. Researchers have addressed the intersection of ICTs, race, gender, and class in diverse ways.

Drawing on Pierre Bourdieu's concept of cultural capital, one researcher (Reza 1998) illustrated that education was the main anticipated factor in access to and use of home computers. Education also mediated the transition from lower to higher socioeconomic class.

Reports by the Pew Internet and American Life Project (Jansen 2010; Jones and Fox 2009) have suggested for some time that Internet penetration may be reaching social limits in the case of groups that do not regard ICTs as advantageous to their lives. The Pew studies have highlighted this among older Americans, but earlier studies by the Tomás Rivera Policy Institute also indicated that many Hispanic heads of families were ambivalent about the Internet (Wilhelm 1998). A Kaiser Family Foundation report (1999) asserted that children who live or attend school in lower-income communities spent more time with most types of media than children in wealthier neighborhoods, but were significantly less likely to use computers. Largely because of income differences, children from minority groups have tended to have substantially less access to computers outside of school. Racial disparities in computer use among two- to seven-year-olds who are not yet in school are particularly pronounced, with white children about twice as likely as African American or Hispanic children to use a computer (Singer and Singer 2005). In 2000, the discussion on the digital divide took mainly a structural point of view, and many analyses pointed to income as a key issue in access. However, we argued then that a fundamental number of aspects of the digital divide persisted above and beyond income and the ability to afford access: notably group disposition (or habitus), based in part on income disparities, but also education, cultural patterns, family trajectories, and the structure of opportunities. Today, those factors still remain in place.

Bourdieu's key concepts of habitus, field, and capital provided us with an opportunity to apply his theory to the area of social practices and digital inclusion and develop new concepts to describe the phenomenon under observation: techno-dispositions, techno-field, and techno-capital. These interrelated concepts refer to people's dispositions toward technology as a variable of how much they know about them and what the perceived role is in their lives. (The concepts are elaborated in more detail in Chapter 1.) As our research progressed, we wanted to achieve a more comprehensive individual-structural interaction perspective, and we focused our attention beyond the sphere of the individual choices into the realm of intergenerational families, using family history as a method of analysis (Bertaux and Thompson 1997; Andorka 1997; González 1997, 2000). By tracking family histories in Austin, it is possible to make sense of the different factors that constitute the structural socioeconomic conditions impacting access and use of new technologies, such as particular processes of migration, social and linguistic capital, generational status, and family transference of cultural and economic capital.

INEQUALITIES AND THE SOCIOLOGY OF BOURDIEU

Bourdieu describes habitus as a set of dispositions that create "durable" and "transposable" practices and perceptions over a long process of social inculcation. The similarity of dispositions and practices experienced by members of the same social class constitutes a class habitus for Bourdieu (Johnson 1993). Such shared orientations help explain why groups acquire and hold dispositions against the use of certain technologies like networked computers, even when those technologies become accessible and receive favorable publicity in the media.

These kinds of dispositions seem specific to groups defined by more than just economic class. Bourdieu highlights that it is the *interrelationship* between different pertinent properties (sex, age, economic and cultural capital, ethnicity, education, and so on) that constitutes a social class, rather than simply a collection of demographic properties. Both this theory and prior empirical work on the digital divide seem to suggest that combinations of interrelated factors or characteristics should be analyzed—notably economic capital, cultural capital, linguistic capital, ethnicity, age, and gender—to understand something as subtle as a disposition toward a technology (Schement 1998; Hoffman and Novak 1998). When these dispositions are held by a number of people in the same class circumstances, we can speak of a class habitus toward technology, or a techno-habitus.

Although the literature on social capital strongly emphasizes its positive consequences, Alejandro Portes (1998) notes that the network of associations that social capital embodies can have negative effects as well. There is a sociological bias "to see good things emerging out of sociability; bad things are more commonly associated with the behavior of *homo economicus*. However, the same mechanisms appropriable by individuals and groups as social capital can have other, less desirable consequences" (Portes 1998, 15). Portes labels this "negative social capital." Social capital within youth gangs, for example, may lead to connections and networks that enable "success" in what would be considered criminal behavior. In a preliminary focus group before our 1999 interviews began, Straubhaar observed that when one minority boy began to talk about computers with some excitement, another scowled and shut him up, as if to say, "Guys like us are not into that stuff," which would be a social network deterrent to the acquisition of techno-capital by the first boy.

AUSTIN AS A WIRED CASE STUDY

Austin should present a best-case scenario for narrowing the digital divide. This dynamic southwestern city has a thriving information economy, as described in Chapters 3 and 4, which tends to pull people toward technologically oriented education as well as training for the new jobs the sector creates. However, Hispanics and African Americans in Austin face more than a digital divide; they face ethnic, gender, education, income, and neighborhood divides too, as described in Chapter 2. In a city with a dynamic information economy, and with strong educational institutions and Internet access in most homes, there is an ever-widening wealth gap that affects working-class residents.

1999–2000 STUDY: JOHNSTON HIGH SCHOOL

The first study was developed during the fall of 1999 and spring of 2000 at Johnston High School in East Austin and included twelve families with children who were students in a ninth-grade algebra class. The parents allowed their children to participate in, and agreed themselves to be interviewed for, a study exploring how ethnic minorities perceived the role of technology in their lives. Members of nine Hispanic families, two African American families, and one white family participated in at least two hour-long interviews. We thought that semistructured in-depth interviews would provide a richer data for the purpose of our study. We wanted to understand how people made sense of what they heard and saw about computers and the Internet, while also probing the origin of the cultural capital and dispositions they employed when deciding whether to make use of these technologies. The interview research was intended to be inductive in the sense of letting participants speak for themselves without an a priori superimposition of theory. Still, the project began by assuming that family trajectories, life experiences, and social structures help to form cultural capital, which in turn affects perceptions and use of new ICTs. Interviews were carried out by a group of twenty-one students, both undergraduate and graduate, enrolled in a research seminar on the digital divide in the College of Communication at the University of Texas in 1999–2000.

Upon completion of the interviews, we proceeded to analyze the transcripts according to the constructs of techno-dispositions, techno-field, and techno-capital. This would be the only time in our longitudinal study in which we would interview only two generations of a family (parents and children). The study of three or more generations emerged later as a necessity to understand in more perspective the interrelation between habitus and the social practices of media and information technology in a historical perspective of the family trajectory.

We started with the assumption that the internal stratification and inequities within Austin were on display in the public schools. After initial contacts and collaborations with administrators and teachers at Johnston High, we defined that campus as the setting for our study. While the Austin Independent School District (AISD) has a number of excellent high schools, Johnston High was routinely portrayed in newspaper accounts as a neglected and troubled school. It was considered one of thirteen "low-performing" schools in AISD, according to standardized test scores (Kurtz and McEntee 2000). After five years of failure under the state's accountability system, the school was closed in 2007. AISD has since repurposed the campus as East Side Memorial High School, which includes three schools: a high-tech vocational high school, an early-college campus, and an international high school (Borget 2008). At the time of our study in 1999–2000, Johnston High—similarly to other poor schools in the United States—did not have a ratio of computers to students that could have assured even a minimum access to new technology. Field notes by Straubhaar from 1999 indicate that Johnston had only six accessible computers in a temporary library in the girls' gym, plus computers in about half of the classrooms for teachers' use. According to Straubhaar's observation, more computers were sitting in boxes awaiting the conclusion of a construction project that had been dragging out for over a year, while comparable construction at upscale Austin High had been finished quickly.

Several research questions guided our first study:

- How do parents and teenagers in disadvantaged communities perceive the importance of ICTs in their lives?
- What attitudes do parents and teenagers in disadvantaged communities have toward computers and the Internet?
- What cultural capital about technology (or techno-capital) do these parents transfer to their children?
- What techno-capital are these children receiving from school and other sources?

FINDINGS

In our first study we found that family resources, class economic habitus, and associated life trajectories form a set of boundaries that place limits on the formation of positive techno-dispositions. Within those bounds, ethnicity seems to powerfully affect different sources of capital that might form techno-capital. Among both the older and younger age groups, ethnicity seemed to frame how gender was constructed. Class, ethnicity, and gender all affected techno-dispositions.

To illustrate the complexity of the various forces at play in the formation of techno-capital, consider the example of a Hispanic mother and her ninth-grade son interviewed for this study. The boy watched his mother work her way up from welfare recipient to Walmart clerk to secretary. She was very proud of having her own office space, desk, and computer. She saw herself as upwardly mobile and wanted to get her son involved in information technology work. Indeed, she would have liked him to focus on technology as a life endeavor. But first she had to try to overcome prevailing attitudes about minorities and technology in East Austin. She was irritated that counselors at Johnston High suggested to her son that he think about going into refrigerator repair, instead of more academic courses, an example of the tendency of school institutions to reproduce class status rather than transform it, as noted by Bourdieu (1977).

The son liked drawing but had trouble getting into art courses at the high school. He seemed to want to be an architect, but didn't realize that drafting and design work was already computer aided. He had little exposure to computers at school, except as a tool for word processing. Nor did he have any adult male role models who used information technology at work or during their off-hours. In a focus group for this study, his friends told him computers and the Internet were for geeks. One boy asked as an aside, "Who would want to be one of those computer geeks?" The same classmate noted in another aside during the group discussion that a billboard for a local Internet service provider, which exhorted passersby to call "1-800-BE-A-GEEK," was off-putting.

If we think about his case in sociological terms, this minority teen was receiving conflicting pieces of both cultural and social capital. On the one hand, his mother pushed him toward acquiring techno-capital and encouraged a positive disposition toward information technology. On the other hand, his school counselor, friends, adult male role models, and, to some degree, the media (at least commercial messages) seemed to be either directly or indirectly telling him to be negatively disposed toward ICTs. (A parallel study of popular radio stations in Austin in 1999 found that black- and Hispanic-oriented stations carried significantly fewer advertisements for computers, software, or Internet services than did white- or general-population-oriented stations [Rupertus, Straubhaar, and LaPastina 2001].)

1999–2000 FINDINGS 1: PARENTS' LIFE TRAJECTORIES AND TECHNO-CAPITAL

Among the nine Hispanic parents interviewed for this research, all but one were of Mexican heritage, either first-, second-, or third-generation immigrants. The one exception was a mother of Puerto Rican descent. Most first-generation-immigrant parents interviewed described their life in this country as one of bare survival and commented on how their parents had little or no schooling. These parents worked as various skilled laborers—baker, truck driver, carpenter, and school janitor, among others. The five poorest families spoke Spanish at home. But even though they were fluent in their native tongue, they all recognized that they had difficulties reading and writing in Spanish. Only three parents had earned a high school diploma; none had a college degree.

Of the two African American mothers interviewed, one was very poor and had been on and off welfare, while the other was working class, with a fairly steady job. The one white, non-Hispanic parent interviewed was a recently divorced woman, a computer professional who ordinarily would be considered middle class. Her residence in the low-income Johnston High district was anomalous, a result of temporary poverty due to the divorce. Most of the parents had married young—during or before their twenties. Five of the couples had been married for around twenty years; one mother had remarried twice, but several remained divorced or single.

Almost all the families interviewed considered education as a highly regarded commodity. Some immigrant families had sacrificed their goal of returning to their country of origin to assure their children's stability in school. All the Hispanic parents interviewed wanted their children to graduate from high school. For several, their immediate concern was to keep their children from dropping out of school. However, with regard to higher education, only two students among the poorest five Hispanic families clearly stated that their goal was to continue on to college, and only one of the Hispanic mothers said she was committed to helping her kids do so. Desire to attend college was clearer among the three Hispanic families slightly higher on the socioeconomic scale (lower middle class). Part of the class habitus that limited most of these families is the perception that high school, rather than college, is the culmination of a formal education. Indeed, the teens we interviewed tended to reflect the educational aspirations that their parents had for them.

Parents, especially from the immigrant families from Mexico, recognized that they themselves had lacked access to the newest communication technologies in their youth, such as radio, telephone, and television. When interviewed, they possessed most of the then-latest consumer technologies, including media and communication devices like cell phones, VCRs, stereos, cordless telephones with caller ID, and video games, as well as household appliances like microwave ovens, washers, and dryers. In most of our respondents' households there also were one or two cars. But despite all this investment in media and technology, there were very few computers. Only four families out of the twelve we interviewed did own a computer. Half of the parents did not have access to a computer at home or work, and only a few parents knew how to surf the Internet. Through television shows and news, several parents were aware of the possible negative consequences of the Internet for teenagers, especially access to pornography, which led to conflicting techno-dispositions among some parents.

1999–2000 FINDINGS 2:
TEENAGERS AND TECHNO-CAPITAL

Comments from the teenage respondents reflected a wider use of media technologies than their parents. Their usage included radio and television, stereos, VCRs, cell phones, pagers, and CD players. The use of multiple media technologies illustrated these teens' capacity to comprehend and appropriate ICTs (excepting computers) in everyday life. Their media savvy constituted an integral part of their techno-competencies; however, their technology use was largely entertainment oriented. The interviews revealed that most of our teenaged respondents were avid video game players. Some of the teens suggested that video games stimulated their interest in new media technology.

Most of our teenage respondents said their awareness about the Internet and computers arose from their social networks, including relatives and classmates. Commenting on the limited appeal of Internet ads on television, they pointed out the commercials' seeming irrelevance to them. Family and friends served as important mediating resources for our respondents' computer competencies. They not only provided some computer access but also conveyed positive dispositions for and familiarity with computer literacy. Immediate family played a particularly supportive role for several of our respondents. Family encouragement for getting out from under their disadvantaged status reinforced the need for education and technological knowledge for social and economic mobility. Several of the boys, as in the example cited earlier, learned about computers from their mothers and aunts, but did not see their "pink collar" jobs as secretaries as something they would aspire to themselves.

Friends also provided much of the discursive and practical space for the introduction and interplay of new technologies in these teens' everyday lives. While few of the families owned a computer or maintained an Internet connection at home, most of our respondents were friends with someone whose parents did. Indeed, many had played computer games or had accessed the Internet at friends' houses. However, they did not really consider this indirect access to technology as their own.

1999–2000 FINDINGS 3: TECHNO-DISPOSITIONS

Although only four of the parents in our group said they worked directly with computers, the parents overall realized the importance of technology for their children's future and seemed willing to acquire their own machine sometime soon. One respondent raised issues of class and socioeconomic status, a Mexican American mother who perceived the new technology to be for the "rich and educated people."

Understanding the parents' and teens' dispositions toward technology requires an appreciation of family dynamics. Like conventional socialization theory, which considers the family to be the key agency of cultural transmission, Bourdieu's conceptual scheme regards the family to be the "primary habitus" (Murdock 1989). The family has "a set of generalized schemes of thought, perception, appreciation and action" through which people think about and respond to the social world (Murdock 1989, 93). Consistent with Bourdieu's idea that a person's class location structures their cultural consumption, it can be argued that families structure the cultural preferences of their members and contribute to the formation of a class ethos.

Poor and working-class families share a class habitus in the sense that they adjust to their social position "either because they feel 'made' for jobs that are 'made' for them . . . or because they adjust their aspirations to their objective chances" (Bourdieu 1984, 110). This process of adjustment and conformity can be analyzed through the concept of class ethos, which designates a "system of implicit and deeply internalized values which, among other things, helps to define attitudes toward cultural capital and educational institutions" (Bourdieu, cited in Swartz 1977, 32). Bourdieu uses this concept to show how parents' educational background affects their children's academic performance. The structures that shape the material world of the parents, and their perception of it, also shape the habitus of their children. This conceptualization of reproduction in part explains why some teenagers and their siblings are at risk of dropping out of school. Bourdieu asserts that whether or not youth stay in school depends appreciably on their perceptions of the probability that people of their social class will succeed academically (Swartz 1977; Bourdieu 1977).

The institutional framework of school likely constitutes the most important arena in which teenage respondents interacted and negotiated with restrictions and resources to develop a repertoire of technological competencies. This repertoire is built through such mechanisms as computer classes that teach basic skills and research assignments that give students the opportunity to apply their knowledge—and learn more on their own. While providing basic instruction in computing and word processing, many computer classes have acquired a "boring" connotation because they focus too heavily on typing skills. For a few of the respondents, the impression that computers were dull had been formed in elementary or middle school, where "keyboarding" was taught on simple machines with monochrome monitors. Some of the male respondents also implied that labels such as "keyboarding" gendered these classes—and computer use generally—as "something girls do." In addition to these social and experiential obstacles, the physical arrangement of computer and Internet access at Johnston High was also problematic. The school district had allowed a construction project, which closed the regular library, to drag on for two years. As a result, the library, ordinarily the point of online access, was "temporarily" housed in a gym with very limited computer network connections.

Respondents' understandings of the Internet reflected their practical encounters with the technology at school and home. From an educational standpoint, the teens perceived the Internet as an efficient tool for researching school projects, whereas for entertainment purposes they regarded it as a medium for following their favorite sports teams and television shows. E-mail and online shopping were also recognized by some of our respondents as relevant ways of using the Internet. Almost all acknowledged computers as important, in one way or another. One female respondent commented, "That's what's going to be it pretty soon, nothing but technology. You're either gonna stay with it or get lost. If you learn about it now, it can help you now and in the future [to get a] better job—if you know how to mess with a computer." However, the idea that the teens we interviewed would use computers in their daily lives seemed somewhat remote to them; it was something they envisioned for the distant future, particularly the boys.

Though rhetoric of the "information age" permeated almost all of the interviews, few of the students had much actual experience with the technology of the Internet. (Some students lived close to a public library branch with Internet access, but they didn't seem curious enough to go.) Even without this experience, the connection between computer skills and upward mobility was something our respondents discursively acknowledged. The students' techno-dispositions were reproduced into practice by way of family encouragement, incentives from school, and, in some cases, motivations from friends. However, as noted above, peers were also discouraging of computer use, particularly for the male students we interviewed. These teens didn't see information technology as occupying a central part, or any part, of their life. This feeling is enhanced in East Austin by the structural arrangements at school and public libraries, where time restrictions and lack of guidance contribute to an unsuccessful experience with the technology.

CONCLUSIONS TO THE 1999–2000 STUDY

The most immediate boundary preventing the poorest of these teens from acquiring techno-capital or a positive techno-disposition was economic class and the formation of a demotivating class habitus that reinforced their social standing, as theorists like Bourdieu (1984) and Vincent Mosco (1996) have suggested. In fact, among the poor and working-class families we interviewed, there appeared to be a homogeneity of dispositions associated with their social position, as posed by Bourdieu. Lack of access to a quality education because of neighborhood placement, the necessity of sustaining a large family on little income, time demands for earning that income, the fact of having a recent immigration history, and the inability of the parents to progress beyond low-paid, unskilled jobs all contributed to the class habitus of the poorest families we interviewed. Deferring their own dreams, many of the parents perceived that they had no option *but* to work as unskilled, manual laborers so their children could perhaps achieve a different position in the social hierarchy.

In the six poorest families we interviewed, computers and Internet access were considered far too expensive for personal adoption; few relatives or friends could afford it either. Further, the cultural capital related to technology (techno-capital) that the parents were able to transfer to their children was minimal or nonexistent—most were barely aware of the new ICTs. These teenagers had little or no knowledge of how computers and the Internet worked, even in the case of those exposed to computers in middle school. Although they recognized a connection between computers and the Internet, they were not able to specify or articulate the relationship. None of the teenagers perceived computers to be of immediate relevance to their lives; despite receiving extra credit for completing school assignments on a word processor, they refused to access the technology at community centers or libraries. Interestingly, even the poorest teens were familiar with household electronics such as VCRs, stereos, microwaves, cordless telephones, and caller ID. Furthermore, all had video games in their homes. Yet, they remained intimidated by computers. None knew the difference, for example, between an IBM-compatible PC and an Apple Macintosh computer. All of our teen respondents had friends who accessed the web for information about their favorite personalities and activities—music, wrestling, sports, and celebrities—but they did not make the connection that they too could access this information if they only visited the community center or library.

Social networks and social capital do not really compensate for this lack of economic and cultural capital in the immediate family. All of the teenagers interviewed for this project knew at least one person or family member who owned a computer. But they did not consider that access their own. Public access didn't necessarily solve the problem either. The connection between libraries and the web "lifestyle" was not established; libraries were just a place to study or get books. Moreover, public libraries were viewed as unfriendly places where people made you be quiet. (The participant observation in libraries in 2009 reported in Chapter 7, however, shows that more minority teens were using libraries for access ten years after our initial study.)

Schools could perhaps introduce new cultural capital for these poorest teenagers, but as Bourdieu (1977) noted, the high school experience tends to reproduce or reinforce the class status, habitus, and social dispositions that children receive from their parents. Regarding the long-term relevance of information technology, our respondents vaguely recognized that it *might* be useful to know how to use a computer at some point in their lives, but for the time being, computing was not something they want to invest effort in.

In the working-class families (those with annual incomes of at least $30,000), greater resources gave parents more possibilities of obtaining computer and Internet access as well as greater cultural capital to work with. Several working-class parents had exposure to computers at work, and some were considering them for home. These parents were more likely to have and to pass on cultural capital and techno-dispositions favorable to computing and Internet use. Indeed, several working mothers were thinking about how to transfer what they were learning at work to their children at home. Within this group, though, parent and child gender mattered, as did social capital from neighbors, friends, and peers about technology. While an African American father could effectively encourage his son, whom we interviewed, to defy peer pressure and pursue his interest in computers, even at the risk of being labeled a "geek," a Hispanic mother we interviewed had a much harder time overcoming her son's peer influences and lack of a male role model to encourage him to develop computer literacy.

In this first study we addressed what Bourdieu calls reproduction of inequalities within a school system that doesn't socially level the students. However, Bourdieu, in the theory of practice, perceives a possibility of change in the tension between agency and structure. This "restricted/constrained freedom" for change comes from the individual who manages to apply strategies (practices) that do not contain the regulatory traces of the structure—that is, they set out to acquire cultural and techno-capital that could be converted to economic capital through improved employment.

In the second study we elaborated more on the role of the family in the transmission of cultural capital and techno-dispositions. In particular, we looked at family trajectory and generational differences across three generations of the same families. Concepts developed in the first study such as techno-field, techno-capital, techno-dispositions, techno-competencies, and techno-habitus remained central in this project.

2009 STUDY: GENERATIONAL CHANGES, TRANSMISSIBILITY, AND SOCIAL MOBILITY

As we laid out in Chapter 1, Austin has become a city in which the field of technology skill, access, and understanding has become the driving force of its economy, and the key to social mobility for families and individuals living there. So we argue here that the techno-field must be at the center of our analysis. How much do people interviewed understand the centrality of the techno-field to work and social mobility in Austin? That perception will greatly affect their techno-disposition and their desire to gain techno-capital. We argue on the basis of these interviews that awareness of the techno-field, the techno-disposition to acquire access, and techno-capital has increased notably from 1999 to 2009 as awareness of the field's centrality moves further into disadvantaged populations. However, many people among the disadvantaged, in particular, are not in positions to do much about it. Furthermore, they may prefer to focus on capitals that are closer to their historical experience, so we want to be very careful to not blame people as individuals or groups for not focusing on the techno-field or techno-capitals. We don't want to fall back into one of the primary pitfalls of the diffusion of innovations model, blaming the victim, the poor or disadvantaged person, for not somehow finding a way to adopt the central new technology (Rogers 1995).

In this study we wanted to expand our analysis of the impact of class and family habitus on the dispositions, use, and knowledge of new technologies of information. We focused on the role families have in the transmission of techno-capital and in the development of techno-competencies across generations. We wanted to know what type of resources (economic, human, cultural, relational) families mobilized to "place" their descendants on desirable social trajectories. How did these resources shape children's trajectory, and what aspects of these intergenerational transmissions were not reappropriated by the children and their siblings?

We conducted intergenerational interviews with four African American and two Hispanic families of college students who had grown up in or currently resided in Austin. This group of families is very different than those interviewed in 1999–2000. Those families lived in one of the poorest neighborhoods and went to the worst high school in Austin. In 2009, we deliberately looked at a group with somewhat different social class profiles and different educational trajectories. We wanted to see what was similar and what was different among minority families who were succeeding in sending at least some of their children to college. This sample lets us see some of the same factors at work as in the 1999–2000 study. Many among these extended families did not finish high school or go to college, but it also allows us to see what kinds of cultural capital and family trajectories made for at least some educational success.

A total of sixteen adult respondents were interviewed twice during the spring of 2009 using a slightly expanded version of the protocol described earlier. Besides participating in the semistructured in-depth interviews, the main informants of each family completed a chart—a socioeconomic genogram—with basic demographic, educational, linguistic, and occupational data from three generations, including maternal and paternal grandparents, parents, and children (Spence 2007). The socioeconomic genograms gave us the socio-historical-spatial perspective for each family, while the interviews allowed us to understand how families participate in games of competition (social mobility) and what children (and later on adults) do with what has been voluntarily or involuntarily transferred to them (Bertaux 1981; Bertaux and Bertaux 1997). Additionally, this qualitative data provided us with a more detailed picture of the access, use, and appropriation of new technologies of information throughout generations.

The study focused on the maternal lineage of six female college students and included interviews with their mothers and grandmothers when available, or a sibling representative of the elder generations. With the exception of one Mexican American father, all the informants were women. Fourteen graduate students participated in the data collection and transcription.

FAMILY TRANSMISSIONS AND TRAJECTORIES

Individuals and families develop different strategies to overcome structural constraints such as poverty, illiteracy, and segregation. Daniel Bertaux and Paul Thompson (1997), delving into Bourdieu's notion of habitus, developed a methodology to study families' social mobility over generations, which they called social genealogies. The approach takes the family as the unit of analysis, the primary site where social status and social mobility is constructed for its members, recognizing that peers, schooling, neighbors, and others have powerful influence as well. Parents attempt to achieve or obtain various capitals (economic, social, and cultural) and other resources, which they try to pass on to their children, but "while the expectations of status achievement that are projected on to the children are obviously related to [the parents'] social status, the concrete resources they are able to pass on to their children, especially key resources of insider's information about the rules of the game and interpersonal connections, are clearly *situs* bond" (Bertaux and Thompson 1997). Bourdieu uses the concept of situs in his explanation of fields and capital, where he frames situs as the present and potential situation of agents or institutions within networks of objective relations (Wacquant 1989, 37).

Family status can be described in terms of the amount of economic, social, and cultural capital accumulated by the family. Families do routinely try to pass on various forms of capital—cultural, economic, social, perhaps even technological—to their children (Bertaux and Thompson 2005). While economic capital may or may not last over generations, there is an argument building that both social and cultural capital are more transmissable between generations, particularly in an emerging information or technology economy in which higher education is increasingly the pathway to well-paid occupations. In fact, Charles Murray (2011) goes so far as to argue that a new kind of class formation, based on what we could call cultural capital, is growing in the USA, as better educated people marry each other and transmit the value of education to their children.

Transmissibility of an element of status as a resource is directly proportional to its degree of objectivation and inversely proportionate to its degree of subjectivation; for example, money has a high degree of transmissibility, whereas parents' personal charisma or prestige has a low degree of transmissibility (Bertaux and Thompson 1997). Because many elements have a low degree of transmissibility, transmissions of status are frequently implemented by transforming a resource into a condition of action, such as choosing to live in a neighborhood with a better school (Bertaux and Bertaux 1997).

The work of Bertaux and Thompson is helpful in applying this concept of capital to family units. Much of their joint research focused on families and social mobility, building on years of intergenerational interviews in Britain and France (1997). These studies have served to demonstrate how "some families transmit particular occupations while most try to maintain their social positions by adaptations, how mobility may be a consequence of family discord as well as ambition, and the different paths followed by men and women" (Bertaux and Thompson 2005, 1).

Bertaux and Thompson (1997) found the distinctions made by Bourdieu between the three main kinds of family assets, or capital (economic capital, cultural capital, and social capital) to be particularly useful in their work. Specifically, transmissibility and the family systems concept lie at the core of Bertaux and Thompson's work (1993, 1997, 2005), and much of how transmissibility functions can be explained by the transmission of the various types of capital from one generation to the next within a family. Not only do parents pass on accumulated wealth—economic capital—to their children, but they also pass on much of their social capital, by introducing their children to the various people they know, and their cultural capital, by exposing their children to various experiences, knowledge, tastes, and habits. Bertaux and Thompson found the family systems approach to be useful in the understanding of transmission in practice.

Jorge González (1997) also used family histories in his research on cultural fields among different publics or social groups in Mexico. The use of family histories allowed for the observation of social trajectories (occupational, spatial, familial, and educational) across at least three generations. Each accumulated family history allowed González to identify and examine dozens of successful and unsuccessful trajectories. In addition to the basic family history, Bertaux and Thompson and also González all used genograms to chart key items of information on ancestors' social mobility—and, in the case of González, information, media, and cultural resource use.

The transference of any form of capital between generations does not follow a continuous line. Likewise, there are ruptures in transmission between generations when new technologies are introduced, like the Internet or cell phones, which permit many new kinds of media use to be taken up, especially by youth. A number of studies, like *Grown Up Digital* (Tapscott 2009), claim that young people have grown up with such intimate familiarity with new media that their overall use of media will be substantially different from that of previous generations. Some (United Nations 2005) acknowledge, however, that poverty and lower educational opportunities will keep some youth away from participation in this generational shift. It is interesting to see in our 2009 study that some parents and grandparents manage to pass along their educational trajectory, a disposition to keep acquiring educational and cultural capital, even though they don't manage to pass on some media habits (which have often been seen as associated with educational and cultural capital), such as reading newspapers and books.

The sociology of stratification and family histories allows us to track the strategies of social mobility where, first, women have a specific place and role; second, family ties matter; and third, generations differ in schooling and vocations. These processes take place under intertwined family-individual relationships within a larger context of the marketplace and collective historical events and structured opportunities (Bertaux and Thompson 1997).

The research questions guiding our study in 2009 were as follows:

- How much continuity is there in educational trajectories (i.e., the disposition to acquire and deploy cultural capital across generations)?
- How much continuity is there in media use between generations? How do parents transmit the importance of new technologies (techno-capital) to the next generations?
- What seems to account for major media habit changes between generations, such as when the children of newspaper readers no longer do so, or when the youngest generation switches both its media and interpersonal communication focus to mobile phones?
- What is the role of gender and kin relationships in the transmission of techno-dispositions and techno-capital inside the family?
- What is the importance of technology in family mobility?
- What is the impact of technology in the social trajectory of different generations?
- How much does the availability of new technology connect to generational differences?
- Are there varying generational similarities and differences in media use between African American and Latino families?

2009 FINDINGS 1: FAMILY TRAJECTORY AND CAPITAL

Although the six families interviewed in this study were all centered in Texas, migration stories permeate their trajectories. Both Hispanic families could track their heritage to Mexican farms or border towns in the great-grandparents' generation. The four African American families had a more steady settlement in Austin or surrounding areas in the past three generations, with internal moves in Texas and some occasional out-of-state migrations by some of their family members. The Mexican American families also had a history of steady residency in the cities of Laredo, Waco, Forth Worth, San Antonio, and Austin. Only one father who migrated from New York and a grandmother who was born in Pensacola, Florida, modified this main pattern of long-established residency in the state of Texas.

Culturally, these families were racially and ethnically homogeneous, with only one white maternal grandparent in a Hispanic family. All the families could be characterized as working class or lower middle class in the majority of the earlier generations, with some upward mobility in the younger generations (grandchildren), although some families had seen earlier mobility through education as well. Over the course of fifty to one hundred years, the families had slowly moved from agricultural and blue-collar jobs to clerical, state, service, and educational jobs. Informants from earlier generations tended to remain longer in the same jobs (e.g., twenty-five years in the day-care business, thirty-three years as an accountant for the Texas Department of Public Safety, and twenty years as a public school nurse before becoming assistant principal for another five years).

Respondents from both the Latino and African American cultural groups had faced experiences of segregation, discrimination, and linguistic prejudice, particularly among the grandparents' and great-grandparents' generations. Their stories indicated the school system as a place where discrimination was enacted, either against themselves or their children, again demonstrating the prevalence of the reproduction of social class in schools (Bourdieu 1977). Respondents also commented on their strategies to cope with the system, such as the case of a Hispanic grandmother who decided (using her own agency) to transfer her children from a public school to a private Catholic school without worrying about how much that would tighten the family budget. That strategy was also repeated later with her granddaughters who are now college students, the siblings with more cultural capital in that line of succession.

The interviews revealed an intense communication between family members in which the current available media technologies, such as telephone, e-mail, and text messages, allowed daily or weekly interaction between parents and children. Beyond mediated communications, most of these family members had regular contact with one another by visiting during weekends, exchanging information, and helping each other resolve problems such as installing programs on their computers. Cell phones played an important role in communicating with family and friends but also in administering their daily lives, particularly in the case of three African American grandmothers who helped raise their grandchildren because the parents worked, went to school, or (in one case) were in prison.

Some grandmothers continued the work of raising children after retirement and were very self-conscious of the importance of their role in the family structure. Grandmothers' homes operated as a hub for family connections, particularly during weekends, holidays, and birthday celebrations. As one African American respondent said, they were the "backbone" of the family. The grandmothers also acted as a buffer against the fast-paced life of urban society. They saw their children and grandchildren struggling to make it in the market society and acted as protective safety nets, devoting their time to preparing their grandchildren for the struggles of life.

The resources these grandmothers transferred to their grandchildren were not necessarily economic or material. Besides love and support, what most parents and grandparents transferred to their children was their expectation for success. The expectation becomes part of an immaterial transfer between generations. As one African American mother put it, "They know that we expect them to find their niche in life. To achieve." Or as a Hispanic grandmother said about her own migrant father's expectations in the 1930s, "He always said that he wanted us to get an education and not to be burros like him. . . . He never told me to meet a nice man and get married. . . . He always encouraged us to get an education. . . . 'You got to get what I didn't get.'"

One fairly consistent thread we noticed among the families interviewed in 2009 compared to those interviewed in 1999–2000 was that more generations, particularly more grandparents, were actively involved in passing along values of social mobility linked to education. As with some of the families studied by Bertaux and Thompson, they tried to transmit values related to education and to create a sustainable trajectory in which many, if not all, of their descendants received a strong valuation of education.

However, not all grandmothers or mothers could count on a husband's or partner's assistance to develop the caring and nurturing work for the younger generation, and ultimately the transmission work that takes place during infancy and school years. There is a notorious absence of fathers in African American families that burdens women's work across generations. Some interviewees expressed their open resentment toward their male parents for leaving their mothers, not being around during childhood, or not contacting them after they had finished paying child support. African American families interviewed for this project presented a more pronounced matriarchal lineage as compared to the Hispanic families. In both cases, the middle-aged and older women, the grandmothers, could better recount the stories and trajectories of the family heritage.

2009 FINDINGS 2: ON GENERATIONAL
TRANSMISSION AND RESOURCES

Parents' expectations do not necessarily determine children's outcomes. Their children's education will also depend on what the younger individuals do with the capital (resources) being transmitted to them. A family's mobility trajectory can take longer than expected to reach the levels desired by previous generations. Depending on the concrete context, the social setting, age, sex, ethnicity, and other factors, different possible destinies will open up for individuals of the same family. Siblings can depart from their parents' trajectory or they can reproduce the family social status. The reception and appropriation of the family resources is variable and depends on the children. Children are best conceived as players in a general social competition, and whatever each child retains will condition to a large extent his or her personality, school career, integration in the working world, and ultimately social integration (Bertaux and Bertaux-Wiame 1997, 66).

The families interviewed here departed from a reproduction pattern in which the same activities or trades are repeated generation after generation. The African American and Hispanic families presented trajectories that included social mobility, change, discontinuity, and rupture. A long-range view of these families reveals successive subdivisions and recompositions at each generation that in no way cancels out the idea of its continuity. A triangulation of the family stories indicates how individual members of different generations struggled to go beyond or at least to maintain the family status that had been transferred to them. The ones who failed to do so in time had other opportunities to improve their lot (e.g., by returning to school after having a teen pregnancy or after raising children) and define a new probable destiny for themselves or for their children or grandchildren.

Education seems to be an essential variable in what sometimes appears to be a contradictory pattern of upward and downward mobility and discontinuities within these families, although it not the only element in explaining upward mobility (Bertaux and Bertaux-Wiame 1997). In a span of fifty years, one Mexican American family went from paternal grandparents having a few years of elementary schooling to six of their seven children obtaining college degrees and seventeen grandchildren obtaining a college education. By contrast, a maternal line from a second Mexican American family—whose illiterate great-grandfather came from Mexico in 1913 to escape the Mexican Revolution—took about seventy years for a great-granddaughter to go to graduate school.

Educational achievement was more prevalent among the African American families interviewed in this study, although this achievement was not evenly distributed among the siblings. Sometimes early pregnancies, the death of one of the parents, the need to enter the labor market early, or lack of interest in the college experience constrained social mobility. Educational cost was mentioned in only one case as a barrier to attend a private college in Austin. Probably as a function of the recruiting process of informants, we found two families with generations of daughters, mothers, and grandmothers who had all attended high school and obtained—or were in the process to obtaining—associate's or college degrees.

Only one African American woman, working as a middle school assistant principal, had obtained a master's degree. In another African American family, a father was working his way up to obtain his PhD while raising one child in college and two in high school. He had obtained his bachelor's degree in New York, his mother was a teacher, and all of his siblings had college degrees. His case appears as an intervention in changing positively the trajectory of his children. Even though his older daughter was unmarried with two children at age twenty-one, and even though she did not know what major or career she would pursue, she was taking courses at Austin Community College in addition to having a full-time job at a state agency. She noted that education was something that was preached about at home. The weight of the transmission of this intangible resource—that is, the value of education—is evident.

Some maternal lineages can be characterized as reproducing traditional trades, such as the reproduction of teachers and educators graduated from the same traditional black college in Austin. A lineage that started with grandparents working as janitors for education offices of the state government continued with three daughters (born in the 1920s) obtaining educational degrees at Huston-Tillotson University to become teachers. Even though the following three generations (born in the 1940s, 1960s, and late 1980s) went on to obtain degrees or some college education, none of them became teachers, disrupting the educational lineage.

However, a stark contrast between siblings' trajectories occurred in that same lineage. Elizabeth (a pseudonym, as are all proper names used here), the daughter of one of the three teachers, was born in 1948. She dropped out of college at twenty. She had six daughters, five of whom got associate's or college degrees. One of those five was working on her master's degree at the time of the study, whereas another one was in jail.

2009 FINDINGS 3: FAMILIES, MEDIA, AND NEW TECHNOLOGIES

Oral communication is central to family socialization processes, and the families studied in this project successfully transmitted the importance of being in close contact. The telephone, a technology that was scarce for much of the grandparents' and great-grandparents' lives, had become a necessity for the parents' and children's generations. Marilyn, fifty-three, the mother of a graduate student and the daughter of second-generation Mexican Americans, first had access to a home phone in the mid-1960s when she was in second grade. She explained the process of introducing the new technology at home as well as in the community:

> It's just that phones were still not seen as a vital necessity in the household. They were seen as, "OK, we can't afford that right now, but maybe someday we'll get it." . . . Just to let you know how new the idea or concept for the common person to have a phone in their home was the time when I was in first grade. It would have been '62, I believe. The Southwestern Bell Telephone Company had agents coming into the elementary school with phones, little pretend phone systems. The old rotary phone, the big blockish phones, and they showed all the kids in the class how to properly use a phone, how to make a call, how to properly answer a phone. Like how to say, "Hello?" And how to, if you call, how to properly say, "Hi, this is so-and-so. May I speak to so-and-so?" We had practice drills, and everyone got an opportunity to be the caller and the recipient of the call with this little fake phone system where the phone would ring. That's how new this idea of everyone having a phone was. It's not that phones were not around. It's just that phones were still not seen as a vital necessity in the household. . . . I know that by the time I was in second grade, we had our phone because [before] my mother would have to go and borrow a phone

that someone else had. Someone else had a telephone that she'd have to say, "Lets walk over there and see if they wouldn't mind us borrowing the phone," and we could make a call. . . . When we lived on Daniels St., we did not have the phone. If she needed to use a phone, she would have to go to a neighbor's or walk down to the store, which was a few blocks away, that had a public telephone. A pay phone that you could put in a dime or a nickel, I can't remember.

Having a phone was a novelty for the grandparents' generation. To-day, phones, and particularly cell phones, represent a familiar commodity for all members of the parents' and children's generations. Without exception, all the parents and children interviewed owned cell phones, which they used in different degrees to talk, send text messages, or, in a more sophisticated use, access the Internet and download materials. This technology presented a reverse trajectory in the life of the grandparents. In many cases daughters and grand-daughters were the ones buying the devices for their grandparents and teaching them how to use them, even though text messaging didn't appear to be a common behavior for the older generations. As one of the mothers (Jennifer, fifty-two) said, "We're not this generation that does a lot of texting, and we mostly call each other on the phone, or we do it by meeting each other at family gatherings."

A similar pattern was observed with computers and Internet access, which in many cases were given as a gift to the grandparents with the expectation that they would learn, even at age seventy-five and above, to send e-mails and search for basic information on the Internet. We found several cases of college-age youth teaching their parents or grandparents how to use computers and the Internet.

When it came to communicating with their parents or grand-parents, the young informants generally used the cell phone. Text messaging was more prevalent in youngest generation, and used more to communicate with peers and siblings of the same generation. Caroline, twenty, a criminal justice major at a university close to Houston, acknowledged sending more than seven thousand text messages each month. "When my phone is off, I want to scream," said the young African American student, who was the only one among her siblings that decided to study away from home. She had a Palm Treo (personal digital assistant) that gave her the ability to take pictures, listen to music, surf the Internet, and even use word processing software such as Microsoft Word. By contrast her mother, a federal employee, didn't send text messages and was more apt to use her phone "as just a phone." Her mother said, "When I'm buying a cell-phone . . . I just want to make sure that I'm able to talk, I don't buy for the camera phone, because I don't take pictures."

For some African American and Hispanic teenagers, telephone communications were so important growing up that some of them got personal landlines to avoid family conflicts over phone usage. This appropriation of the technology, in which adolescents would talk hours over the phone, was abandoned or reduced in use when they went to college, became parents, or gained work responsibilities.

Cell phone and Internet (e-mail and instant messaging) have become the preferred technologies for many, especially youth, to be in touch with friends and family. According to some respondents, even when they had a computer at home, many of the family interactions (and also the communications with friends) via e-mail or chatting took place while they were at work. In some cases, work was a place to develop techno-competencies, and younger generations continued their personal communications there because the structure of the job allowed for it. Consider the case of Rebecca, twenty-two, who worked processing student loans for a state agency, took courses at a community college, and was also raising two children. She described her work and use of information technology:

> [I] process e-mails, loans, and that's it. Take payments, answer questions, like people need, or change stuff on their student loans. That's it, real boring . . . and I talk on the phone. That's it. Surf the web most of the time. . . . I use Craigslist all the time. . . . It's a place I use to look for a job. [She was looking a job for her boyfriend.] I guess he felt I could do it, plus it gave me something to do at work, otherwise I'd be bored at work. Because I can just look on the Internet, because we are not busy, like ever, hardly. So in between calls I would just look on Craigslist. "Oh, I found this job what do you think?" and I would just IM [instant message] him at our home.

Rebecca's work computer was also the place to get news and information. She claimed that she was so busy with school and her children that by the time she arrived home, she was too tired to even turn on the computer. In addition to watching the local TV news while getting ready to go to work, she described her media routine as follows:

> While I'm at work I'll just get on Statesman.com [the website of the local newspaper], just to see, that's probably the first thing I log into when I get in—after I log into my computer, just to see what's going on, looking at classifieds, looking at a whole bunch of stuff. Just for anything, just to give myself something to do . . . just to see what's going on. . . . I don't know why it's important, just so I know what's going on in the world.

2009 FINDINGS 4: EDUCATION, THE MAIN TRANSMISSION

The three generations of women interviewed in this study agreed that the main thing parents transferred to them was the importance of education and the value of being good human beings. For some of them it was never an option not to go to college. Caroline, an African American college student whose mother was a postal worker, said that her mother, aunt, and uncle all went to Huston-Tillotson University and that she knew, "I was gonna go to college." She said that her older sister graduated with an accounting degree and that the next sister started college and got pregnant twice but was still talked into returning to college both times by her mother. She said she always had As and Bs and that she was "kind of like the nerd out of my sisters." Caroline had watched how her sister had to stop going to college and decided she would do things differently: "I don't want to be that person that stops. I want to go on and keep going."

Comparing achievements was a recurring theme in families that presented discontinuities. Beverly, an African American sophomore who was studying accounting and working two part-time jobs, indicated that her older stepsister, despite being sweet, was "going towards the wrong crowd and the wrong time." She commented that her younger sister, who was in eighth grade and on probation, "wants to fit in so much so she tries and does things to fit in, and I guess she starting to sway towards the wrong also. I guess she just wants to be bad."

Even in cases in which there was discontinuity regarding the goal of education, respondents acknowledged the importance of getting a college degree. In some cases, younger generations took longer in appropriating resources that parents had promoted several years earlier. For example, the story of Rebecca, presented above, shows a different angle when we look at her new interest in reading. Her mother, who ran a day care at home, had an associate's degree, and was married to a college teacher working on his PhD, had long insisted on the value of formal education as well as on constant reading. Rebecca said,

My mom, she's always been a big reader, always, and now I've started reading a lot. So that's one thing I did pick up that she does a lot. . . . I just read romance. Like I read those Twilight books, those are so good. And now, I am getting into vampire books. I have been reading this new vampire series [House of Night], and I really like it. . . . After I read those Twilights, she was like, just try this one, try this book. . . . I got hooked on it, cause I haven't even had the books that long, it's four books and I'm on the last one, I probably got them last week. So I just really love it. And I used to read, before these, I would just read romance, any kind of romance I could buy from Walmart or Target . . . probably like two years ago I started reading. Yeah, about two years. Cause at first, I didn't even read the book. Me and my mom went to see the movie. And then, she's like, you have to read the books. She'd already finished reading them. So I read those, so good. And another lady at work, she had already read them, and when she saw me reading them, we would talk about it and stuff that's going on in the book, and I'd be like, what's happening next? What's happening next? . . . I read those at work. When I wasn't surfing the web I was reading them.

Rebecca's mother, Theresa, was transferring resources, cultural capital, and a disposition focused on the pleasure and importance of reading. Decades ago, her aunt provided her with books when she was a child, and she wanted to be a librarian growing up. Theresa regularly bought children's and educational literature for her day care. However, when it came to newer technologies such as computers, she was very dependent on Rebecca and her other two high school children, who received and handled in their accounts the e-mails sent to their mother. This lack of techno-capital contrasted with her husband's capital in that he knew how to use computers, bought the first computer for the home, and introduced their three children to the new technology. This more restrictive pattern of ICT use was also found in the case of another mother, a postal worker (fifty-two, second-generation Mexican American), who only used the Internet at home for two hours a week, mainly to pay her bills and for general information like news and traffic routes. According to one of her daughters—a college major in Houston—she needed to memorize 1,292 city streets.

Computer use among the parents interviewed seemed to be related to the type of job that they currently performed or that they had before retirement. This finding echoes the pattern in a related study on communities, social capital, and media use in which computer use started at work (Rojas et al. 2005). Sara, sixty-one, was retired from the Boy Scouts of America, had a computer at home, and used it daily to read the news and check e-mails. She also played games, researched jobs, submitted applications, and typed letters. Leslie, forty-seven, who worked as an assistant principal, had a laptop that kept her "connected to the world and allows me to do my job at home, and it allows the kids to do their work at home as well." Besides her eldest daughter, who was in college and worked as a "network troubleshooter," she had three other children between five and fifteen years old.

Marilyn, who was Mexican American and high school educated, used computers and the Internet every day in her work as a ticket auditor for an airline company. She checked her personal and work e-mails on the job, followed news stories, and also checked the Discovery website for images of "what's happening in the Earth, such as natural disasters. . . . That's one of my immediate links off of my homepage."

2009 FINDINGS 5: TRANSFORMING THE FAMILY TECHNO-HABITUS

The introduction of the television set and the computer in the family household followed different paths. The grandparents' generation considered television as a home entertainment appliance that was important to have for their own and their children's leisure. The contents offered by this medium were clear to them—news and entertainment (movies, soaps, and series)—and they could easily relate to them. The computer, by contrast, was a more challenging technology to this older generation, and its use required techno-capitals the grandparents did not possess; hence the introduction of this new technology can be traced in more detail in the parents' generation.

Home video games appear as an intervening element between the two media technologies of television and computers, in that their initial simplicity (e.g., Pong) attracted the older generations (parents and grandparents) but their later sophistication and complexity has made them favorites among the younger generations, with particularly high penetration rates among minority households (Anderson 2008).

The grandparents interviewed clearly remembered the advent of television in their homes. The life story of Georgina, a Mexican American grandmother whose first language was Spanish, might help us to understand how families negotiate and appropriate new ICTs in the household. Georgina couldn't finish high school in 1950 because her father passed away. She had to start working to help her mother and brothers. She remembers buying a black-and-white TV for the family:

> We didn't go to the movies. My mother didn't go to the movies, but I know there were programs she could watch, even if she couldn't understand them. And she would get together with my mother-in-law after we were married, and they would discuss the story of what they thought they had understood! And then it was more interesting, *their* stories, than the stories that were happening on the screen. It's like what they did to the stories, you know? And it was just on body language. They knew when the person got angry. They didn't understand the lingo! [*laughs*]

By contrast, Georgina's daughter, Marilyn, who completed high school and worked for an airline company, grew up with a TV at home. Her very first memory of TV is "black and white, big round face with little tubes in the back that you'd replace when they burned out. You could go to any store, any 7-11 or any little store, and pick up your replacements and test your tubes." She recalls watching many shows from "what they call the golden age of TV." She said that growing up, all the way to her teen years, "TV was a big part of life. It was the main source of entertainment." Today, she tends to watch TV alone, and most of it is "home and garden based."

Marilyn experimented with several other media technologies and together with her husband—a professional photographer—introduced more technologies in their home than their minority neighbors in Forth Worth (Mexican, African American, and Vietnamese). Her family was the first one to have a huge satellite dish in the late 1980s, and her children had access to home computers at a very young age. She explained this by saying that since high school, she had been interested in science and innovations at a different level: "I was at a technical school and chose a 'major' that had to do with computers." Marilyn and her husband knew that their children would use computers at school and didn't want them to go somebody else's house to use them. (Their eldest daughter, today a graduate student, was in third grade then.) They got their first two computers in an auction with the hope that Marilyn would be able to become a computer programmer. For almost $2,000, they got two non-IBM personal computers, several parts, keyboards, cables, and one of the first computers games, "Adventures in Heaven," which came on a disk.

Marilyn presented other examples of techno-capital she had accumulated since her adolescence. Being interested in music, she transitioned through different models of mobile media players, starting with a radio transistor she got as a child and passing through record players, 8-track tape players, portable tape players, and Walkman and personal CD players: "And then, of course, I graduated to my iPod." She also ventured very early into video game technology: "Since I was twenty, video games have been one form of entertainment that has been in my life, so that's a long time, that's been over thirty years." She elaborated on her transition from arcade to console to online games, which she played on at least three different websites, either alone or in company of her youngest son.

The question that might arise here is where this third-generation Mexican American woman who attained only a high school education got the techno-capital and techno-dispositions that prompted her interest in all these media innovations. In order to understand the development of her techno-dispositions, we need to look at her father's work while she was growing up. Marilyn attributed her interest in technology and scientific advances in general to all the books and magazines her father used to bring home when she was a teenager. Her father worked for a distribution company of books and magazines and was allowed to take home publications that did not sell or were considered losses, "leftover or trash, much the same way that I guess a restaurant . . . might let their workers to take that stuff home." Some of her favorite magazines were *Popular Science, Popular Mechanics, Popular Electronics, Video Gamer, Guitar Player,* and others. In her interview she reasons that this was "one of the biggest services" done for her:

> It really opened our world to so many books, so many types of periodicals, and so many types of printed medias. . . . Without that exposure, I can't really say we would have been the same peo-

ple. . . . My generation might not have had all university educations, but the wealth of information that we got from the information that was brought to us by Dad . . . it acquainted us with the rest of the world. It opened our minds to types of living, of so much more than just what we knew in our little corner of the world. . . . It's putting up the world to you. It's saying, "OK, these are the latest innovations, here's what's coming." . . . So it was a very future thinking. . . . Because of that we got to be the kind of people that would pick up a copy of something like that in a newsstand when Dad didn't work there anymore and say, "I wonder what's happening?"

In addition to Marilyn's paternal influence, we might add that her husband worked as a photographer for Lockheed Martin, and that they as a couple once owned a photography business, before the advent of digital photography made them search for other types of employment.

At this point, let's introduce Marilyn's daughter and Georgina's granddaughter, Roxana, a graduate student in a communication-related program. Seventy years after her maternal grandfather migrated from Mexico, she was the first one to get a college degree in her family. She attributed her interest for film and media to her grandfather's work in a stereo system factory and then in a magazine distribution company, and to her parents' photo studio. All of these resources seemed decisive for Roxana's techno-capital. Additionally, she stated that there was musical inclination running in the family that could have influenced her own academic and artistic interests. Her mother, Marilyn, played the guitar, the violin, and the drums. Her grandfather was also a musician, and had played the saxophone since he was a teenager and in bands during the 1940s and 1950s.

Roxana had her own interpretation of the slow process of social mobility in her family. She spoke of a series of "missed opportunities":

When I think about my family history, there was also a missed opportunity or opportunities that were not even provided. My grandfather was actually taken out of school; he was drafted into the Korean War. He could not finish high school. My grandmother left high school to support her mom and her brothers when her dad passed away. Her brothers ended up leaving school too. At least, for where my parents were involved, they finished high school. I know that my dad had an inclination to college, but it never happened. My mother, actually, had a scholarship and offers to go to particular colleges, but she decided to dive in the workforce. When I hear these stories, all these missed opportunities, I knew I did not want to be like that. . . . That being said, my family had a lot of missed opportunities, but they also decided to make opportunities for them. My grandmother went back to school in her thirties, forties. My Uncle Robert just went back to school four months ago. He quit his job, and he is a freshman college student. My Uncle Edward and my Aunt Caroline have also taken some classes together at school. So, my family had missed opportunities, but they went back and have tried to pursue those paths in their own personal ways. Not only for the degree, but for them.

The transference of technological resources in the three generations of this family indicates a progressive techno-disposition toward the adoption of innovations. It is evident from the stories that none of the women in these generations were early adopters or innovators, but with different strategies (e.g., buying used computers), at least one mother—Marilyn—brought the new technologies to their children, including satellite TV, computers, mobile music players, and audiovisual games. Even though her daughter Roxana said that the computers they got at home when she was in elementary school were "kind of crappy computers . . . monochrome and . . . really not that fun," these devices might have developed her own techno-dispositions and techno-capital. She went from having only a game called "Paint" as a child to today having expertise on video game systems such as Xbox 360, in addition to regularly using her laptop, Internet, cable TV, and iPod. She also noted that her mother taught her to play video games as a fun thing to do together. Without being deterministic we might propose here that the resources were at the family home and that it was up to the children, with parental encouragement, to appropriate them and reinvent their usage in their own lives.

CONCLUSION

The more fully multigenerational approach used in 2009 allowed us to trace in more detail the transference of cultural capital between generations. In each case, these working- and lower-middle-class families presented a more pronounced use of media technologies in the younger generations. All grandchildren interviewed in this project were familiar with different applications of the Internet, iPods, cell phones, cable TV on demand, and online gaming. These young adults grew up with cable and satellite television and semiprivate availability of landline phones, and in 2009, without exception, they all owned cell phones or other integrated phone devices. Their usage of these devices was more sophisticated than the elder generations. They were the ones explaining and teaching the new technology to their grandparents and occasionally to their parents. Also, they had learned from their parents to watch or listen to news, but they incorporated that practice into their daily routine through different means. The Internet was most commonly how they found out "what's going on."

Compared to the first- and second-generation immigrants of the Latino families presented in the 1999–2000 study, the African American and Hispanic respondents interviewed in 2009 did not seem to be constrained by the same class ethos of being minorities and children of recent immigrants. Perhaps as a function of their longer settlement in Austin and in the state of Texas, dating back more than one hundred years in most cases, the 2009 respondents appeared to have a more consistent tendency toward upward mobility. The majority of the siblings had at least a high school education, and despite some discontinuities, many in the parents' generation, particularly in the African American families, had college degrees. This indicates to us that the educational goal and trajectory established several generations ago tended to be sustained by the new generations. It also suggests that recent immigrants and their offspring should be specially considered in intervention programs promoting media access and use. First- and second-generation immigrants face more difficulties in establishing themselves in the new U.S. and urban context (because of their lack of cultural capital, social networks, linguistic capital, and other entitlements), which makes them more vulnerable in their negotiations with the structure. They have to work longer hours and are less prepared to transfer cultural capital to their children. In many cases the only immaterial form of capital they have to transfer is values and expectations about the importance of education.

Overall, as the research in this project developed over ten years, the role of economic capital and literal access to ICTs became secondary to the role of education and techno-habitus in relation to both shifts in family trajectory and proclivities toward access and use of ICTs. One of the main differences between the two groups we studied is that the second group had been stable in a larger city in the United States much longer than the first group. Other interviews done for a related project in the early 2000s indicated that migration to the rural United States from rural Mexico had much less transformative impact than the move a generation or two later to Austin from rural areas. Once established in a city with more educational and work opportunities, the parents' generation was able to achieve better work and material conditions, which enabled their children to achieve more education. So stability in the urban setting may account for part of the difference, permitting new trajectories that focus more on higher education.

We also noticed more of a generational difference in ICT use between the youngest generation and the parents and grandparents in the 2009 study. Even though several different generations in 2009 were using mobile phones, computers, and the Internet, the youngest generation was using them more extensively and had integrated them more fully into their lives. One exception, perhaps, is the last Latino family discussed above, that of Marilyn and Roxanna, who displayed similarly extensive use of ICTs.

Comparing the two studies, we find a more consistently high techno-disposition among the young in the second study. Directly relating to our principal research question of whether there would be a durable class habitus against ICT use, we find more evidence in 2009 to say that social capital impacts among the young have changed, in that young people are more likely to resemble each other in their techno-capital, techno-disposition, and group habitus than they are to follow in a family-based class habitus received from their parents. There seems to be some evidence in this study for a strong critical mass effect among youth and young adults (under thirty) now, so that even disadvantaged youth are being pulled into the "digital generation" (described Tapscott 2009 and others) by a strong consistent pull of social capital tied to ICT use among their fellow young people.

APPENDIX 9.1. INTERVIEW GUIDE FOR THE 1999 STUDY

A slightly updated version of this guide was applied in 2009 to include questions on cell phones and other newer technologies.

General (recommended first interview questions)

- Tell me about yourself.
- Where are you from?
- How long have you lived in Austin? Why did you move here?
- Where did you live before?
- What direction do you see yourself going in the future?
- What direction do you see your family going in the future?

- What would you most like to do when you are about twenty?
- If you could change anything in your life right now, what would it be?
- What kind of information do you need for your life right now?
- How are you different from your mom (or dad) in where you go for information you need?
- How do people in your family get the information they need?
- How do you get your information?
- Who or what supports you in seeking information?
- What do you teach your family about how to get the information they need?
- What are some memories you have about technology from when you were growing up?
- What kinds of technology are important to you?
- Do you feel that technology benefits you?
- *(For immigrants)* What things caught your attention the most when you arrived in the United States?
- How do you like Johnston High for your children?

Questions about specific media use

- Do you watch TV? What kind of things do you watch?
- Do you play video games? What kinds? Why do you like them?
- Do you like radio? What do you like best?
- If you had a computer, would you play on it?
- Of TV, radio, video games, computers, and stuff like that, which do you like most?
- What kinds of stuff are cool to you?
- What technologies are cool?
- What kinds of things would you most like to have?
- Have you ever heard of the information superhighway?
- What does the information superhighway mean to you?
- When did you first hear about computers?
- What is your earliest/first memory of a computer?
- Who are computers for?
- Who is the Internet for?
- How do you feel toward computers?
- Do you get the feeling that computers are for people like you?
- Do you get the feeling that the Internet is for people like you?
- Do you need a computer?
- Do you need the Internet?
- Would your friends think having a computer was cool?
- What do you need to use the Internet?
- What do you think of the Internet?
- What comes to mind when you see someone using the Internet?
- How do you see yourself in relation to the Internet?
- Do you think the Internet is/would be useful to you?
- Do you consider the Internet a vital part of your everyday life? If yes, why and how so?

- How do you keep in touch with relatives out of town (e.g., in Mexico)?
- Would the Internet help you get ahead?
- Do you have any interest in using computers or the Internet?
- Do you see the Internet as a useful source of information?
- What kinds of information do you need from the Internet?
- Does the Internet help everybody?
- Do you have a computer at home?
- How old were you when you first had a computer in your home? (Or how old were you when you first saw a computer?)

Specific Internet questions

- Have you seen ads about the Internet?
- What did they tell you about it?
- How did they make you think about it?
- Did they make you want to use it?
- If you needed to use the Internet, where would you go?
- How has your family encouraged or discouraged your involvement with the Internet?
- Is the Internet easily available for people in your community?
- Would you use the Internet more often if it were in Spanish?
- Rank how important these different technologies are to you according to how often you use them: (*specifically name phone, computer, etc.*)
- How do minorities use the Internet? Do they want to take advantage of what it can deliver?
- Is the Internet important to your culture?

If you know about the Internet:

- Where did you hear about the Internet?
- What kind of things can people do with the Internet?
- Do people in your family use the Internet?

If you have used the Internet:

- Where do you (or would you) get access to the Internet?
- What do you like on the Internet?
- What do you personally like most on the Internet?
- Why do you not want to use the Internet?
- When you see an ad for the Internet, what are the images usually shown?

REFERENCES

Anderson, D. (2008). Honey, we acculturated the kids: Key influences on Hispanic buying behavior. *Nielsen Consumer Insight* 11 (October). Retrieved October 11, 2009, from www.us.nielsen.com/pubs/index.shtml.

Andorka, R. (1997). Social mobility in Hungary since the Second World War: Interpretations through surveys and through family histories. In D. Bertaux and P. Thompson, *Pathways to social class*, pp. 259–298. Oxford: Clarendon Press.

Benton Foundation. (1998). Losing ground bit by bit: Low-income communities in the information age. Retrieved January 29, 2002, from http://www.benton.org/Library/Low-Income/.

Bertaux, D. (Ed.). (1981). *Biography and society: The life history approach in the social sciences*. Beverly Hills, CA: Sage.

Bertaux, D., and M. Bertaux-Wiame. (1997). Heritage and its lineage: A case history of transmission and social mobility over five generations. In D. Bertaux and P. Thompson (Eds.), *Pathways to social class: A qualitative approach to social mobility*. New York: Oxford University Press.

Bertaux, D., and P. Thompson. (1993). Introduction: In between generations: Family models, myths and memories. In D. Bertaux and P. Thompson (Eds.), *International Yearbook of Oral History and Life Stories*, pp. 1–12. New York: Oxford University Press.

———. (1997). *Pathways to social class*. Oxford: Clarendon Press.

——— (Eds.). (2005). *Between generations: Family models, myths and memories*. New York: Oxford University Press.

Borget, J. (2008). Johnston campus now Eastside Memorial High School. News 8 Austin, August 21. Retrieved September 30, 2009, from http://news8austin.com/content/top_stories/default.asp?ArID=217821.

Bourdieu, P. (1977). *Outline of a theory of practice*. Cambridge, UK: Cambridge University Press.

———. (1980). *The logic of practice*. Trans. Richard Nice. Stanford, CA: Stanford University Press.

———. (1984). *Distinction: A social critique of the judgement of taste*. Cambridge, MA: Harvard University Press.

———. (1985). The forms of capital. In J. G. Richardson (Ed.), *Handbook of theory and research for the sociology of education*, pp. 241–258. New York: Greenwood Press.

———. (1993a). *The field of cultural production*. New York: Columbia University Press.

———. (1993b). *Sociology in question*. London: Sage.

Brubaker, R. (1993). Social theory as habitus. In C. Calhoun, E. LiPuma, and M. Postone (Eds.), *Bourdieu: Critical perspectives*, pp. 212–234. Chicago: University of Chicago Press.

Educational Testing Service. (1997). Computers and classrooms: The status of technology in U.S. schools. May. Retrieved January 23, 2002, from http://www.ets.org/research/pic/pir.html.

Garnham, N. (1986). Extended review: Bourdieu's *Distinction*. *Sociological Review* 34 (2): 423–433.

González, J. (1986). Y todo queda entre familia. *Revista Estudios Sobre las Culturas Contemporáneas* 1(1): 135–154.

———. (1997). The willingness to weave: Cultural analysis, cultural fronts and the networks of the future. *Media Development* 44(1): 30–36.

———. (2000). Cultural fronts: Towards a dialogical understanding of contemporary cultures. In J. Lull (Ed.), *Culture in the information age*. London: Routledge.

Heritage Foundation. (2000). How free computers are filling the digital divide. April 20. Retrieved December 10, 2001, from http://www.heritage.org/library/backgrounder/bg1361.html.

Hoffman, D., and T. Novak. (1998). Bridging the digital divide: The impact of race on computer access and Internet use. February 2. Retrieved March 21, 2002, from http://elab.vanderbilt.edu/research/papers/html/manuscripts/race/science.html.

Holstein, W. (2000). A tale of two Austins: How one boomtown is coping with the growing wealth gap. *U.S. News and World Report*, February 21. Retrieved March 21, 2002, from http://www.usnews.com/utils/search.

Jansen, J. (2010). The better-off online. Pew Research Center Publications. Retrieved March 29. 2011, from pewresearch.org/pubs/1809/internet-usage-higher-income-americans.

Johnson, R. (1993). Editor's introduction. In P. Bourdieu, *The field of cultural production*, pp. 1–25. New York: Columbia University Press.

Jones, S., and S. Fox. (2009). Report: Generations, digital divide, seniors, teens, email in generations online in 2009. Pew Internet and American Life Project. Retrieved August 8, 2009, from http://www.pewinternet.org/Reports/2009/Generations-Online-in-2009.aspx.

Kaiser Family Foundation. (1999). Kids and media @ the new millennium. Retrieved March 19, 2011, from http://www.kff.org/entmedia/1535-index.cfm.

Kurtz, M., and McEntee, R. (2000). Hard times at Johnston. *Austin American-Statesman*, January 23.

Mosco, V. (1996.) *The political economy of communication*. Thousand Oaks, CA: Sage.

Murdock, D. (2000). Digital divide? What digital divide? Cato Institute, June 16. Retrieved December 10, 2001, from http://www.cato.org/dailys/06-16-00.html.

Murdock, G. (1989). Class stratification and cultural consumption: Some motifs in the work of Pierre Bourdieu (1977). In F. Coalter (Ed.), *Freedom and constraint: The paradoxes of leisure: Ten years of the Leisure Studies Association*, pp. 90–101. London: Comedia/Routledge.

Murray, C. (2010). The tea party warns of a new elite: they're right. *Washington Post*. http://www.washingtonpost.com/wp-dyn/content/article/2010/10/22/AR2010102202873.html.

NTIA (National Telecommunication and Information Administration). (1995). Falling through the Net: A survey of the "have nots" in rural and urban America. July. Retrieved January 23, 2002, from http://www.ntia.doc.gov/ntiahome/fallingthru.html.

———. (1998). Falling through the Net 2: New data on the digital divide. July 28. Retrieved January 10, 2002, from http://www.ntia.doc.gov/ntiahome/net2/.

———. (1999). Falling through the Net: Defining the digital divide. July 8. Retrieved August 7, 2000, from http://www.ntia.doc.gov/ntiahome/fttn99/contents.html.

———. (2000). Falling through the Net, toward digital inclusion. October. Re-

trieved March 12, 2002, from http://www.ntia.doc.gov/ntiahome/fttn00/con
tents00.html.

———. (2002). A nation online: How Americans are expanding their use of the
Internet. February. Retrieved March 21, 2002, from http://www.ntia.doc.gov/
ntiahome/dn/index.html.

Pew Internet and American Life Project. (2000). Who's not online. September 21.
Retrieved March 15, 2002, from http://www.pewinternet.org/reports/index
.asp.

Portes, A. (1998). Social capital: Its origins and applications in modern sociology.
Annual Review of Sociology 24:1–24.

Reza, N. (1998). Social origins, social statuses and home computer access and use.
Canadian Journal of Sociology 23(4): 427–450.

Rogers, E. M. (1995). *Diffusion of innovations.* New York: Simon and Schuster.

Rojas, V., J. Straubhaar, M. Fuentes-Bautista, and J. Piñon. (2005). Still divided:
Ethnicity, generation, cultural capital and new technologies. In O. Jambeiro
and J. Straubhaar (Eds.), *Políticas de informação e comunicação, jornalismo
e inclusão digital: O local e o global em Austin e Salvador (Information and
communication policy, journalism and digital inclusion: The local and global in Austin and Salvador)*, pp. 297–322. Salvador, Brazil: Federal University
of Bahia Press.

Rojas, V., J. Straubhaar, J. Roychowdhury, and O. Okur. (2004). Communities, cultural capital and the digital divide. In E. Bucy and J. Newhagen (Eds.), *Media
access: Social and psychological dimensions of new technology use*, pp. 107–
133. Mahwah, NJ: Lawrence Erlbaum.

Rupertus, J., J. Straubhaar, and A. LaPastina. (2001). *This Internet is NOT for you:
Mismarketing the Internet to minorities.* Paper presented at the 51st International Communication Association Conference, Washington, DC.

Schement, J. R. (1998). Thorough Americans: Minorities and the new media. In
A. Korzick (Ed.), *Investing in diversity: Advancing opportunities for minorities and the media*, pp. 51–84. Washington, DC: Aspen Institute, Communications and Society Program.

Singer, D., and J. Singer. (2005). *Imagination and play in the electronic age.* Harvard, MA: Harvard University Press.

Spence, J. (2007). Socioeconomic genograms: Methodological experimentation in
the study of social mobility and cultural assimilation. Master's thesis, University of Texas at Austin.

Strover, S., and J. Straubhaar. (2000). E-government services and computer and
Internet use in Texas. Telecommunications and Information Policy Institute,
University of Texas at Austin, May. Retrieved December 10, 2001, from http://
www.utexas.edu/research/ti2e/tipi/resources/reports/full.htm.

Swartz, D. (1977). Pierre Bourdieu: The cultural transmission of social inequality.
Harvard Educational Review 47(4): 545–555.

Tapscott, D. (2009). *Grown up digital: How the Net generation is changing your
world.* New York: McGraw-Hill.

Tomás Rivera Policy Institute. (2002). Latinos and the information technology:
The promise and the challenge. Retrieved March, 21, 2002, from http://www
.trpi.org/PDF/Latinos%20and%20IT.pdf.

United Nations. (2005). World Youth report 2005: Young people today and in 2015. United Nations, Department of Economic and Social Affairs.

Wacquant, L. (1989). Towards a reflexive sociology: A workshop with Pierre Bourdieu. *Sociological Theory* 7(1): 26–63.

Wacquant, L. (1996). Reading Bourdieu's "capital." *International Journal of Contemporary Sociology* 33(2): 151–170.

Warschauer, M. (2004). *Technology and social inclusion: Rethinking the digital divide.* Cambridge, MA: MIT Press.

Wilhelm, A. (1998). *Closing the digital divide: Enhancing Hispanic participation in the information age.* Claremont, CA: Tomás Rivera Policy Institute.

CONCLUSION

This book has examined some important questions, both for those studying digital inequality, technology, and urban development and for those attempting to make policy about it or simply live and work more effectively in one of the many rapidly emerging technology cities, or technopolises, of the world (Boucke et al. 1994). Why did Austin, Texas, try to become a technopolis? What were the problems it had to face, particularly as a city where education had very recently been racially segregated? How broadly have gains actually been shared in terms of jobs, income, education, and social mobility under Austin's emergence as a technopolis? Who has benefited as well as been left behind, and how does such neglect occur?

How important are new digital technologies like the Internet and computers to questions of social change and social equity? In particular, we (notably in Chapter 4) were interested in how it would impact both work and the educational opportunities that prepare people to work in a new field like information technology. How much do the impacts of these new technologies depend on earlier patterns of who gets a good education and who does not? As we found in Chapter 2, this is a key point in a once-segregated city like Austin, but it is also an important point wherever educational inequalities exist—that is to say, everywhere.

In terms of policy in Austin, the book examines the impact of digital inclusion programs that were created in the 1990s nationally and for the state, as well as what happened when those programs were gradually cut back by conservative administrations after 2000. It also examines how the City of Austin persisted in its own efforts toward digital inclusion, working with its public libraries and a number of local nonprofits, like the Austin Free-Net, and the positive impact those programs had.

How much impact did these efforts to restructure the technopolis from below, to make its benefits more widely accessible, actually have on those who needed them most? Another main question for this book is how to understand the struggle within the fields of education and technology in Austin by a variety of people, not only to gain to digital tools but also to develop what we call techno-capital (the knowledge and skills required to use digital media capably), as well as an understanding of its usefulness, what we call techno-disposition. (These questions are addressed particularly in Chapters 7 and 9.)

STRUCTURING AUSTIN AS A TECHNOPOLIS FROM ABOVE AND BELOW

Theoretically, the book examines the structuring of cultural geography in the city. One group of planners created segregation in 1928, which had lasting effects in restricting and hampering access to the field of education for most African American and Latino residents. Then other planners from companies, the city government, and the university worked to create an economic technopolis from the 1950s on (before school segregation had even ended). This created a new economic field of information and communication technology (ICT), which became the key arena for people in Austin in their competition for resources and social mobility. Meanwhile other groups and individuals reworked the structures of access to computers and the Internet from below to make them more livable.

Our findings agree with Michel de Certeau's (1984) argument that the cultural geography of a city is defined and gradually constructed from both above and below. Politicians, planners, industrialists, and university leaders made many strategic decisions from the top down. The first major one that we examined in Chapter 2 was the deliberate reinforcement of segregation by city planners in 1928.[1] To trace its effects, we created maps, using the methodology of Jorge González (1995), which show very clearly how much both housing and schools were changed from 1910 (before segregation) to 1940 (after the 1928 enactment of formal segregation). The next major restructuring of Austin occurred in the 1970s, with desegregation (discussed in Chapter 2) and the top-down planning of Austin as a technopolis (discussed in Chapter 3). Desegregation did not really change the earlier structuring, but the creation of the technopolis had powerful impacts on the city.

Chapter 2 of this book observed how the public school system in the Austin area evolved, before and after segregation. It also reflected on the larger set of problems facing schools in the United States as they try to adapt to new ICTs and train people for industries that increasingly use or even focus on those ICTs. It found a strong continuity of historic inequities between schools in more and less affluent, majority and minority parts of town. Building on the maps of residences by racial group, we then looked at where resources like schools and libraries were placed. The allocation of ICT resources clearly follows the lines of segregation, with poorer, minority schools getting fewer resources and inadequate help to use the resources they did receive. This pattern is shown as prefiguring the digital divide. Chapter 2 concluded with an examination of one particular case, Johnston High School, one of the poorest schools in the district, where some of the fieldwork discussed in Chapter 9 was based. It showed just how powerful and lasting the racially based structuring of Austin in 1928 was. It also showed how a lastingly segregated school system created a paradox in a city whose subsequent growth as a technopolis supposed a necessary and rapid growth in education as a base for the techno-capital and techno-dispositions that its citizens would need to navigate the new, crucial field of information technology. The structural problems uncovered in Chapter 2 helped explain the difficulties poor students at Johnston were having in learning techno-capital at school that we observed in Chapter 9.

In Chapter 3 we looked at the history of Austin's development as a technopolis, a city with an economy based largely on information technology and digital media. That guided the strategies that Austin city planners used to bring the city out of an economic slump in the 1980s and into an initial period of economic boom through the 1990s, particularly through a strong university-private-public (city) partnership. However, the success of the technopolis strategy has also brought new concerns about a declining quality of life and unequal distribution of the benefits of the technology economy. We found both realized potential as well as very real pitfalls in the Austin private-public partnership led by the technology community, and its intention to tackle social issues such as the digital divide. A key problem was that many groups, such as the Latino and African American populations, have been largely left out of technology and economic planning, even though, as Chapter 6 shows, the City of Austin itself did an outstanding job of focusing on and providing resources for digital inclusion. This indicates that planning from above (de Certeau 1984) is not a singular process but also reflects what Gramsci would call a competition between elites in a given place or space to set the terms of a policy consensus or hegemonic frame of reference.

FOCUSING ON THE FIELD OF TECHNOLOGY

To better examine and theoretically interrogate the transformation of Austin into a technopolis in which the prime focus of development is the field of technology, we have proposed and examined the concept of the techno-field. Pierre Bourdieu (1984) used the term *field* to describe specific, concrete social formations or situations in which people and institutions as agents act and compete, accumulating and using different forms of capital—economic, cultural, social, linguistic, and technological. A particular field, like the techno-field, is defined by the specific form of capital it requires, as people struggle to acquire or maintain that capital. Austin's planners restructured the city's economy as a technopolis, which emphasized the field of technology as the primary field of economic growth.

In order to succeed in the new dominant field of information technology, Austinites must build techno-capital, building on Bourdieu's idea of cultural capital, which is related to techno-disposition, a sense of priority (or not) that leads people to invest their own resources, time, and energy into learning about technology. In an emerging technopolis, it becomes imperative to gain competencies and resources to negotiate within the techno-field. We found that techno-dispositions are delineated by such indicators as social practices, perceptions and attitudes, technical education, awareness of technology, desire for information, job requirements, social relations, community interactions, and geographic location.

In other words, people are led by various aspects of their individual and family lives to have greater or less interest in learning skills for the techno-field. For example, in a focus group held just prior to the interviews in 1999 reported in Chapter 8, a fourteen-year-old Latino boy at Johnston High School looked at me (I was conducting the group) and said, "I think computers are women's work." That statement seemed extraordinary, contrary to what we thought we knew about the gendering of computers as a largely male activity at that time. But further conversation revealed that the only Latino adults he knew who used computers professionally were women who were secretaries, including his mother. To understand his statement, you had to understand his social geography in a working-class Latino neighborhood, where women were indeed becoming computer-qualified secretaries but working with computers was not something men were doing yet. That entails understanding the notion of masculinity that he was growing up with, as well as his class position among a group where men tended to work with their hands. (His high school guidance counselor was suggesting that he take up refrigerator repair.)

This kind of social positioning is also dynamic. By the time we observed and interviewed people again in 2009, Latino boys considerably outnumbered girls in going to libraries to use public access computers. The gendering of computers as a cool male thing to do had caught up with these youth by then (see Chapter 7). Indeed, young Latinos had been caught up in a kind of critical mass of computer-, game-, and smartphone-oriented youth culture that began to pull them into much greater similarity to the rest of their generation (Watkins 2009).

According to their class techno-habitus, people make specific investments in the fields in which they participate, such as different kinds of work, education, or computer technology skill. Bourdieu defined the habitus as a set of dispositions that generate practices and perceptions among members of the same class. However, we would like to expand the idea of the group habitus based on class to include critical aspects of race/ethnicity, gender, and age, in order to better explain the conjuncture of forces which act together as a combined group habitus in cases like that of the Latino boy described above in 1999. Bourdieu notes that a group's habitus is a product of the history of the group and is internalized in the mind of the actors who participate in it and perform it in their daily lives, creating what Anthony Giddens (1984) would call a structure in their own lives. Habitus implies a certain knowledge and recognition of the stakes in the field and generates the strategies of action with which people participate in the field (Bourdieu 1993b); this is key to our understanding of how people in Austin have dealt with the rapid growth of the techno-field.

The focus by Austin planners on building the technopolis, creating a crucial high stakes field of competition in and around information or digital technology, has certainly transformed the city. Its population doubled between 1980 and 2005, accompanied by a striking shift in the types of jobs people have in the city, with many moving into the field of technology, especially the ICTs. However, many of those jobs turned out to be less transformative and less well paying than most of the analysts and promoters of the information society and technopolis had predicted, as Chapter 4 documented.

Chapter 4 of this book delved more deeply into specific discourses about the technopolis, focusing on the discussion that surfaced among educators, the business community, and the government on how best to address the perceived shortage of high-skilled workers for both the real technopolis and the anticipated information society. Concerns in the 1990s about the shortage of skilled workers shared the assumption that the structure of the economy of the new millennium was to be postindustrial, and that our current society would be best characterized as an information society where, it was further assumed, significant social and economic mobility could be achieved through the acquisition of high-tech skills and information literacy. This chapter questioned the axiom that equitable distribution of educational opportunities for acquiring these skills would result in a more equitable social stratification. If the inequalities of society, particularly in the new digital city, could be bridged by imparting high skills to larger numbers of today's youth, who would employ them? The chapter digs into the Austin data to show that the jobs are not really there, even in the technopolis, and makes a somewhat controversial argument about the real job-market prospects in Austin—many of which are low paid and low skilled.

ADDRESSING THE DIGITAL DIVIDE

So far we have addressed three key top-down structuring moments: the creation of segregation, attempted desegregation, and the structuring of the technopolis. A fourth key moment in Austin of top-down planning and attempted restructuring started in the 1990s, to remedy some of the problems caused by the new economy of the technopolis. At the national, state, and local levels, a number of decision makers, from President Clinton and several of his advisors to state legislators to the staff of the City of Austin, became concerned that the overall shift in the United States toward an information economy and technology use was creating a new layer of social stratification between social classes, races, genders, and ages—a digital divide (Irving 1999). Chapter 5 examined how this policy debate was supported by research showing a racial divide in computer access and use.

Returning to our initial theoretical framework, we see that those who live in the city and use its resources make tactical decisions on the ground that can, to a substantial degree, redefine what practices evolve (de Certeau 1984). That is particularly feasible if people in positions of some power in the city work with those nonprofits and other grassroots forces who are trying to ameliorate the negative aspects of earlier decisions. Many people in Austin fought against segregation, as described in Chapter 2, and worked to undo it, although de facto segregation of housing, schools, work, and access to digital resources remains in many parts of the city (Orum 2002). Although the technopolis economy was planned by city, university, and business officials, drawing resources from national planners who wanted to see such development (Smilor, Gibson, and Kozmetsky 1988, xiii), others in the community were worried about how to implement this idea in a way that mitigated some of its potential downsides, which culminated in the local, state, and national dialogue about the digital divide, as discussed in Chapter 5.

By the late 1990s, one of the main ways of addressing the question of the digital divide was to provide computer and Internet access, training, and skills. Chapter 6 of this book discussed how a variety of groups began to plan and implement local programs, often calling on resources that were becoming available through national and state programs. Chapter 7 focused on how libraries in particular came to be a focus of access to new digital resources and education. Chapter 8 discussed how enthusiasm for wireless Internet began to draw attention away from more traditional community access programs, perhaps reflecting a return to worrying about the young, mobile creative people who were seen as critical to the technopolis project. Chapter 9 looked at how a variety of people responded to access and training as it became available.

All of these chapters in different ways looked at what de Certeau would call the structuring or modification of structures from below, by those actually living in the planned technopolis. The chapters used historical analysis, policy analysis, and interview research about the nature of the digital divide, and participant observation in libraries and community centers to see who used public access.

Chapter 5 looked first at the history of U.S. thinking about the digital divide issue and how that affected U.S. policy making. It then considers the programs that came out of those policies in some detail to show what resources Austin organizations had to work with. There were three major federal programs that responded to the problems of the digital divide. The first was the E-Rate program, which still subsidizes the cost of connectivity to the Internet for schools and libraries. The second was the U.S. Department of Commerce's Technology Opportunities Program (TOP), which gave competitive grants for applications of information technology that helped empower low-income communities. The third was the U.S. Department of Education's Community Technology Center (CTC) Program, which gave money to create or expand community technology centers located in economically distressed urban and rural communities. The state of Texas, for its part, created a Telecommunications Infrastructure Fund (TIF) that was somewhat parallel to the E-Rate for Texas schools, libraries, and public health facilities. Chapter 5 discussed each program in terms of its origins and goals, beneficiaries, and effectiveness. The chapter concluded that the four programs taken together played a distinct and important role in addressing the underlying issues of the digital divide and helped to move the nation toward the goals of social equity and economic growth. Finally, the chapter noted major policy changes made under the Bush administration that cut TOP and the CTC Program, and equivalent changes in Texas that cut TIF. The chapter shows that the debate over the digital divide at the national and state level was dominated by skeptics after 2000, who urged cutting programs.

Chapter 6 analyzed the history of what was done in a variety of Austin locations by many kinds of groups to provide digital access and training. This chapter built on the issues of universal service detailed in the previous chapter by reviewing and comparing a number of initiatives in Austin to address the digital divide. The chapter examined the histories of several of the major initiatives in both access and training programs in East Austin based on interviewing at programs in 2003, updated in 2009. The chapter focused on the goals, target clienteles, and approaches of the programs, and how those evolved. It particularly focused on the impact of various sources of funding, as well as the grassroots initiatives of local activists. The primary programs relied heavily on public funding streams designed to increase public access to computer and Internet resources, particularly the federal TOP, the statewide TIF, and U.S. Department of Education funds, as well as City of Austin support and some foundation support, reflecting the very real local impact of some of the programs described in Chapter 5. In some measure, this chapter gives a sense of the impact of a variety of digital divide initiatives in East Austin. It also shows how those programs struggled after the cutoff of federal and state funds from 2000 to 2003, with those that survived depending on a strong local base of support, like the City of Austin's own library program.

We should note that after 2008, the Obama administration began to restore some programs to address digital inclusion and a variety of broadband programs, including a revised Broadband Technology Opportunity Program within the U.S. Department of Commerce to promote extension of broadband connectivity and to create programs to reach and train potential users. Several of the programs in Austin described in Chapter 6, such as the Austin Free-Net and the University of Texas Telecommunications and Information Policy Institute, received one of these grants to support and extend public access and training in Austin and several other parts of Central and South Texas. This renewed federal funding reflects how ideology and policy can affect top-down structuring (de Certeau 1984) via funding. The Austin case shows that local institutions such as nonprofits, the City of Austin, and the Austin Public Library can resist changes in structure via policy from the top, but obviously do better when supported by top-down federal policy rather than opposed by it.

Chapter 7 detailed the efforts of Austin city libraries and other centers to become more friendly and inclusive, particularly to children, teenagers, and immigrants. It explored how public libraries in Austin restructured access to the Internet in disadvantaged and minority communities, from our first examination in 1999 to our follow-up examination in 2009. Numerous public access sites were made available to community residents, allowing researchers to look beyond typical access challenges and focus instead on experiential aspects of Internet use in these settings. Through interviews and observations, the chapter highlighted how several factors at the local level enable and constrain access to and use of the Internet, and how those changed between 1999 and 2009.

Findings suggested that while public libraries are a favored site for many federal and foundation programs designed to bridge the digital divide, they may not always offer the best settings in which to engage those considered vulnerable to that divide. Results from 1999 suggested that a wide variety of centers, beyond just libraries, were useful. Findings from 1999 and 2009–2010 confirm that seniors particularly benefit from centers oriented toward their needs, for example.

Chapter 7 specifically examined both city initiatives and the Wired for Youth grant initiative by the Dell Foundation and focused on whether libraries had become more friendly to minorities in East and South Austin. It found that by 2009, the libraries had substantially transformed their physical space to incorporate more computers, including whole new spaces for Wired for Youth programs, and their sense of mission as they increasingly defined themselves as centers for access to and training for the use of a wide variety of media, including books and magazines, but also DVDs, CDs, Internet access terminals, laptop checkout programs, and wireless hotspots.

Overall, Chapters 6 and 7 both reinforce two key arguments of this volume. First, despite the politics that led to a radical restructuring of policy at the federal and state level in 2000–2003, local actors (including city government officials) and activists were able to continue to structure their own programs from below, a possibility predicted by de Certeau (1984). Second, there was local demand for, and local response in providing, resources to help those who lacked techo-capital in Austin, both in terms of access to and knowledge about how to use ICTs. The evolution of the city programs detailed in Chapter 7 showed that potential users of computers and the Internet increasingly turned toward the library as a place of access and learning. Surveys of ICT users and nonusers in the state of Texas (Straubhaar et al. 2005) also showed disadvantaged users turning toward public access at libraries and other public centers between 2000 and 2004. A later study (Straubhaar et al. 2008) found similar results for two small, largely poor Latino towns in South Texas.

Chapter 8 evaluated the shift of policy attention and resources to wireless access by the City of Austin and many of the nonprofit actors involved in digital inclusion. The authors also mapped out where public free wireless was available, based on research from 2004, showing that it was concentrated heavily in West Austin and that almost the only providers in the minority areas of East Austin were, once again, the public libraries. That observation reinforces one of the overall arguments of this book, that almost every new technology creates immediate layers of potential stratification (who owns a laptop, who lives near the coffeehouses with Wi-Fi, and who does not?). It also shows that government programs like public libraries tend to be the programs that most consistently step into such gaps to close them, at least somewhat, until infrastructure like Wi-Fi and the technologies to access it move through the market to reach less advantaged populations.

Finally, we were very interested in looking directly at the formation of techno-dispositions, techno-capital, and techno-habitus among different groups of individuals and families. Chapter 9 sought to understand the formation of those qualities and the general social construction of information technology in the lives of Latinos and African Americans in Austin. It looked at a group of working-class and poor families based around a ninth-grade class in a poor, largely minority high school in 1999–2000 and at a somewhat more affluent group of minority families in 2009. It examined the economic and social causes for why many people do not have, do not seek, or do not use access to new technologies: combinations of class, ethnic status, age, geographic isolation, and gender-role influences. It focused on the sources of the cultural capital (or techno-capital) and on the techno-dispositions that these families employ as they decide whether and how to make use of technology in their lives, and on the class habitus about technology that is formed among them.

The first set of interviews in 1999–2000 was with a group of twelve teenagers, their parents, and, in some cases, their siblings. The second set of interviews in 2009 focused on a set of six three-generation families, four black, two Latino. Conceptually, the second study still builds on Bourdieu's ideas of cultural, social, and symbolic capital, as well as elaborating on the concept of linguistic capital, particularly. It also uses the generational perspectives of Daniel Bertaux and Paul Thompson, looking at how generations of families work toward social mobility using their capital and struggling to compete in fields that they are not always very familiar with.

The chapter found that several distinct groups use technology quite differently, based on their levels of formal education and their language skills, more than other aspects of their human capital. But it also found distinct family patterns that sometimes defy expectations coming from an analysis of class and language, showing that some families build their own techno-habitus that departs from the larger habitus of their social class.

We found particularly useful, as reported in Chapter 9, the idea of interviewing multiple generations of the same families. Many of the authors involved in this book are now doing a follow-up study look-ing at media, ICTs, and migration, examining how migrants use me-dia to adapt to life in Texas. Again, in this new work, we find the approach of in-depth interviews across multiple generations to be particularly useful.

Theoretically, we find that Chapter 9 reinforces for us the impor-tance of understanding how families and individuals struggle and compete over time to acquire and to attempt to pass on a series of capitals: cultural or educational, economic, social, linguistic, and technological. We found that families were showing some success in increasing their techno-capital. We found a small indication of a pattern that we are examining now in subsequent work, that among poor and minority families, youth are frequently those who introduce technology to the household, who explain it to older generations, who help older generations learn to use it, and who find things for them when they can't use information technology for themselves.

Comparing 1999 and 2009, we found that the techno-disposition of minority youth has changed considerably. As Chapter 7 pointed out, minority boys were much more in evidence in using library public access in 2009 than they were in 1999. Minority youth interviewed in 2009 also showed considerably more disposition to engage ICTs and learn techno-capital than did minority youth in 1999. To some degree, that reflects their changed appreciation of the continuing, ris-ing importance of the techno-field, particularly in Austin. To some degree, it also reflects the growth of a youth culture of digital media use, in which minority, poor, and Spanish-speaking youth are drawn into digital media use by the critical mass of their contemporaries who use it (Pew Research Center 2010, 2011).

NOTES

1. The 1928 decision to formally segregate Austin, taken in the context of a na-tionwide push for segregation under Jim Crow laws, created the most lasting plan-ning intervention, one which proved very difficult to restructure later, whether from above with federal-ordered desegregation or by activism from below.

REFERENCES

Bertaux, D., and P. Thompson. (1997). *Pathways to social class*. Oxford: Claren-don Press.

Boucke, C., et al. (1994). "Technopolises" as a policy goal: A morphological study of the Wissenschaftsstadt Ulm. *Technovation* 14(6): 407–418.

Bourdieu, P. (1984). *Distinction: A social critique of the judgement of taste.* Cambridge, MA: Harvard University Press.

———. (1993b). *Sociology in question.* London: Sage.

de Certeau, M. (1984). *The practices of everyday life.* Berkeley: University of California Press.

Giddens, A. (1984). *The constitution of society: Outline of a theory of structuration.* Berkeley: University of California Press.

González, J. (1986). Y todo queda entre familia. *Revista Estudios Sobre las Culturas Contemporáneas* 1(1): 135–154.

———. (1995). Coordenadas del imaginario. *Revista Estudios Sobre las Culturas Contemporáneas,* Época II I(2).

Irving, L. (1999). Falling through the Net: Defining the digital divide. National Telecommunications and Information Administration. Retrieved from ntia .doc.gov/ntiahome/fttn99/introduction.html.

Orum, A. (2002). *Power, money and the people: The making of modern Austin.* Austin: Resource Publications.

Pew Research Center. (2010). Millennials: A portrait of Generation Next. Pew Research Report. Retrieved February 10, 2011, from http://pewresearch.org/ millennials/.

———. (2011). Latinos and digital media technology, 2010. Pew Research Center Report. Retrieved February 10, 2011, from http://pewhispanic.org/reports/report .php?ReportID=134.

Reich, R. (1991). *The work of nations: Preparing ourselves for 21st-century capitalism.* New York: Knopf.

Smilor, R. W., D. V. Gibson, and G. Kozmetsky. (1988). Creating the technopolis: High-technology development in Austin, Texas. University of Texas at Austin.

Straubhaar, J., S. Strover, M. Fuentes, and Nobuya Inagake. (2005). Critically evaluating market diffusion policy and the digital divide in Texas, 2000–2004. Paper presented at the Communicating and Technology Division, International Communication Association Conference, New York, May.

Straubhaar, J., S. Strover, N. Inagaki, R. Larose, and J. Gregg. (2008). Broadband divides of age, immigration and language in two rural Texas communities. Paper presented at the Communication Policy and Technology Section, International Association for Media and Communication Research, Stockholm, Sweden, July 20–25.

Alexander Cho is a doctoral student in the Department of Radio, TV & Film at the University of Texas at Austin.

Miyase Christensen, PhD, is an associate professor (docent) in the Department of Media and Communication Studies at Karlstadt University, Sweden. She is the editor of the book *Understanding Media and Culture in Turkey* and is currently conducting research on a project titled "Secure Spaces: Media, Consumption, and Social Surveillance."

Carolyn Cunningham, PhD, wrote a dissertation titled "Technological Learning after School: A Study of the Communication Dimensions of Technological Literacy in Three Informal Education Programs for Female and Minority Youth." She is currently an assistant professor of Communication Arts at Gonzaga University, Spokane.

Holly Custard is a PhD candidate in the College of Communications at the University of Texas at Austin. Her main areas of study are globalization, ICTs and media, and development communication.

Stuart Davis is a PhD candidate in media studies in the Department of Radio-Television-Film at the University of Texas at Austin. He is working on Brazilian media culture and ICTs.

Laura Dixon is a Michener Fellow at the University of Texas at Austin, working toward her MFA in poetry, with a secondary concentration in fiction.

Martha Fuentes-Bautista, PhD, wrote a dissertation titled "Space Reconfiguring Public Access in the Post-Convergence Era: The Social Construction of Public Access to New Media in Austin, TX." She is currently an assistant professor at the University of Massachusetts, Amherst.

Dean Graber is senior program coordinator at the Knight Center for Journalism in the Americas at the University of Texas at Austin.

Karen Gustafson, PhD, wrote a dissertation titled "Deregulation and the Market in Public Discourse: The AT&T Divestiture, the 1996 Telecommunications Act, and the Development of a Commercial Internet." She is currently a lecturer at the University of Texas at Austin.

Lisa Hartenberger, PhD (U.S. Agency for International Development), wrote a dissertation titled "Mediating Transition in Afghanistan, 2001–2004."

Nobuya Inagaki is an assistant professor in the Communication and Leadership Studies Program at Gonzaga University, Spokane. His teaching and research interests include the social significance of digital communication technologies, international communication, and research methods.

Antonio LaPastina, PhD, is an associate professor in the Communication Department at Texas A&M University in College Station. His research interests are on media reception, the representation of otherness in mainstream media and its role on diasporic cultures as well as the implications of the digital divide to peripheral communities.

Ed Lenert, PhD, teaches media law at the University of San Francisco. He recently completed a term as professor at the Reynolds School of Journalism, University of Nevada, Reno, and held the Fred W. Smith Chair in Critical Thinking and Ethical Practices. He was also director of the Laboratory for Innovation and Ethical Practices at the Center for Advanced Media Studies at the University of Nevada.

Roberta Lentz (McGill University, Montreal) is an assistant professor in Media and Communications in the Department of Art History and Communication Studies, specializing in the area of media and public policy.

Bethany Letalien, PhD, is Presidential Management Fellow on detail at the U.S. Office of Personnel Management.

Ozlem Okur was a doctoral candidate at the University of Texas at Austin and an International Dissertation Research Fellow with the Social Science Research Council. She passed away in November 2006 after a lengthy battle with cervical cancer.

Juan Piñon wrote a dissertation titled "The Incursion of Azteca America into U.S. Latino Media." He is currently an assistant professor of culture and communication at New York University.

Viviana Rojas, PhD, is an associate professor of communication at the University of Texas at San Antonio. She has conducted research on media and immigration, migrant families and new technologies, and cultural adaptation of U.S. retirees in Mexico and the Philippines.

Debasmita Roychowdhury (University of Texas at Austin) is a senior product manager at Crossroads Systems.

Jeremiah Spence, MA (University of Texas at Austin), is a senior doctoral student in the Radio-Television-Film Department with a focus on ICTs, both in segregated communities and in Brazil. He is also the editor-in-chief of the *Journal of Virtual Worlds Research*.

Joseph Straubhaar, PhD (University of Texas at Austin), is the Amon G. Carter Centennial Professor of Communications in the Department of Radio-TV-Film at the University of Texas at Austin. He is also Associate Director for International Programs of the Telecommunication and Information Policy Institute at the University of Texas.

Zeynep Tufekci is an assistant professor at the University of North Carolina, Chapel Hill, in the School of Information and Library Science with an affiliate appointment in the Department of Sociology. She is also a Fellow at the Berkman Center for Internet and Society at Harvard University. Her research revolves around the interaction between technology and social, cultural, and political dynamics. She is particularly interested in collective action and social movements, complex systems, surveillance, privacy, and sociality.

www.ingramcontent.com/pod-product-compliance
Ingram Content Group UK Ltd.
Pitfield, Milton Keynes, MK11 3LW, UK
UKHW042309280325
456870UK00001B/38